COMPUTER-AIDED GRAPHICS AND DESIGN

MECHANICAL ENGINEERING

A Series of Textbooks and Reference Books

EDITORS

L. L. FAULKNER

*Department of Mechanical Engineering
The Ohio State University
Columbus, Ohio*

S. B. MENKES

*Department of Mechanical Engineering
The City College of the
City University of New York
New York, New York*

OTHER VOLUMES IN PREPARATION

COMPUTER-AIDED GRAPHICS AND DESIGN

Second Edition, Revised and Expanded

Daniel L. Ryan
Clemson University
Clemson, South Carolina

MARCEL DEKKER, INC.   New York and Basel

Library of Congress Cataloging in Publication Data

Ryan, Daniel L.,   [date]
  Computer-aided graphics and design.

  (Mechanical engineering ; 38)
  Bibliography: p.
  Includes index.
  1. Computer graphics.   2. Computer-aided design.
I. Title. II. Series.
T385.R9 1985   001.64'43   85-7019
ISBN 0-8247-7305-5

MARCEL DEKKER, INC.
270 Madison Avenue, New York, New York 10016

Current printing (last digit):
10 9 8 7 6 5 4 3 2 1

PRINTED IN THE UNITED STATES OF AMERICA

Preface

This second edition reflects the many changes that have been requested. These requests have come from the thousands of readers who are presently using the first edition of this classic approach to computer-automated graphics and design instruction. The theory of presentation has remained the same—that is, the beginning level has not changed—but the applications and illustrations have all been updated to reflect the current state of the art in hardware and software. The premise of this book is that beginning readers will want to read and understand the material presented. Therefore, a common sense approach has been used throughout. For example, the use of advanced mathematical transformations has been kept to a minimum, with emphasis on the *use* of programs containing these concepts and *not* the reinvention of these.

Computer-Aided Graphics and Design, then, is a text for engineering and technology students because the computerized approach to engineering graphics is an indispensable supplement to the manual/analytical methods taught in traditional graphics courses. Producing graphics by computer for many types of applications, especially those involving massive amounts of data or repetition, is much more efficient than by traditional manual methods. Portions of the first edition now appear in traditional textbooks published since 1979 and, as an author, it is always gratifying to see one's ideas accepted by colleagues. There remain, however, many CAD graphical problems that can be easily analyzed and automated. These now appear in this second edition. No attempt has been made to replace all engineering graphics subject matter with computer/automated methods. Only those graphical procedures which are felt to make a definite contribution to the effective graphical communications area are presented.

iii

The selection of material for this second edition is based on the premise that the readers and users of this text are the best judge of what is needed. Nearly 50 percent of some chapters have been rewritten, edited, expanded, or deleted so that basic situations are explained in the clearest terms. Thanks to the many letters, telephone conversations, and meetings detailing these changes for the second edition, the emphasis remains on computer graphics usage in engineering problem solving. The expanded methods of using software procedures are stressed, as is the procedure for writing new procedures. The emphasis here, as in the first edition, is on use rather than on how to create software. It is the author's belief, supported by the users of the first edition, that this delimitation is necessary in a first course in computer graphics, because CAD requires more ingenuity, inventiveness, imagination, and patience. Anyone who has ever tried to teach computer graphics to freshmen knows this.

The unique features of the second edition are:

1. It is a complete study of engineering graphics, not a computer or mathematics textbook.
2. Types of modern CAD equipment are demonstrated and explained in lay terms.
3. The book has a substantial amount of illustrative examples with computer solutions explained in step-by-step fashion.
4. Common computer languages (BASIC and FORTRAN) are used side-by-side.

The author makes no claim to the originality of the illustrations presented; most were completed by students at Clemson University during the last five years. Most illustrations reflect the presentation technique taught throughout the book, and represent a pioneer effort in the computerization of heretofore manual methods. The references consulted during the editing of the second edition are listed in the bibliography and in various foonotes. The unique character of this second edition lies in its industrial orientation, its use by leading colleges, and the user-oriented manner in which topics are presented.

To present this industrial orientation, a number of industrial organizations and manufacturers have generously assisted the author by supplying appropriate materials and information needed in developing certain topics. The author deeply appreciates the kindness and generosity of these companies and the personnel who found the time to consult and allow the author to visit their various manufacturing plants. Special appreciation must be expressed to the other members of the engineering graphics staff at Clemson University for their continuing support and patience during the creation of this second edition. Not to be forgotten are the many students and users of the first edition who made valuable contributions to this edition. The author's indebtedness to excellent, intelligent students is hereby reaffirmed.

Daniel L. Ryan

Contents

COMPUTER-AIDED
GRAPHICS AND DESIGN

1

Introduction to Automated Graphics

A complete study of engineering graphics must include something about the age of computerization and how it affects work done by a designer or engineer.

The human is smart, creative, and slow, while the computer is stupid, uncreative, and very fast. The problem then is to allow human and machine to work well together as a team. Certainly their characteristics complement each other, but their languages are very different. We think in symbols and pictures, while the computer understands only simple electrical impulses. Computers and automated graphics are playing an increasingly large part in our lives. Over the past decade, automated graphics applications, particularly for computer-aided design, have been justified because they can save money and time and can improve the quality of the drawings. Dollar savings of from 3:1 to 6:1, and time savings of from 20:1 to 50:1, are typical of those quoted in applications explained later in this text.

Automated graphics or computer graphics is a way of converting the computer's impulses into engineering documents and, conversely, to translate the operator's instructions into electronic data. In many of the more sophisticated systems, we need know little about computer programming in order to control the human-machine effort. In general, computer graphics includes any device that converts computer language to people language, or any device that converts people language to computer language, with the intent of solving problems by creating graphical images.

QUALITY OF COMPUTER-GENERATED DRAWINGS

Most automated graphics devices are easy-to-operate, self-contained, automated systems for the direct translation of rough sketches into high-quality finished ink on vellum drawings. The system is designed for simple, real-time operation by drafters or designers and is particularly useful for producing drawings containing repetitive symbology and text. It can be used in a drafting room since it does not depend totally on an outside processing source. Applications include logic diagrams, illustrations, technical schematics, detailed drawings, technical layouts and many other drawings where speed and accuracy are a must.

An example of an automated system and how it works can be studied by examining a typical block diagram as shown in Figure 1.1. The quality of a computer-

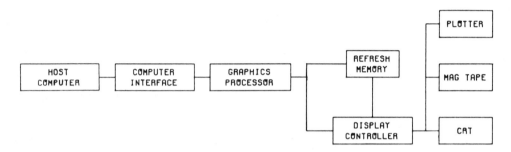

```
C  **************************************************************
C  *   IT SHOULD BE NOTED IN THE TYPICAL AUTOMATED GRAPHICS SYS-  *
C  *   TEM BLOCK DIAGRAM THAT DATA CAN ALSO BE ROUTED FROM THE    *
C  *   DISPLAY CONTROLLER TO THE HOST COMPUTER.  IN MANY CASES    *
C  *   THE HOST COMPUTER EMPLOYS A LINE PRINTER THAT WILL PRO-    *
C  *   VIDE A HARD COPY OF THE DISPLAY PROGRAM UPON COMMAND FROM  *
C  *   THE USER.  IN ADDITION, A JOY STICK WHICH CONTROLS A DVST  *
C  *   SCREEN CURSOR IS USED TO ALLOW THE USER TO ENTER DATA AT   *
C  *   SPECIFIC LOCATIONS.  THE HOST COMPUTER MUST BE ABLE TO     *
C  *   OBTAIN THE DISPLAY CODE AT ANY GIVEN TIME FROM THE DISPLAY *
C  *   CONTROLLER AND MUST ALSO BE ABLE TO OBTAIN JOY STICK OR    *
C  *   OTHER POINTER LOCATION INFORMATION FOR DATA ENTRY.  THE    *
C  *   DISPLAY CONTROLLER, UPON REQUEST FROM THE HOST COMPUTER,   *
C  *   ROUTES DATA TO THE COMPUTER FROM THE DISPLAY MEMORY VIA    *
C  *   THE COMPUTER INTERFACE.                                    *
C  **************************************************************
```

Figure 1.1 Typical automated graphics system.

generated drawing can also be noted since the diagram produced for Figure 1.1 was produced by a digital computer (IBM 370/3081) and plotter (online Cal-Comp). The typical offline plotter is brought online as shown in Figure 1.1 by the addition of the controller shown in Figure 1.2. This controller is a micro-processor-based data control system which functions as an online interconnecting device between a CalComp plotter and host computer. Both a pen plotter, shown in Figure 1.3, and an electrostatic plotter, shown in Figure 1.4, may be simultaneously attached to the controller. The controller has a simple-to-use operator control panel for using the same display coding technique for pen plotting and raster vector plot data via an RS-232-C or a bisynchronous serial interface from the host computer as shown in Figure 1.1.

Every illustration, diagram, and drawing using in this textbook was produced by a computer with the help and instructions of a human operator.

An automated method, then, would be the combination of these two elements to produce synergy, or united action. The logical basis for this concept lies in the fact that the human mind tends to solve problems heuristically (trial and error), while a mechanical system solves by the use of algorithms (error-

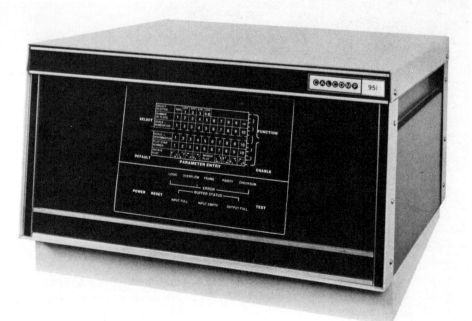

Figure 1.2 Online CalComp controller. (Courtesy CalComp Corp.)

Figure 1.3   Model 960 pen plotter. (Courtesy CalComp Corp.)

free sequences of logic). By letting each (mind/machine) work to its best capacity, a new and better method can be automated. How this human-machine process is automated is rather simple. Strictly speaking, the automation of any process means the improvement or elimination of certain or all parts of the manual labor involved in doing a job. This does not mean the elimination of humans from the scene, for we have to start and stop the process, either directly by pushing a button or indirectly by programming another machine device such as a host computer. Modern automated graphics terminals, for in-

Figure 1.4 Model 5105 electrostatic plotter. (Courtesy CalComp Corp.)

stance, can be programmed so that all the data in a computer file can be displayed by pushing a single key on a typewriter keyboard. The signal of the depressed key releases a set of data points that can describe an entire engineering drawing or something as simple as a circle.

To demonstrate this, suppose the host computer used in Figure 1.1 was contacted from the keyboard of the graphics terminal through the computer interface as:

LOGON
—enter userid—

where the drafter entered the instruction LOGON and the host computer responded with —enter userid. The user would then enter:

USERID/PASSWORD

and the host would respond with the current date, time, and messages useful for the drafter. The user would then enter the instructions for the preprogrammed output, for example

CE .PFK1

which stands for CREATE a PROGRAMMED FUNCTION KEY called one. Next the drafter enters the list of instructions for that function as:

```
INPUT
00010   C   THIS IS A LIST OF OUTPUT COMMANDS TO BE PROCESSED
00020   //USERID1 JOB (0923-1-003-TB-I,:01,1)
00030   //S1 EXEC FORTCLG, PLOTTER = VERSATEC
00040   //C.SYSIN DD *
00050
00060   EDIT
SAVE
```

Now when the 1 key is depressed, the list of instructions are automatically routed to the VERSATEC plotter.

The first drafting machine to come onto the market eliminated the need for the drafter to push and pull a triangle and T-square around the drafting table. The first step in automating the drafting procedure, then, would be the elimination of the pencil or pen from the drafter's hand. A good example of these types of automated drafting machines is shown in Figure 1.5. These are commonly called precision plotters for they are very accurate, usually with a resolution of 0.0002 inch. The model shown in Figure 1.5 is capable of speeds up to 42 inches per second with liquid ink. A full range of line widths can be used. The four-pen pressure inking system provides consistent line quality. In addition to liquid inks, dry ink (ballpoint) pens can be used. The system goes beyond pen and ink plotting, however. Various papers and synthetic drafting materials can be used on the large flatbed plotter surface as well as scribe-coated and the strippable films. Vacuum holddown is standard. A scribing and cutting head attachment is provided.

Using the controller shown in Figure 1.2 adds flexibility in online modes of operation. In the offline mode, it includes a magnetic tape unit that reads plot data from the host computer shown in Figure 1.1. Software is loaded from a magnetic tape cartridge or a disk as demonstrated in Figure 1.6. This software processes the plot data, generates plotter commands, and gives the user complete control over plotter acceleration, maximum speed and pen delays, as well as

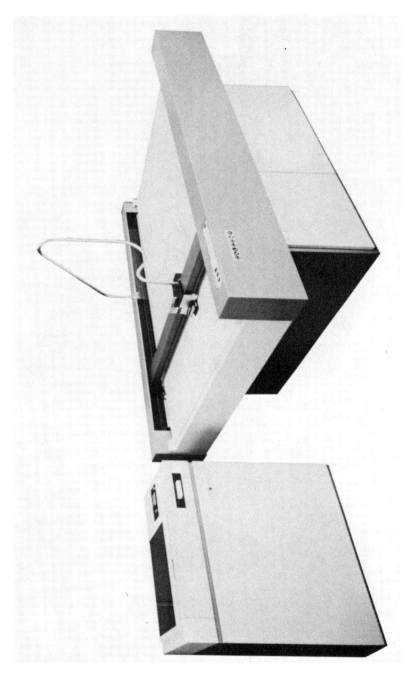

Figure 1.5 Model 7000 high-performance drafting system. (Courtesy CalComp Corp.)

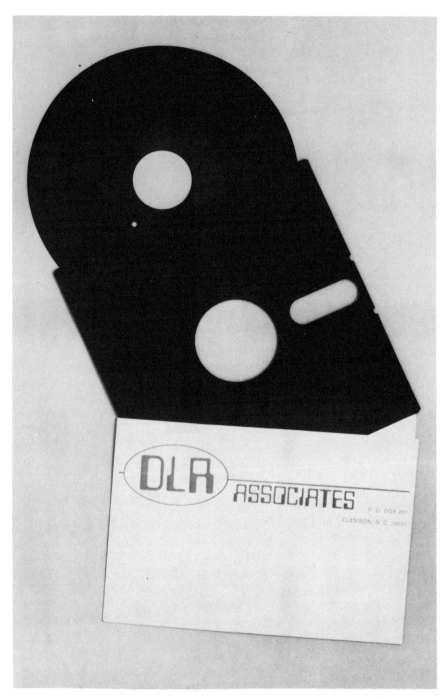

Figure 1.6 Software loaded on a disc.

plot scaling. After loading the software, the user simply dials in parameters appropriate for the drawing to be produced.

The user operating an automated graphics system as diagrammed in Figure 1.1 describes the drawing, and then a permanent electronic record is kept in computer storage. In addition, an offline record is often kept as a backup. Changes in the design drawing are made by editing the stored database. The host computer can display the new drawing information on a digital plotter (Figure 1.3 or 1.4), an automated drafting machine (Figure 1.5), or other suitable device. An engineer may choose to send the information by telephone to another office before it is displayed and while it is still a form of computer data. The electronic information is received at the new location and then displayed. Automated graphics systems produce good quality documents and in the final desired location.

DEFINITION OF TERMS

Computers and automated graphics are playing an increasingly large part in engineering efforts. After some initial problems, we have learned to work with them. To many of us, the computer is a genie that can produce monumental results, either technically wonderful or technically fouled up. Our uneasiness is due largely to a basic lack of understanding of what a computer can and cannot do. Used improperly, almost any mistake can be blamed on the computer. To gain acceptance some products are labeled computer-designed when in fact the design of the product had nothing to do with a computer. And when we know too little about a computer, we do not protest when some badly thought-out feature of a computer-designed system subjects us to inconvenience.

Unfortunately, a person who tries to learn more about computers quickly encounters a problem. A language full of colorful terms has evolved with computers. Slang, technical terms, and phrases used by computer manufacturers all contribute to the problem. To the professional engineer, it is a natural medium for expressing ideas, but to the uninitiated it is a puzzle to be solved. To help solve the puzzle the author offers this section of Chapter 1.

Fortunately, understanding what automated graphics is all about does not require more than ordinary language. But being able to understand technical names for different processes is a big help. With Table 1.1 as a starting point, automated graphics devices can be categorized as shown in Figure 1.7. That is, the devices are either graphic or nongraphic, and they are either interactive or batch. The implication of batch systems is that there is a significant time lag between the moment the information is sent to the automated graphics system and the point at which an answer is received. For example, if the drafter wishes to make a change in response to the displayed drawing, an interactive display

Table 1.1   Glossary of Automated Graphics and Computer Graphics

Term	Definition
Active graphics	A system that is directly human-machine-related in which the graphics operator designs a figure or drawing with a computer device such as a light pen. This is often referred to as *real-time* operation
Algorithm	An error-free system or plan for solving a problem or plotting a figure such as an orthographic view
Analog computer	One-half of a hybrid system for plotting real-time graphics, usually used in a simulation or a mechanical system
ANSI	American National Standards Institute
Application-oriented langauge	The language which is primarily used in template descriptions for engineering graphics
Architecture	The collection of the computer memory, CRT display, light pen, graphics tablet, a floppy disk, magnetic tape unit, and plotter into a system for doing drafting
Argument	The variable located inside the subroutine header list that the computer works on to produce pen movement
Arithmetic program statement	A variable followed by an equals sign and an expression. The expression is completed and stored inside the variable
Array	The most important concept in computer graphics storage of continuous database. The array must be *dimensioned* prior to use by the computer
Arrow	A graphic shape preprogrammed for use as a geometric construction
ASCII	American Standard Code for Information Interchange
Automatic drafting machine (ADM)	A computer-assisted device for the production of high-quality ink drawings

Table 1.1 (Continued)

Term	Definition
Basic	A programming language used for small-scale computers in an engineering graphics laboratory
Baud	The data transmission rate of 1 bit per second. A teletypewriter has a baud rate of 110, or ten characters per second
BCD	Binary coded decimal
Block	A section of information stored on magnetic tape or floppy disk
Byte	Eight bits of information or computer word
CAD	Computer-aided design
CAM	Computer-aided manufacturing
Cathode-ray tube (CRT)	A display screen for viewing graphics or drawing new graphic shapes to be stored by the computer
Central processing unit (CPU)	The brain of the computer where calculations are done
COM	Computer output of microfilm by exposure of a CRT screen onto microfilm for storage
Computer-assisted graphics	A technique known as off-line batch processing of a graphical data base
Database	To display information as pictures instead of numbers the computer must have a set of coordinate locations for the end points of lines, planes, or solids. The total collection of these coordinates is referred to as the database
Digitize	To transform a graphical shape into a digital signal for storage in a database
DVST	Direct-view storage tube
EBCDIC	Extended Binary Coded Decimal Interchange Code
END	The last statement in a graphics program
Flowchart	A picture-type logical path of the graphics program

Table 1.1 (Continued)

Term	Definition
Format	The method or style of data read into or printed out of a graphics program
FORTRAN 77	The most popular graphics language because of its strong relationship to descriptive geometry
Function	A special subroutine kept in computer memory because of its high use factor, e.g., square roots, trigonometric functions, logs, etc.
GOTO	A branch statement in a computer language used to separate graphic functions
Hollerith	The inventor of the punched card
IF	A branch statement in a computer language that tests a situation and branches based on true/false or arithmetic values
Interactive graphics	The most common form of graphics done on CRT displays
IOCS	Input/output control system
Keyboard	An input device for computer graphics typewriters
Light pen	Detects the presence of light when held to a CRT screen
List	A data structure where each coordinate of the database is represented
Macro	A set of sequences of instructions used frequently that are grouped together and labeled for use in a CAM program
Merge	To combine two graphics programs and keep the correct order of each
Microprocessor	The compression of a minicomputer onto a single chip of memory. A major breakthrough for reducing the size of graphic processors in stand-alone ADMs
Minicomputer	A small special-purpose computer with a word length of 18 bits or less and about 4000 of memory

Table 1.1 (Continued)

Term	Definition
Mnemonic	An abbreviated name for a graphics package or set of instructions
Modem	The telephone translation of computer pulses for long-distance graphic data transfer
N/C	Numerical control or digitally encoded numeric data is one means of CAM
Offline	A batch method of communication, or not in contact with the computer on a turn-around basis
Online	An interactive method of communication with the computer
Passive graphics	An offline method of engineering drawing by computer
Plotter	A device which allows the computer to control a pen moving over a piece of paper to make an engineering drawing
Printer	An output device such as a matrix printer, line printer, teletype, or video terminal
Program	Set of instructions designed to make the computer output an engineering drawing
Punched card	An input device containing eighty columns and twelve rows which can be punched out to create a communications code
Queue	A date structure that resembles a list. In a list items are merged, whereas in a queue things are added end to end
RAM	Random-access memory
Remote	Refers to graphics equipment located a distance from the computer
ROM	Ready-only memory
RS-232	The most widely used standard for serial data transmission
Simulation	A computer is used to imitate the behavior of a process or system

Table 1.1 (Continued)

Term	Definition
Stand-alone	Refers to a piece of graphics equipment that is capable of doing its job without being connected to anything else
Subroutine	When a graphics shape is used many times in a program it is made into a miniprogram and called when needed
Syntax	Rules for operation of a computer graphics language
Teletype (TTY)	The most popular computer terminal; it looks like a typewriter
Video graphic display	A CRT for doing engineering drawing

method should be used. Graphic devices use points, lines, curves, circles, characters, and combinations of these to create a drawing, while nongraphic devices use a combination of characters, spaces, and line feeds to generate a nontextual shadow image. The Snoopy posters in every office are a good example of these shadow plots as indicated in Figure 1.8.

A nongraphic batch device is a matrix or line printer, as shown in Figure 1.9. The output is alphanumeric (A/N) and, except by building up a picture by a series of "X" or "." characters, the presentation is A/N oriented. The output is

	NONGRAPHIC	GRAPHIC
BATCH	LINE PRINTER	PLOTTER, COM
INTERACTIVE	TTY, CRT (A/N)	CRT GRAPHICS

Figure 1.7 Automated graphics devices.

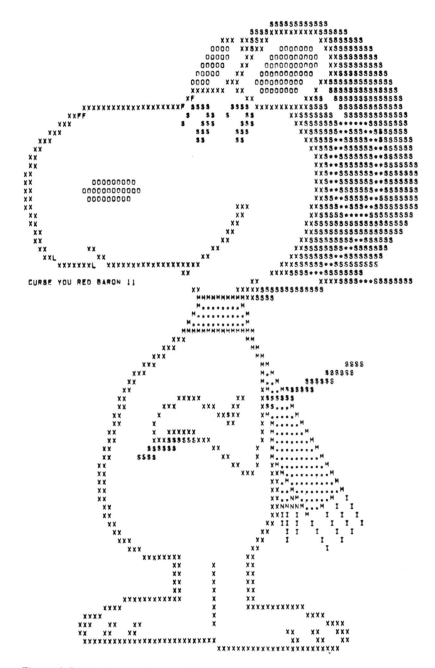

Figure 1.8 Shadow plot example.

Figure 1.9 Matrix printer. (Copyright 1985 Tektronix, Inc. Used with permission.)

generally processed in a batch computer mode because the printer is used to list both the programming instructions and the result of the computation as shown in Figure 1.10.

The most widely used graphic batch device is the incremental digital plotter, such as CalComp, manufactured by California Computer Products, Inc. Figure 1.11 illustrates just a few of the many types of plotters available from CalComp. Along with the many models of plotters currently in use, microfilm units like that pictured in Figure 1.12 are used for computer output on microfilm (COM). William Porter, director of marketing for Datagraphix, was quoted by *Computerworld* as saying:

> COM is an inexpensive peripheral system from the point of view of total capital outlay, but the savings which can be derived from its use can be quite significant. So, if the users look at the savings, there is a high priority for its installation.

In the field of automated drafting and design, COM is a natural output medium. Engineering graphics has used microfilm to record and store drawings for years. With the introduction of computer automation for microfilm the automated drawing is now stored at the same time. Computer-produced magnetic tapes are fed through a tape-to-film recorder. Electronic impulses are converted to visual images on microfilm at speeds 10 to 20 times faster than line printing.

The microfilm is processed in an automated film developer. Duplicators make as many copies of the developed microfilm as needed. A 4 X 6 inch microfiche can hold up to 690 11 X 14 inch drawings plus indexing, depending on reduction. Drafters can easily locate desired drawings through oversize titles and indexing along the top of columns. The retrieval of information can be done in a matter of seconds with a standard desk-top viewer. When paper copies are required, a reader-printer provides full-size prints at minimal cost.

One of the advantages of COM is that a user can make as many high-quality prints as needed, so it is possible for companies with small printing jobs and big distribution problems to justify a COM unit on less than 100,000 original drawings a month.

The best example of the nongraphic interactive device is the A/N-CRT terminal shown in Figure 1.12. Another market authority estimates that in automated graphics environments alone there are 175,000 to 200,000 CRTs installed. The CRT in most environments is interactive because the drafter carries on a running dialog with the computer. The drafter types computer statements, and the computer responds with appropriate programmed answers.

```
C    ***********************************************************************
C    *  DAMPED OSCILLATION GRAPHING BY SHADOW PLOT ROUTINE               *
C    *  BLANK = BACKGROUND OF PLOT, ENTER CHARACTER OR SPACE BAR         *
C    *  DOT = GRADUATION OF X AND Y AXIS                                 *
C    *  X = POINT ALONG THE CURVE OF THE GRAPH                           *
C    *  JCYCLE = NUMBER OF CYCLES BEFORE CLOSED LINE APPEARS             *
C    *  NPC = NUMBER OF POINTS PER CYCLE                                 *
C    *  Q,R,C,XL = VARIABLES WITHIN THE CIRCUIT SO THAT RESISTANCE       *
C    *            CAPACITY, INDUCTANCE CAN BE CHANGED                    *
C    ***********************************************************************
      DIMENSION XLINE(100)
      READ(1,*) BLANK,DOT,X,JCYCLE,NPC,Q,R,C,XL
      IF(R**2-4.*XL/C)9,13,13
    9 DO 101 J=1,61
  101 XLINE(J)=DOT
      WRITE(3,102) (XLINE(J),J=1,61)
  102 FORMAT(1H,61A1)
      DO 103 K=1,61
  103 XLINE(K)=BLANK
      FO=.1591549/SQRT(XL*C)
      F1=.1591549*SQRT(1./(XL*C)-R**2/(4.*XL**2))
      TEMP=NPC
      DELT=1./(TEMP*FO)
      XIM=6.2831853*FO**2*Q/F1
      C1=R/(2.*XL)
      C2=6.2831853*F1
      T=0.
      LIMIT=JCYCLE*NPC
      DO 11 L = 1,LIMIT
      X1=XIM*EXP(-C1*T)*SIN(C2*T)
      J=30.*(X1/XIM+1.)+1.5
      XLINE(J)=X
      WRITE(3,104) (XLINE(J),J=1,61)
  104 FORMAT(1H,61A1)
      DO 105 J=1,61
  105 XLINE(J)=BLANK
      XLINE(31)=DOT
   11 T=T+DELT
   13 STOP
      END
```

Figure 1.10a Programming instructions for shadow plot of damped oscillation.

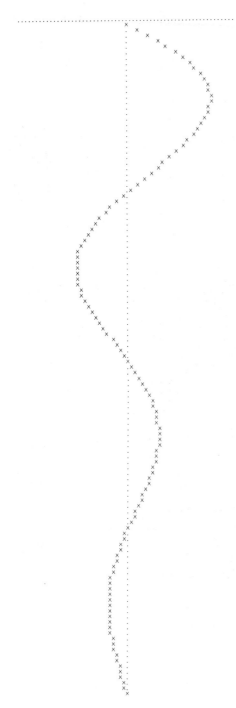

Figure 1.10b Output of program showing shadow plot.

Figure 1.11   Types of digital plotters manufactured. (Courtesy CalComp Corp.)

Figure 1.12 Model 1581 COM plotter and CRT based control console. (Courtesy CalComp Corp.)

Two examples of graphic interactive devices exist for us to examine.

1. *Hewlett-Packard.* The 2647A graphics display terminal shown in Figure 1.13, has a microprocessor-based system design and raster scan technology. By offering many system-independent features, it helps take the burden off both the user and the host computer to make graphics applications more effective and productive.

2. *Tektronix.* The family of Tektronix terminals is the largest single manufactured item that can be found in nearly every computer graphics application. For this reason Tektronix terminals are included as the major example of DVST interactive displays. The range of devices manufactured is excellent, from an inexpensive 4014 model to the system-designed 4107. Peripherals such as joy sticks, hard copy units, data tablets, small interactive plotters, and added storage make this line of products extremely flexible and useful for the engineer. Figure 1.15 illustrates the complete line of hardware available.

Figure 1.13 Model 2647A intelligent graphics terminal. (Courtesy Hewlett-Packard Company.)

22

Figure 1.14 Graphics display terminal.

TYPES OF EQUIPMENT

The graphics process can be automated by establishing a cycle where we begin and end a specific task such as drawing a line. The cycle should be as follows:

1. A command is given by the designer to draw an image as shown in Figure 1.15.
2. The computer responds to this command.
3. An output device displays the image as shown in Figure 1.14.
4. The designer may modify the image displayed.

The common types of equipment that a designer may use to issue a command or instruction are keyboard (Figure 1.16), tape reader (Figure 1.17), magnetic disk (Figure 1.6), CRT controller (Figure 1.12), graphic tablet, and related items shown in Figure 1.18. All of these input methods tell the computer what to do and how to do it. The automated graphics device displays the drawing image according to the output device used: the plotter (Figure 1.11), matrix printer (Figure 1.9), drafting machine (Figure 1.5), COM (Figure 1.12), or CRT (Figure 1.13).

Figure 1.15 Computer display devices for engineering drawings. (Copyright 1985 Tektronix, Inc. Used with permission.)

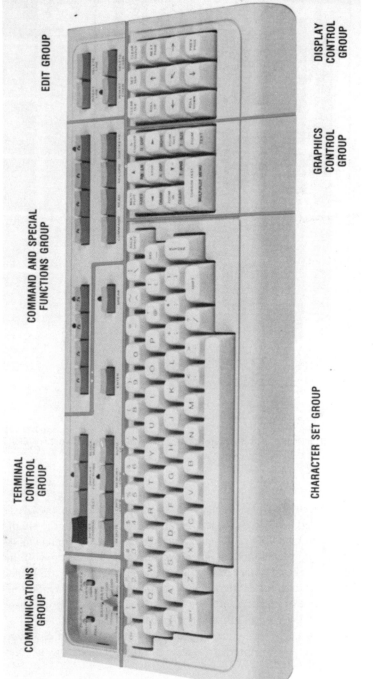

Figure 1.16 Typical terminal keyboard. (Courtesy Hewlett-Packard Company.)

25

Figure 1.17 Tape reader for automated drafting machine. (Courtesy CalComp Corp.)

Halfway between the two extremes of passive, batch versus interactive graphics (see Figure 1.19) is the low-cost micrographics terminal. With the aid of a microcomputer and a software graphing package, an English command structure can be used by nonprogrammers. It is a conversational relationship with the micro computer. By using a library of prompt messages, the drafter can launch into a straightforward system of database construction. Although elementary in its execution, this type of graphics software has a lot of computing power backing it up. Examples of these types of packages are listed in Table 1.2.

From these three types of equipment (host computer-based batch, microcomputer active, and host-based interactive) a system for doing drafting and design

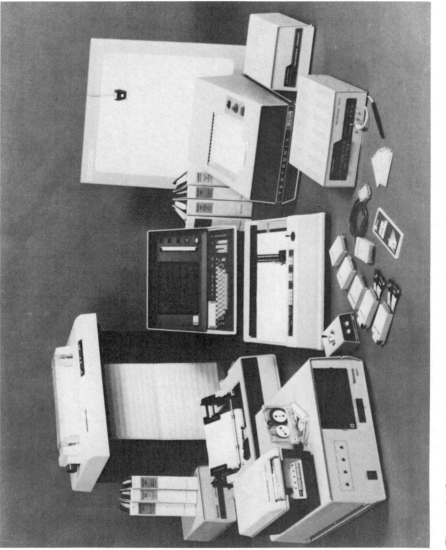

Figure 1.18 Graphics tablet and related items for I/O. (Copyright 1985 Tektronix, Inc., used with permission.)

Table 1.2 Commercially Available Software For Mini/Micro Computer-Aided Engineering Graphics Applications[a]

Supplier	Coding language	Number of routines	Hardware supported	Internal processor	Color	Initialization
Adage	FORTRAN	80 images 45 options	Peripheral for any mini	yes	yes	none required
Apple	BASIC, FORTRAN	84 images 86 AGII	CRT, plotter, tablet	yes	yes	set at system
Amcomp	APL, BASIC, FORTRAN	128 images 4 options	Keyboard, lightpen, ball	yes	no	call to buffer
CalComp	FORTRAN	10 + 43 9 options	COM, plotter, CRT, tablet	no	yes	call to plots
Commodore	BASIC	32 programmable keys	PET micro and peripherals	yes	no	set at system
DEC	FORTRAN	96 images 16 options	PDP series of minicomputers	yes	yes	call to device
Disspla	FORTRAN	206 subpicture parts	CalComp, Xynetics, IBM, DEC	no	no	call to COMMON
E & S	FORTRAN	96 images 8 options	PDP series of minicomputers	yes	yes	call to device
GCS	FORTRAN	96 images	Burroughs, CDC, Honeywell	yes	no	sets default
GINO-F	FORTRAN	231 subpicture parts	Nova, UNIVAC, Prime, Varian	no	yes	select device
GPGS	FORTRAN	116 images 2 options	IBM, Harris, UNIVAC, DEC	no	no	buffer size
H-P	AGL, BASIC, FORTRAN	127 images	2648a via DMA interface	yes	no	window size
Hughes	FORTRAN	96 images [variable]	Nova, DEC, HP	yes	no	hardware mode
IBM	FORTRAN	63 images 2 options	IBM, Tektronix 618, Sanders	yes	yes	alloc file space

IG	ASSEMBLY	97 routines	AMDAHL, IBM	no	no	alloc file space
IMLAC	FORTRAN	555,555 image points	PDS-4	yes	no	set at system
Info. Dis.	FORTRAN	128 images 2 options	Most 32 bit minis	no	yes	call to buffer
Interstate	FORTRAN	96 images [variable]	Most minis	yes	no	set at system
Lundy	FORTRAN	192 routines	DEC, CDC, IBM	yes	yes	call to buffer
Megatek	FORTRAN	84 images 86 AGII	Nova, most minis	yes	no	call to COMMON
Numagraphics	FORTRAN	64 images 2 options	Intel, most micros	yes	no	set at system
Princeton	FORTRAN	128 images 3 options	Most minis	no	no	call to device
Ramtek	FORTRAN	64 images 4 options	DEC, Nova, HP	no	yes	call to option
Sai Tech	FORTRAN	[uses plasma panel]	Most 32 bit minis	optional	no	alloc file space
Sanders	FORTRAN	96 + 32 4 options	IBM, DEC/VAX	yes	yes	call to device
Tektronix	APL, BASIC, FORTRAN	84 images 86 AGII	Most 32 bit minis	optional	yes	call to init
TRS-80	BASIC, FORTRAN	36 w/color option	Most micro peripherals	yes	yes	set and reset
Vector Gen.	FORTRAN	192 images 32 options	Most minis	yes	yes	set at system
Wang	FORTRAN	112 conic/cubic images	Wang	yes	no	set at system

[a]Supplier offering: FORTRAN only, 24; BASIC only, 1; BASIC/FORTRAN, 5; APL, AGL, and others, 3.

Figure 1.19 Typical interactive graphics system. (Courtesy Auto-trol Technology Corp.)

work can be built. So far we have examined the batch-based system items and the micro-attached items, leaving the host- or minicomputer-based interactive systems. An ideal system would contain one or more of the following items:

1. A host computer for construction of a data base and storage
2. A digital plotter, drum, or flat bed for finished drawings
3. A graphic display terminal for preview of design intent:
   a. A hard copy unit for DVST copies of design stages
   b. A joy stick for graphic manipulation
   c. A graphic tablet or digitizer for existing drawings
4. A matrix printer for shadow plots and a preview of plotter output
5. A disk drive for off-line storage

A current list of manufacturers for this type of equipment is shown in Table 1.3. This list was limited to those who currently produce computer graphics equipment and who responded to a survey form mailed to them. Some companies were not included because of this selection process. The author wishes to point out that these types of manufacturers are the backbone of the industry. The majority of manufacturers listed in Table 1.3 make several peripheral devices such as plotters, digitizers, or the like. The number is increasing almost at a daily rate. The reader should be aware that the list in Table 1.3 is representative of the total number of companies, not the total.

Another classification used in Table 1.3 is the interactive graphics system (IGS). These are self-contained graphics systems usually containing one or more of the following items:

1. General-purpose 32-bit minicomputer
2. Microprocessor-based CRT terminal
3. Ten-megabyte disk storage units
4. 36 X 48 inch graphics tablet (digitizer)
5. Small flat bed plotter
6. Hard copy unit for CRT
7. High-level language compiler
8. Database management software systems

It would be impossible, within the framework of this text, to give a detailed working description of each of the manufactured systems listed in Tables 1.2 or 1.3.

As we progress through this textbook, many examples of input and output peripheral devices will be explained in detail. The CalComp plotter is a classic example of a well-known computer graphics peripheral device. It is not designed for engineering graphics use solely. It is a general-purpose device. The author makes us of it throughout the text by modification to the basic, general-purpose software. Whenever change has been made, it has been noted with comment statements before the software listing.

Peripheral devices describe the character of the automated graphics system chosen. Automated graphics systems are used for drafting, mapping image analysis, or business applications. The scope of this text is limited to graphic applications. The systems outlined in Table 1.3 include all aspects of automated graphics.

Now the user must decide how to communicate with the system chosen. The most common types of languages used in programming graphics systems are mathematical- formula-based ones. FORTRAN is the most popular, and the following section of Chapter 1 is based on a sound understanding of FORTRAN 77.

Table 1.3 Current Automated Drafting Equipment Manufacturers[a]

Manufacturers	Type of device
Adage, Inc.	Interactive graphics systems
Altek	Digitizer
Amcomp	CRT
Applicon, Inc.	Interactive graphics systems
Artronix	Digital plotter
Auto-Trol	Digitizer, plotter
Bendix	Digitizer
Broomall	Digitizer, plotter
Caima	Interactive graphics, CRT, digitizer
CalComp	Digital plotter
Comarc	Interactive graphics systems
Compunetics	Digitizer
Computex, Inc.	Digitizer
Computer Research Corp.	Interactive graphics systems
Computervision Corp.	Interactive graphics systems
Control Data	CRT
CPS, Inc.	CRT
De Anza Systems	CRT
Dest Data	Digitizer
Digital Equipment	Interactive graphics systems
Dimensional systems	Interactive graphics systems
Evans & Sutherland	CRT
EMR Photoelectric	Digitizer
Foster	Digital plotter, digitizer
Geo Space	Digital plotter
Gerber Scientific	Interactive graphics systems
Glaser Data	Digital plotter
Gould	Electrostatic plotter
Graph Data	Digitizer
Grinnell	CRT
Hewlett-Packard	CRT, plotter
Houston Instrument	Digital plotter
Hughes Aircraft	CRT
IBM	CRT
Image Graphics	Digital plotter

Table 1.3 (Continued)

Manufacturers	Type of device
IMLAC Corp.	Interactive graphics systems
Industrial Data	CRT
Information Displays	Interactive graphics systems
Instronics	Digitizer
Intellent Systems	CRT
Interstate Electronics	CRT
Litton	Digital plotter
Lundy	CRT
Megatek Corp.	CRT
Nugraphics	CRT
Numonics	Digitizer
Optronics Inter.	Digitizer, digital plotter
Princeton	CRT
Ramtek	CRT
Ruscom	Digitizer
Sai Tech	CRT
Sanders	CRT
Science Assoc.	Digitizer
Spatial Data	Digitizer
Summagraphics	Digitizer
Synercom	Interactive graphics systems
Sysdyne	Digital plotter
Talos	Digitizer
Tektronix	Systems hardware
Terak	Interactive graphics systems
Time Share	Digital plotter
United Computing	Interactive graphics systems
Varian	Digital plotter
Vector General	CRT
Versatec	Digital plotter
Wang	CRT, plotters
Whew	Digitizer
Xerox	Digital plotter
Zeta	Digital plotter

[a]Automated drafting seminar survey respondents of November, 1982.

No matter which type of language is chosen, the steps in problem solving remain the same:

1. Formulate the problem.
2. Construct a mathematical model by the use of graphical methods.
3. Set up the model in the form of one or more equations that satisfy the model constraints.
4. Draw a flowchart of the logical problem solution.
5. Write the language required, such as FORTRAN 77 or BASIC.
6. Prepare the data for input to the program.
7. Trial-run the program and data on the computer.
8. Analyze the results and modify the program.

LANGUAGES

A design language can best be described as a method by which we, the designers, supply raw information to a computer and the computer in turn assists us in finding an answer to one or more problems. A language for engineering graphics implies a uniform, easily understood, organized procedure for feeding information into and out of the design cycle. The design cycle would involve setting up the goal, defining the task to be done, constructing a certain concept of analysis, and then utilizing the routine for solution and documentation. This indicates that a designer produces a program. It is inside of this program that the design language is most useful, for here the speed and accuracy of the computer can be harnessed.

The two main parts of a design program are data and instructions. Data consist of the numbers and characters which are to be used by the instructions to produce an engineering drawing. The main types of data used are numeric and alphanumeric, plus special characters. A list of the characters allowable in most design languages is:

```
0 1 2 3 4 5 6 7 8 9
A B C D E F G H I J K L M N O P Q R S T U V W X Y Z
= ( ) $ ! " # % & ' * / + − ↑ ← \ ; . [ ] < > ?
```

Each line of the program is divided into positions, each of which may contain one character or space. Positions 1 through 5 are used for line numbers, which are labels to identify a particular line. If no statement number is assigned, then the first five spaces are left blank. The design command is entered in positions 7 through 72. A character C in the position 1 indicates that the command on that line is a designer comment. Comments do not affect the program and may be used for explanatory purposes. Each of the lines that are used by a designer is one of the following types:

1. *Arithmetic*: specifies computation to be completed
2. *Control*: commands which specify flow of machine operations
3. *Input/Output*: governs the movement of data between man and machine
4. *Declaration*: supply of descriptive information about programs

The computer langauge for an automated drafting system is usually mathematical-formula-based. FORTRAN 77 is the most popular; however, others such as BASIC and AGL are used. The designer uses the language to produce a series of commands which move the pen in such a manner that the end result is a properly drawn design or working drawing. The particular graphic display device accepts these commands only when received in the proper sequence and in a specific format. The designer must be able to write a computer program in a language such as FORTRAN or BASIC and must also know how to construct subroutines for the display of the standard drawing parts.

Arithmetic Quantities

The three basic arithmetic elements used in coding calculations are constants, variables, and functional references, all of which represent numerical quantities. The two modes of numerical quantities allowed are integer and real. Integer quantities represent whole-number values and are treated as fixed-point numbers within the computer. They may have a value between 0.99999999999 and 99,999,999,999. Real quantities represent real numbers, i.e., those which may have a fractional component. They are treated as floating-point numbers within the computer and have a range between $10^{**}(-150)$ and $10^{**}(147)$. Both integer and real quantities carry eleven significant digits.

Identifiers are used to name the variables, subprograms, or subroutines which appear in a coded program. An identifier is a string of letters or digits, the first of which must be a letter. The string may be any desired length, but only the first six characters will be used. Identifiers are implicitly declared to be one of two types (integer or real), according to the following:

1. Identifiers beginning with the character I, J, K, L, M, or N are assigned integer type.
2. Identifiers not included in the above classification are assigned real type.

Constants

Constants are integers or real numbers which appear in a source program in explicit form. Integer constants are written as a string of decimal digits. Leading zeros are ignored, e.g., 0,1,123. Real constants are written as a string of decimal digits which include a decimal point, e.g., 10,1.,2.768. Real constants may be given a scale factor by appending an E, followed by an integer constant, which indicates the power of ten by which the number is to be multiplied. This scale factor may be preceded by a plus or minus sign to indicate positive or negative powers of ten. If no sign is given, it is assumed to be positive; e.g., 1.E-5 means 0.00001 or .00314E+3 means 3.14.

Variables

Variables represent quantities which may assume many different values during the execution of a program. Each variable has a name and a type. The type of variable corresponds to the type of the quantity it represents. Variables of either type may be scalar or array variables.

Scalar Variables

A scalar variable represents a single quantity and is written as a simple identifier, e.g., AMOUNT, X, K2.

Array Variables

An array variable represents a single element in an array of quantities. An array variable is denoted by the array identifier followed by a subscript list enclosed in parentheses. The subscript list is a sequence of arithmetic expressions separated by commas. Each expression corresponds to a subscript, and the values of the expressions determine which element of the array is referenced, e.g., X(1), K2(M), LINE(Q(INDEX,LINE(Y))+Y). Any valid expression may also be used as a subscript. The value of each subscript expression will be converted to an integer value before it is used as a subscript. The value of a subscript must lie within the limits specified for the array.

Function References

A function is a subprogram which acts upon one or more quantities, called arguments, and produces a single quantity, called the function value. Function references are denoted by the identifier which names the function followed by an argument list enclosed in parentheses.

Function type is assigned by the type of the identifier which names the function. The type of a function is independent of the types of its arguments. A function reference represents a quantity, namely, the function value, and will act as a variable. The type of function corresponds to the type of the function value, e.g., SIN(X), BESSEL(N,Z*SQRT(ALPHA)), DAY(6,7,41).

Arithmetic Expressions

An expression is a sequence of elements separated by operational symbols and/ or parentheses in accordance with conventional mathematical notation. An expression has a single numeric value equaling the result of the calculation specified by the numeric quantities and arithmetic operations comprising it. The arithmetic operational symbols are +, -, *, /, and **, denoting addition, subtraction, multiplication, division, and exponentiation, respectively.

An expression may be as simple as a single element, e.g., -3.146, OMEGA(T), COS(THETA). Compound expressions may be formed by using arithmetic operational symbols to combine basic elements, e.g., -Z+2, SUM/N, SQRT(B**2+A). Any expression may be enclosed in parentheses and considered as a basic element, e.g., -A*(3.14*THETA). Any expression may be preceded by a plus or minus sign, e.g., +TEN, -(A+B), -SIN(THETA). *However, no two operational symbols may appear in sequence.* The expression X*-Y is not allowed in a computer language. The use of parentheses will give the correct form, X*(-Y).

If the precedence of arithmetic operations is not included explicitly by parentheses, it is implicitly interpreted to be as follows, in order of decreasing precedence:

Symbol	Operation
**	Exponentiation
* and /	Multiplication and division
+ and -	Addition and subtraction

For example, the expression U*V+W/X**Y+Z is taken to be (U*V)+ (W/(X**Y))+Z. Since sequence of operations of equal precedence can result in ambiguities, they are resolved by grouping from the left. Thus A**B**C and X/Y/Z are interpreted as (A**B)**C and (X/Y)/Z.

The numerical value of any expression may be integer or real as determined by the types of its elements. There are three possible combinations: All elements are integer (integer expression), all elements are real (real expression), or both real and integer elements occur (mixed expression). All combinations are permissible.

Integer Expressions

An integer expression is evaluated using integer operations throughout to give an integer result. Fractional parts arising in division are truncated, not rounded; e.g., 5/3 gives 1 and 4/7 forms 0.

Real Expressions

Mixed expressions are evaluated by converting all integer values to real values and then treating the expression as if it were real. The result is given as a real quantity, e.g., $Z*2*(I+L)$, $R*(THETA+I)$, and $R(K+2)*TAN(I)$.

Declaration Statements

A declaration describes certain properties of a coded program. Several statements are reserved for the purpose of supplying the system with declarative information. These statements are primarily concerned with the interpretation of identifiers occurring in the source program and with memory allocation in the object program.

Each identifier in a source program is classified in accordance with the element it identifies. Four main classifications are recognized: (1) scalar, (2) array, (3) subprogram, and (4) dummy. Classification is made according to the context in which the identifier makes its first physical appearance in the source program. This first appearance amounts to a declaration, explicit or implicit, of the proper interpretation of the identifier throughout the program.

Allocation Statements

Memory allocation statements are used to supply the graphics system with supplemental information regarding the storage of scalar variables and arrays.

Dimension Statements

The dimension statement is used to declare an identifier to be an array identifier and to specify the number and limits of the array subscripts. As many arrays may be declared in a dimension statement as will fit one line of coded program. Any number of dimension statements may be used in a program. The information provided by a dimension statement is required for allocation of storage for arrays. Each array variable appearing in a program must represent an element of an array declared in a dimension statement. The array variable must have a number of subscripts equal to (or less than) those declared for the array, and the total number of each subscripted variable must not exceed those specified by the dimension statement; e.g., DIMENSION $X(10)$, $Y(10)$, $Z(10)$ gives the array name and the maximum number of storage locations each may assume. Therefore LINE(25,50) is a 2-dimensional array-named line having a maximum storage of twenty-five locations in one direction and fifty in the other. If LINE (I,J) were to be plotted and storage location I contained one to twenty-five sets of data and J contained one to fifty sets of data, a minimum of twenty-five plotted lines would appear on the printout.

Common Statements

The identifiers in a common statement may be either scalar or array identifiers. The common statement specifies that the scalar and array identifiers appearing in the list are to be stored in an area that will also be available to other graphic users. By using the common statement, the same storage area may be shared by a program and its graphic subroutine.

Each array name appearing in a common statement must also appear in a dimension statement in the same program. Quantities whose identifiers appear in common statements are allocated storage cells in the same sequence in which their identifiers appear in the common statement, beginning with the first common statement in the program.

Storage allocation for identifiers appearing in a common statement begins at the same location for all programs. This allows the programmer to establish a one-to-one correspondence between quantities used in several programs even when those quantities have different identifiers within various programs. For example, if a graphics program contains COMMON X,Y,Z as its first common statement and a subroutine has COMMON XPAGE, YPAGE, ZPAGE as its first common statement, X and XPAGE will refer to the same storage location. A similar correspondence will hold for the pairs Y and YPAGE and Z and ZPAGE. Identifiers that are linked through the common statement must agree in type (real or integer).

Equivalence Statements

The equivalence statement allows more than one identifier to represent the same quantity, e.g., EQUIVALENCE (R1,R2, . . . ,Rn), where R denotes a location reference. The location references of an equivalence statement may be simple scalar or array identifiers appended by an integer constant enclosed in parentheses. All location references enclosed within the same parenthetical expression share the same storage location; such a group is known as an equivalence set; e.g., EQUIVALENCE(RADIUS,ARC) states that the identifiers RADIUS and ARC refer to the same storage location.

To reference a specific location in an array, that location must be appended to an array identifier as an integer constant. For example, if A is a scalar variable and B is an array, the statement EQUIVALENCE(A,B(5)) specifies that A and the fifth location of the array B share the same location.

Subprogram Definition Statements

The subprogram is classified as external of the main graphics program and is defined separately from the graphics program calling them. Subprograms are complete and autonomous programs within themselves. There are two types of subprograms which may be declared: function subprograms and subroutine subprograms. The use of the FUNCTION and SUBROUTINE commands and their definitions are illustrated in Chapter 2.

Any subprogram may call other subprograms; however, recursion is not allowed. All subroutines constitute closed subroutines; e.g., they appear only once in the source program regardless of the number of times they are called.

Assignment Statements

An assignment statement specifies an expression to be evaluated and a variable called the statement variable, to which the expression value is to be assigned, e.g., VARIABLE = EXPRESSION.

Note that the "equals" sign does not mean equality but replacement. Consider the following examples:

$$Y=2*Y \quad M=M-S*(M-1) \quad Z(I)=SIN(THETA)$$

These examples are not equations but valid assignment statements. The first example means take the value of Y, double it, and assign the resulting value to Y. In the second example, 1 is subtracted from M, the result is multiplied by S, and that quantity is subtracted from M; the total result is assigned to a storage location called M. In the third example, the sine function is operated on the variable THETA, and this result is assigned to a subscripted variable Z.

Control Statements

In a coded graphics program, control normally passes sequentially from one statement to the next in the order in which they are presented to the computer. Control statements allow the designer to alter this normal program flow. To implement this, source statements may be given statement numbers which are referenced by control statements. A statement number consists of an unsigned integer constant comprised of up to five digits.

Although statement numbers appear in the source program as integers, they must not be confused with numeric quantities. They represent a distinct type of quantity in a graphics program, and no two statements may have the same number. The most common form of control statement is the unconditional GOTO statement. It is used as GOTO n, where n is a statement number. This statement transfers control to the statement numbered n, e.g., GOTO 41.

If Statements

Another type of control statement is the if statement. The if may be used to test a true or false state (logical if) or test the value of an expression for negative, null, or positive responses, e.g., IF(X-1)n1,n2,n3, where n1, n2, and n3 are statement numbers. This statement transfers control to statement n1 if the operation X-1 has a negative result. n2 would receive control if the operation X-1 were also zero, while n3 would receive control if the operation were positive in its result. Any valid expression may be used as the test IF(EXPRESSION), and any statement number arrangement can be used, e.g., IF(TEST+SUM)1,4,4. Here both the zero and positive results are sent to the same statement number.

Do Statements

The do statement allows a series of statements to be executed repeatedly under the control of a variable whose value changes between repetitions, e.g., DO N scalar variable = integer1,integer2,integer3. N is a statement number, and the scalar variable is in integer form. The do statement causes the following statements up to and including statement N to be executed repeatedly. This group of statements is called the range of the do and is located where integer2 is shown. Integer1 is the location of the index or starting point of the do, while integer3 is the incremental value of the index. The values of integers 1, 2, 3 are called the index, range or limit, and increment.

The initial execution of all statements within the range is always performed with the initial value assigned to the index, regardless of the value of the limit and increment. After each execution of the range the increment is added to the value of the index and the result compared to the limit. If the result is not greater than the limit, the statements within the range are again executed using the new value of the index. After the last execution, program control passes to the statement immediately following statement N.

Continue Statements

The general rules of graphics programming state that the range of a do statement cannot end with a transfer instruction. The continue statement is a dummy, or no operation, statement that may be used to end the range of a do statement.

Stop Statements

This statement terminates execution of the graphics program and returns control to the designer for other functions of the ADM system.

Call Statements

This statement is used to call, or transfer control to, a graphic subroutine or subprogram. The identifier is the name of the subroutine. The arguments may be given as constants or subscripted variables. Unlike a function, a subroutine has more than one result and may use one or more of its arguments to return these results to the calling program (the main line). A subroutine may require no arguments at all, e.g., CALL TITLE, where the sole function of the subroutine is to plot a title block for a drawing sheet. However, the general use is with an argument list, e.g., CALL PLOT(XLINE,YLINE,IPEN), where the XLINE is the data required to plot a straight line in the x direction, YLINE is the data required to plot a straight line in the y direction, and IPEN contains an integer for pen control.

Return Statements

This statement returns control from an external graphics subroutine to the calling or graphics mainline program. Therefore, the last statement executed in a subroutine will be a return statement.

Data Statements

A data statement provides a quick method for inputs of *limited* amounts of the database for a graphics procedure, e.g., DATA X/3.14,8.9,5.6/. This statement provides for X_1 to contain 3.14, X_2 to contain 8.9, and X_3 to contain 5.6. X must be contained in a dimension statement in order for the data statement to take effect. Any number of pieces of data may be entered in this manner, provided the variable is an array.

Read Statements

For large amounts of data the read statement is most useful. This causes information to be read from batch, or interactive, sources. It is used in several different ways, e.g., READ(n1,n2) (an IBM method, where n1 is a reader control and n2 is a format statement), READ n, VARIABLE (where n is the format statement), and READ VARIABLE (called a free-format method where data are separated by commas and are not formatted into spaces).

Write Statements

A write statement can also be used as PRINT. The write statement provides a method for output of data in the reverse manner from a read statement. It is used in graphics programs to provide a data base for plotting points as finished geometry.

SAMPLE PROGRAMS AND DRAWINGS

The sample programs illustrated in Figures 1.20 through 1.25 show how language would appear on a standard computer printout sheet. The purpose of the programs is to call a series of subprograms from computer storage to draw a de-

```
LOGON
ENTER USERID:  CEERYAN
ENTER PASSWORD:CAD/CAM
CE .SAMPLE1
INPUT
00010//CEERYAN JOB (0923-1-001-DR- ,:01,1),'MAILBOX 38'
00020//STEP1 EXEC FORTCLG,PLOT=1812,PLOTTER=CALCOMP
00030//C.SYSIN DD *
00040C  THIS STATEMENT ALERTS THE CALCOMP SUBROUTINE PACKAGE
00050      CALL PLOTS
00060C  ENTER ALL SUBROUTINE NAMES NEEDED TO CREATE THE DRAWING
00070C      CALL -----(WHERE NAME OF DESIRED SHAPE IS PLACED)
00080C  THIS STATEMENT DUMPS THE GRAPHICS BUFFER
00090      CALL PLOT(18.,0.,999)
00100C  THIS STATEMENT STOPS THE HOST COMPUTER INSTRUCTIONS
00110      STOP
00120C  THIS STATEMENT ENDS THE EXECUTION OF THE PROGRAM
00130      END
00140//
00150EDIT
SAVE
```

Figure 1.20 CalComp program for simple graphic output.

sign on a digital device. The mechanics of writing graphics programs will be covered in Chapter 2. It is presented here only to indicate the manner in which a designer may use the language needed to operate a graphics system.

This text was developed for student use with a digital computer, graphic tablet, CRT graphic terminals, and digitally controlled plotters. These basic pieces of hardware can be operated together to form either an automated drafting or a design system. The sample programs are written so that the host computer may be any of those listed below.

1. DEC VAX 11/780
2. Interdata 7/32, 8/32
3. D/G Nova series
4. HP 2100, 3000, 9810, 9825, 9830
5. IBM 370 with ASCII Interface
6. CDC 6000 series
7. UNIVAC 1108
8. Wang 2200

```
LOGON
ENTER USERID:  CEERYAN
ENTER PASSWORD:CAD/CAM
CE .SAMPLE2
INPUT
00010//CEERYAN JOB (0923-1-001-DR- ,:01,1),'MAILBOX 38'
00020//STEP1 EXEC FORTCLG
00030//C.SYSIN DD *
00040      CALL PLOTS
00050C  ENTER ALL SUBROUTINE NAMES FOR ELECTROSTATIC OUTPUT
00060      CALL PLOT(0.,0.,999)
00070      STOP
00080      END
00090//G.PLOTPARM DD *
00100 &PLOT MODEL=1200 &END
00110//STEP2 EXEC VTECP, DEST=VER11
00120//
```

Figure 1.21 Electrostatic plotter program for simple graphic output.

```
LOGON
ENTER USERID:  CEERYAN
ENTER PASSWORD:CAD/CAM
CE .SAMPLE3
INPUT
00010//CEERYAN JOB (0923-1-001- ,:01,1),'MAILBOX 38'
00020//STEP1 EXEC PREVIEW,PDS='CEERYAN.LOAD',NAME=SAMPLE3
00030//C.SYSIN DD *
00040      CALL PLOTS
00050C  PROGRAM TO BE PREVIEWED ON DVST BEFORE CALCOMP PLOTTING
00060      CALL PLOT(0.,0.,999)
00070      STOP
00080      END
00090//
```

Figure 1.22 CalComp preview program for viewing plotter output on Tektronix screen.

```
LOGON
ENTER USERID:  CEERYAN
ENTER PASSWORD:CAD/CAM
CE .SAMPLE4
INPUT
00010//CEERYAN JOB (0923-1-001- ,:01,1),'MAILBOX 38'
00020//STEP1 EXEC TEK,PDS='CEERYAN.LOAD',NAME=SAMPLE4
00030//C.SYSIN DD *
00040C  THIS STATEMENT ALERTS THE TEKTRONIX SUBROUTINE PACKAGE - PLOT-10
00050      CALL INITT(960)
00060C  ENTER ALL SUBROUTINE NAMES NEEDED TO CREATE THE DRAWING
00070C      CALL ----(WHERE NAME OF DESIRED SHAPE OR SCREEN FUNCTION IS PLACED)
00080C  THIS STATEMENT RETURNS THE TERMINAL TO ALPHA MODE
00090      CALL FINITT(0,0)
00100      STOP
00110      END
00120//
```

Figure 1.23 Plot-10 program for display of screen graphics.

```
LOGON
ENTER USERID:   CEERYAN/CAD/CAM
CE VECTORS
INPUT
00010 ■■■■■■
00020 EDIT
SAVE
ALLOC DA('CEERYAN.VECTORS') FI(FT10F001)
CALL 'ACS.COTTON.DEMO(VECTORS)'
```

Figure 1.24 Interactive program for creation of screen graphics.

Undoubtedly, other host/plotter arrangements are possible. The author recommends the CalComp shown in Figure 1.11 to ensure compatibility.

EXERCISES

1. Begin a course notebook divided into the following sections: (A) classroom notes, (B) operational instructions for automated drafting devices, (C) sample set of programming instructions for ADM devices, and (D) sample outputs from ADM devices.
2, Obtain handouts for section B above from your local computing center. Read each pamphlet or manual and paste index tabs for easy location of each section. Subdivide section B so each device can be described separately.
3. Prepare a sample set of instructions for each device found in section B. Submit these instructions along with the proper JCL (job control language) so that each of the cases shown in Figure 1.7 can be documented. Section C can be subdivided into the following cases: non-graphic batch, nongraphic interactive, graphic batch, and graphic interactive.
4. Save the outputs from each of the cases listed above, label each, and place them in section D of your notebook.
5. Select one of the current automated drafting manufacturers listed in Table 1.2 or 1.3 that you are *not* familiar with. Locate the proper mailing address in the Thomas Register and prepare a business letter requesting up-to-date operational information. Include these materials in your notebook.
6. Write a short equipment description based on the materials received from the manufacturer selected in exercise 5. You may use the descriptions in your text as guides.

```
    CALL PLOTS
    READ(1,1)NPTS
  1 FORMAT(I4)
    DO 10 I=1,NPTS
    READ(1,2)X,Y,IPEN
  2 FORMAT(2F6.3,I2)
 10 CALL PLOT(X,Y,IPEN)
    CALL PLOT(9.0,0.0,999)
    STOP
    END
```

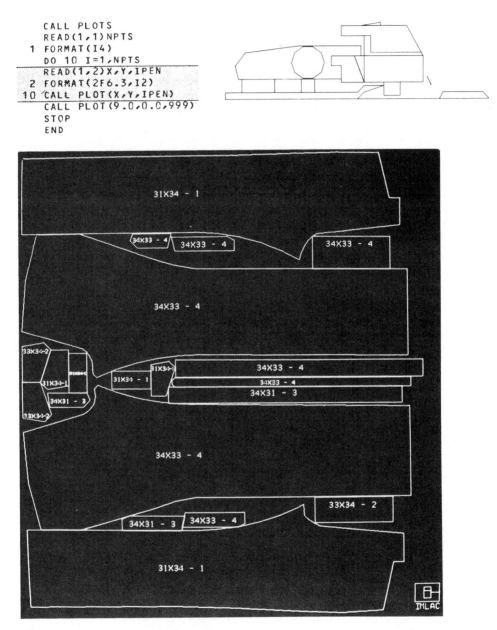

Figure 1.25   Sample automated graphics display outputs.

7. Select one of the programs written from exercise 3. Beside each line of the program, indicate whether it is arithmetic, control, input/output, or declaration in nature.

8. The drafter shown in Figure 1.15 is seated at a Tektronix 4051 DVST. List the names and locations of the other hardware items shown in this figure.

9. The device shown in Figure 1.13 is a stand-alone graphics CRT found in many small offices. List some of the important features of this device when it is used in a system like that shown in Figure 1.1.

10. The image displayed on the CRT in Figure 1.19 is called a wireform. Prepare a list of uses for a display of this type in drafting and design.

11. Input the program shown in Figure 1.20. Make the necessary additions so that a wireform object may be displayed ona CalComp plotter.

12. Input the program shown in Figure 1.21. Make the necessary additions so that a wireform object may be displayed on an electrostatic plotter.

13. Input the program shown in Figure 1.22 so that the wireform object may be viewed on a DVST before CalComp plotting occurs.

14. Input the program shown in Figure 1.23 so that the object may be displayed on the face of a Tektronix screen.

15. Input the program shown in Figure 1.24 so that you may construct any object for display on the screen.

16. Store the database created in exercise 15 under the drawing file name .DATAPT.

17. Prepare a new program for the equipment shown in Figure 1.12.

18. Input the program shown in Figure 1.10 and process it to produce the output as shown in Figure 1.10.

19. List each of the equipment items shown in Figure 1.18.

20. Prepare a section in your notebook called "new terms," and include all terms that are new to you and that are not included in Table 1.1.

2

Principles of Automated Graphics

Automated graphics is a fundamental form of engineering graphics. This concept is applicable to any kind of drawing that must be done in an architect's office or engineering firm. Automatic methods for doing graphics are not new; as early as 1807 a 6-inch paper tape was used to control textile loom needles for sewing monograms or labels in many different graphic shapes and colors. Other early forerunners were the printing and machine tool industries, where this concept was used for etching patterns or tracing template work.

The engineering profession was slower in its use of automated graphics. In the early 1950s the U.S. Military used an interactive CRT graphic system called SAGE. In this system, the controller pointed at a target or aircraft of interest with the light pen, and the computer immediately presented information regarding that target. In a different environment, the TX-1 computer at the Massachusetts Institute of Technology (MIT) in the late 1950s and early 1960s featured a similar type of graphics console. About 20 years ago, General Motors began its work in the application of computer graphics to computer-generated design drawings. One of the milestones in the development of computer graphics and automated drafting was the work done by Dr. Ivan Sutherland. His 1963 MIT thesis describing "Sketch-Pad" contains some of the core data structures, laying the theoretical basis for computer graphics and automated drafting.

In the mid-1960s, large aerospace companies such as Lockheed, McDonnell-Douglas, Ryan, and Boeing began to explore the use of computer graphics for aircraft and missile design. Uniformly, they reported dollar and time savings. At the same time, other industries such as Motorola, Fairchild, and Bell Laboratories began to use computer graphics for the design and production of printed circuit boards and integrated circuit patterns. The 1980s have seen a rapid increase in

49

the use of computer-aiding manufacturing techniques, which include computer graphics display along with computer-generated instructions for machine tool operations. As a result of this work, it is probable that most paper tape readers for N/C (numeral control) machines are now obsolete and have been replaced with mini- or microprocessors that are linked to a larger computer for control.

Recently the U.S. Forest Service developed a computer graphics and mapping system called TOPAS. It is a package of computer programs to collect, manipulate, and analyze digital terrain data. The input is from existing topographic maps, aerial photography, or satellite pictures. The output products are graphic plots which are used by land managers to evaluate impacts of land uses. Typical drawings include scan profiles for orthophoto production and cross-section evaluations for road design or cable logging analysis.

The use of computer graphics by engineers to produce drawings began about 30 years ago. From this beginning, the field has grown until today every major industry has some sort of automated drafting capability.

STRAIGHT LINES

An automatic drafting system accepts symbolic numerical values from a computer and converts this input into physical values through electrical signals that are translated into pen movement. These signals are either digital pulses or analog varying voltages depending on the equipment manufacturer.

There are two major types of digital signals. One supplies incremental data and tells how much pen motion has occurred. In other words, each motion begins with a zero reading and ends with the distance traveled by the pen. The second type of digital signal is absolute. In this case each pulse signal corresponds to a specific location. More than one move in a sequence is added end to end, or the last move of the drawing is a sum total of the distance traveled since motion began. Each method is used by drafting machine manufacturers, and some allow either to be used on the same device. The operator selects the best type of display for the type of data being generated from the computer.

The analog signal is usually in the form of an electric voltage which varies according to the numerical values sent from the computer. The digital signal from the computer is converted to a voltage signal for use by the display device. In the case of a plotter, the pen motion is measured by comparing the input signal or command voltage with the output of generated voltage. The input is digital and is converted to an analog voltage to drive stepping motors which are attached to the horizontal or vertical plotting axis.

Regardless of the method used to display a straight line, most drafting applications require the generation of horizontal or vertical lines to show the relationship between two or more orthographic views. Usually these views can be produced easily and quickly by a suitably programmed combination of pen control subroutines. These graphic subroutines produce display commands that define the desired pen location, in the case of a straight line, or pen motion, in the case of an arc or circle.

When unique plotting requirements cannot be satisfied by using the existing computer subroutines, the designer can resort to writing a special-purpose sub-program, which gives direct control of pen motion and generation of data files. By calling the graphic subroutines, however, the drafter may do 90 percent of the work. The straightline subroutine is stored as the command PLOT in most graphic systems manufactured. The PLOT subroutine is used primarily to move the pen in a straight line to a new position, with the pen either up or down during the movement. It converts the designer's data to the appropriate sequence of plotter commands.

The calling sequence has three designer inputs:

CALL PLOT(XLINE,YLINE,IPEN)

The XLINE is the distance in the horizontal direction from the current pen location to the desired new location where the pen will be moved. Likewise, the YLINE is the desired distance in the vertical direction. The IPEN data specify the pen in an up or down position during the movement. If the drafter has need of the PLOT subroutine in a graphic program, the CALL PLOT command is used followed by the proper X, Y, and pen control data. The computer searches for a preprogrammed subroutine called PLOT and sends the proper display signals to the output device. A subroutine for plotting a straight line on the interactive DVST shown in Chapter 1 would contain the lines of FORTRAN in Figure 2.1.

```
C    ******************************************************************
C    *  THIS SUBROUTINE DISPLAYS A STRAIGHT LINE BETWEEN ANY TWO      *
C    *  POINTS ON THE PLOTTER OR THE DVST SCREEN.  THIS ROUTINE       *
C    *  SHOULD BE USED IN CONNECTION WITH THE PROGRAM LISTED IN       *
C    *  FIGURE 1.24.                                                  *
C    *                                                                *
C    ******************************************************************
     SUBROUTINE PLOT(XLINE,YLINE,IPEN)
     IX=XLINE*130.
     IY=YLINE*130.
     IF(IPEN.EQ.2) CALL DRWABS(IX,IY)
     IF(IPEN.EQ.3) CALL MOVABS(IX,IY)
     IF(IPEN.EQ.-2)CALL DRWREL(IX,IY)
     IF(IPEN.EQ.-3)CALL MOVREL(IX,IY)
     RETURN
     END
```

Figure 2.1 Display subroutine for drawing a straight line.

```
2000 REM SUBPROGRAM PLOT
2010 IF P = 2 THEN DRAW IX,IY
2020 IF P = 3 THEN MOVE IX,IY
2030 IF P =-2 THEN RDRAW IX,IY
2040 IF P =-3 THEN RMOVE IX,IY
2050 RETURN
```

Figure 2.2 Display subroutine written in BASIC.

The term *interactive* means that the designer may want to modify the drawing during execution. In a *real-time* mode of operation a BASIC language subprogram could also be used. It would contain the lines of BASIC shown in Figure 2.2.

ANGLES

Any system that accepts a symbolic numerical value as an input and converts it to a physical value, such as a line, as an output is providing automatic graphics. Whether the distances are put into the system by push buttons, dials, encoders, magnetic tape, or disk (and whether or not the system requires feedback) are secondary functions and are not part of the basic concept.

The particular type of drawing format is under the control of the operator, who performs as many as eight functions:

1. Select the pen style called for (ink pen, scriber, knife).
2. Set the origin or "home" position.
3. Select the pen routines (color, width).
4. Activate the plotter functions.
5. Position the drafting vellum on the plotting area.
6. Start and stop the control processor.
7. Activate the joy sticks, hard copy units, and graphic tablets.
8. Return to home after plot.

The basic concept of the call statement **PLOT** has been explained only insofar as point-to-point motion of the pen was concerned. If a combination of horizontal and vertical input commands are fed from the computer, the pen will produce a slope or angle line. The ability to move the axis at different speeds is a built-in function of most flat bed plotters. This feature allows smooth-flowing line segments at slopes other than 45 degrees. Also the plotting time can be reduced 500 times for each inch of travel in the desired output.

CIRCLES AND ARCS

A complete set of drafting subroutines would naturally include a calling method
for circles of different diameters or portions of these circles to form anywhere

```
C    ****************************************************************
C    *  THIS SUBROUTINE DRAWS AN ARC OR A FULL CIRCLE WITH RADIUS  *
C    *  OF ANY REAL VALUE ANYWHERE ON THE DISPLAY SURFACE.  THE    *
C    *  DEGREE OF ARC MAY VARY AND MAY BE USED WITH EITHER THE     *
C    *  CALCOMP SERIES PLOTTERS OR THE TEKTRONIX INTERACTIVE DVST  *
C    *     X      THE CENTER OF THE ARC IN XLINE                   *
C    *     Y      THE CENTER OF THE ARC IN YLINE                   *
C    *     R      RADIUS OF THE ARC                                *
C    *     SANG   STARTING POINT OF THE ARC IN DEGREES             *
C    *     N      NUMBER OF STRAIGHT LINE INCREMENTS               *
C    *     THETA DEGREES IN EACH SEGMENT                           *
C    ****************************************************************
         SUBROUTINE CIRARC(X,Y,R,SANG,N,THETA)
         X=X-R
         SANG=3.14/80.*SANG
         XX=R*(1-COS(SANG))
         YY=R*(SIN(SANG))
         DX=X+XX
         EY=Y+YY
         CALL PLOT(DX,EY,3)
         THETA=3.14/180.*THETA
         THETA1=THETA
         DO 2 I=1,N
         FEE=SANG+THETA
         PX=R*(1-COS(FEE))
         SY=R*(SIN(FEE))
         DX=X+PX
         EY=Y+SY
         CALL PLOT(DX,EY,2)
       2 THETA=THETA+THETA1
         RETURN
         END
```

Figure 2.3 Subroutine for display of circles and arcs.

from 1 to 360 degrees of arc. The designer needs to have a high degree of flexibility when using such a subroutine, yet it should be fairly simple to use. Figure 2.3 is an example of such a stored computer routine.

You will note that the circle subroutine has been written for either a FORTRAN-based CalComp-type plotter or a DVST interactive device. As in the case with straight lines, the designer may want a real-time, oriented BASIC subprogram, which would contain the lines of code shown in Figure 2.4.

In both examples twenty lines of coding are required to send the proper data points for plotting a circle or arc. The designer need not know how to write the subroutine or subprogram, but must supply the size of radius, the location of the arc, and the smoothness of line. Remember that the subroutine or subprogram has been stored for use by the drafter. It operates from a main-line program and the graphic shapes create the desired drawing geometry. An example of a main-line program which uses both straight-line and circle routines to create drafting geometry is shown in Figure 2.5 along with the plotter output for this program.

```
2200 REM SUBPROGRAM CIRARC
2210 LET X=X-R
2220 LET S=3.14/180.*S
2230 LET X3=R*(1-COS(S))
2240 LET Y3=R*SIN(S)
2250 LET D2=X+X3
2260 LET E2=Y+Y3
2270 MOVE D2,E2
2280 LET T=3.14/180.*T
2290 LET T1=T
2300 FOR I = 1 TO N
2310 LET F=S+T
2320 LET P2=R*(1-COS(F))
2330 LET S2=R*SIN(F)
2340 LET D2=X+P2
2350 LET E2=Y+S2
2360 DRAW D2,E2
2370 LET T=T+T1
2380 NEXT I
2390 RETURN
```

Figure 2.4 Subroutine for display of circles and arcs from microcomputers.

```
      DIMENSION X(3),Y(3),R(3),SANG(3),N(3),THETA(3)
      CALL PLOTS
      DATA X/3.,4.5,6./
      DATA Y/4.,5.5,4./
      DATA R/.875,1.245,.875/
      DATA SANG/270.,225.,45./
      DATA N/45,18,45/
      DATA THETA/3*5./
      DO 10 I=1,3
10 CALL CIRARC(X(I),Y(I),R(I),SANG(I),N(I),THETA(I))
      CALL PLOT(3.,3.125,3)
      CALL PLOT(6.002,3.125,2)
      CALL PLOT(0.,0.,999)
      STOP
      END
```

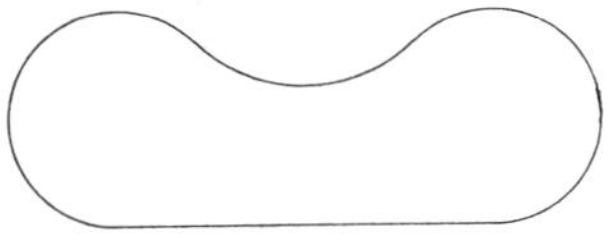

Figure 2.5 Program and output using CIRARC and PLOT.

GEOMETRIC CONSTRUCTIONS

The drafter or designer who elects to use computer graphics in the documentation of a design is seeking a better way to display the engineering data: better,
because it will be quicker, cheaper, and more accurate than manual methods.
To accomplish this a library of standard geometric constructions have been developed by several manufacturers. To date there has not been a national standardization of these routines, and a complete listing would vary from office to
office. However, a rule of thumb might be

AROHD	draws arrowheads
ARROW	draws lines terminated with an arrow for leaders
AXIS	draws and labels X and Y axes
BAR	draws bar graphs
CIRCL	draws a circle or arc
CNTRL	draws a centerline
CURVX	plots a function of X over a given range
CURVY	plots a function of Y over a given range
DASHL	draws a hidden line connecting several points
DASHP	draws a single hidden line
DIMEN	draws annotated dimension lines
DFACT	determines the current scaling factor
DWHR	determines the current scaling factor and location of the pen

ELIPS	draws an ellipse or an elliptical arc
FACTOR	enables the designer to enlarge or reduce a portion of the drawing
FIT	draws a curve through three points
FLINE	draws a smooth curve through a set of points
GRID	draws a linear grid
LABEL	annotation between specified points
LINE	plots a line through several points
NEWPEN	selects the pen to be used for the plot
NUMBER	provides numerical annotation
OFFSET	sets distances from plotter origin
POINT	plots data as a series of points
PLOT	plots data as a series of lines
PLOTS	name of entire set of geometric constructions stored in computer
POLY	draws an equilaterial polygon
RECT	draws a rectangle
ROTATE	rotates a series of points about a center axis
SCALE	automatically determines scaling factors
SHADE	draws section lines between designated lines
SMOOT	smooths data through sequential points
SYMBOL	provides character annotation
WHERE	determines location of the pen
WOFST	determines current offsets and scaling factors

Each of the geometric construction subroutines has a list of calling parameters known as arguments. They are as follows:

AROHD(X,Y,XTIP,YTIP,ALEN,AWD,ICODE)
ARROW(XARAY,YARAY,NPTS,INC,ITYPE)
AXIS(X,Y,IBCD,NCH,AXL,DEG,FIRV,DELV)
BAR(X,Y,THETA,HT,WD,SH,IHAT,NPI)
CIRCL(X,Y,SANG,EANG,SR,ER,CODE)
CNTRL(XARAY,YARRAY,NPTS,INC)
CURVX(X,X1,COEF,EXP,COEF2,EXP2,COEF3,EXP3,COEF4,EXP4)
CURVY(Y,Y1,COEF,EXP,COEF2,EXP2,COEF3,EXP3,COEF4,EXP4)
DASHL(XARRAY,YARRAY,NPTS,INC)
DASHP(X,Y,SIZE)
DIMEN(X,Y,DIME,THETA,SCALE)
DFACT(XFACT,YFACT)
DWHR(X,Y,XFACT,YFACT)
ELIPS(X,Y,RMAJ,RMIN,THETA,SANG,EANG,IPEN)

```
FACTOR(SIZE)
FIT(X1,Y1,X2,Y2,X3,Y3)
FLINE(XARRAY,YARRAY,NPTS,INC,LINTYP,INTEQ)
GRID(X,Y,DX,DY,NXSP,NYSP)
LABEL(X,Y,X2,Y2,IBCD,NCHAR,HT,ISIDE,DSTFIN,FPN,NDEC)
LINE(XAR,YAR,X,Y,NPT)
NEWPEN(IPEN)
NUMBER(X,Y,SIZE,FLNUM,THETA,NDIGITS)
OFFSET(XOFF,XSCALE,YOFF,YSCALE)
POINT(XARRAY,YARRAY)
PLOT(XLINE,YLINE,IPEN)
PLOTS
POLY(X,Y,SLEN,SN,THETA)
RECT(X,Y,HT,WD,THETA,IPEN)
ROTATE(X,Y,Z)
SCALE(AR,AXL,NPT,INC)
SHADE(X,Y,XARAY,YARAY,DLIN,THETA,NPTS,INC,NPTA,INCA)
SMOOT(X,Y,IPEN)
SYMBOL(X,Y,SIZE,MESAGE,THETA,NCHAR)
WHERE(X,Y,FACTOR)
WOFST(XOFF,XSCALE,YOFF,YSCALE)
```

In many of the geometric constructions the first two parameters refer to the starting position for that figure. In the case of RECT, for example, the X and Y refer to the lower left-hand corner of the rectangle. When convenient all graphic shapes are started from this position.

As can be seen, the list of geometric construction techniques are used in both automated drafting and general-purpose computer graphics applications. The thirty-five listed here can be used to create special-purpose drafting subroutines for template-type work. Before a special routine for plotting an electronic symbol can be written, for example, an understanding of how the basic geometric construction routines are used is important.

AROHD(X,Y,XTIP,YTIP,ALEN,AWD,ICODE)

The arrowhead subroutine will display an arrowhead at the end of a line segment. It is used within a program as:

    CALL AROHD(X,Y,XTIP,YTIP,ALEN,AWD,ICODE)

where   X,Y   are the coordinates of the starting point of the line segment
                  that determines the direction of the arrowhead

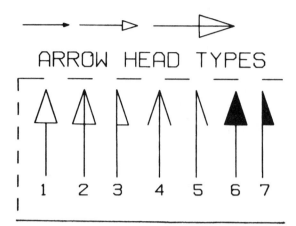

Figure 2.6   Display of subroutine AROHD.

XTIP,YTIP	are the coordinates of the tip of the arrowhead
ALEN	is the arrowhead's length
AWD	is the width
ICODE	is the type of arrowhead desired as illustrated in Figure 2.6.

ARROW(XARRAY,YARRAY,NPTS,INC,ITYPE)

The arrow subroutine will display a line through a series of data points and places an arrow on the end. It is used within a program as:

   CALL ARROW(XARRAY,YARRAY,NPTS,INC,ITYPE)

where XARRAY,YARRAY	are the names of dimensioned arrays containing the data points to be displayed
NPTS	is the number of data points in the arrays
INC	is the increment between array elements, normally all the data points are to be plotted and 1 is used

ITYPE	selects the type of arrowhead from AROHD that is displayed at the end. Choices are:
	    ITYPE = 1 selects AROHD 5
	    ITYPE = 2 selects AROHD 7
	    ITYPE = 3 selects AROHD 2
	    ITYPE = 4 selects AROHD 2 plus extension line used in dimensioning an object as shown in Figure 2.7

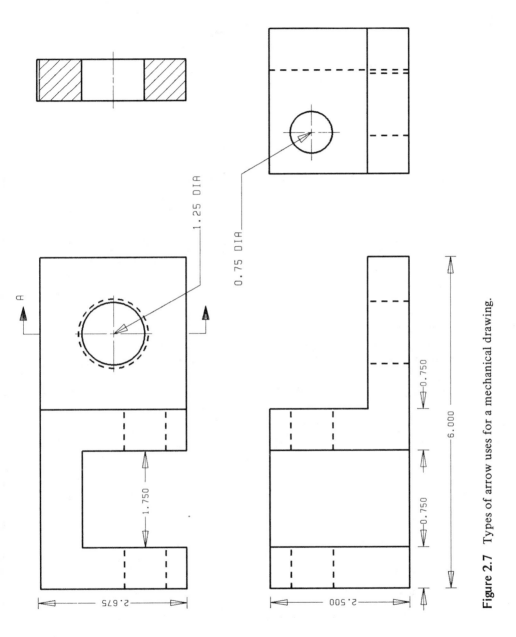

Figure 2.7 Types of arrow uses for a mechanical drawing.

AXIS(X,Y,IBCD,NCH,AXL,DEG,FIRV,DELV)

This subroutine is used to display and annotate the axes for both X and Y. It is used within a program as:

   CALL AXIS(X,Y,IBCD,NCH,AXL,DEG,FIRV,DELV)

where   X,Y   are the coordinates of the axis starting point
           IBCD   is the alphabetic data to be used as the axis title
           NCH   is the number of characters to be displayed in the title.
           AXL   is the axis length to be displayed
           DEG   is the angle of rotation to be displayed for the axis
           FIRV   is the value of the annotation at the first tick mark of the
                      axis
           DELV   represents the distance between tick marks on the axis as
                      shown in Figure 2.8

CIRCL(X,Y,THO,THF,RO,RF,DSHI)

This technique is widely used when constructing figures of all types. It has already been introduced in the preceding section as CIRARC. This is one version of this subroutine used for minicomputers. Table 2.1 compares the use of this subroutine for all three types of computers (mainframe, mini, and micro).

CNTRL (XARAY,YARAY,NPTS,INC)

This construction technique displays centerlines between successive data points stored in XARAY and YARAY. Each construction is a line pattern consisting of alternating long and short dashes as illustrated in Figure 2.9. The long dashes are 4/11 and short dashes 1/11 of the distance between points. NPTS is the number of points in the storage location XARAY and YARAY, while INC is the increment of the connection. If INC=1, then the pattern shown in Figure 2.9 is generated for a single point stored in XARAY, YARAY.

BAR(X,Y,THETA,HT,WD,SH,IHAT,NPI)

This subroutine draws the bars for a chart as shown in Figure 2.9. It is used in chapter 9 but is introduced here because it is considered a basic geometric construction as well. X and Y are the lower left-hand coordinates of the bar. The angle of rotation for the bar stem may be placed in THETA, but normal usage is zero. HT is the height of the overall bar, while WD is the width of the bar stem. SH is the shaded height of the bar. It is possible to shade only a portion of the bar by setting SH less than HT. IHAT is an integer for shading the SH of the bar

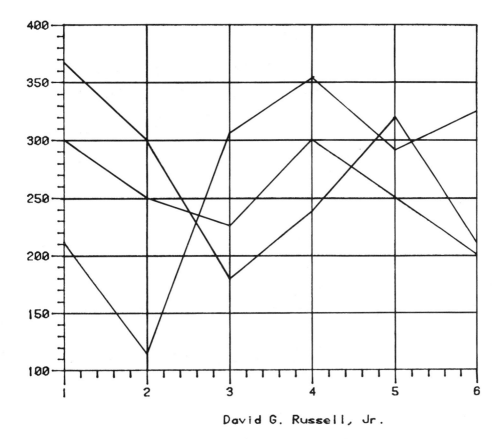

Figure 2.8 Display using the subroutine AXIS.

stem. 1 = no shade, 2 = section line from left to right, 3 = section line from right to left, and 4 = crosshatch of SH. NPI is the number of lines of shading per inch along the base of the bar.

CURVX(X,X1,COEF,EXP,COEF2,EXP2,COEF3,EXP3,COEF4,EXP4)

This subroutine plots a function of X over a given range. The form of the function is a polynominal $Y = COEF*X^{EXP} + COEF2*X^{EXP2} + COEF3*X^{EXP3} + COEF4*X^{EXP4}$ for values of X from the variable X to X1, where delta X = 0.01. The ability to plot functions is important in the design of machine parts such as cams. CURVY is identical to CURVX except the function is graphed along the Y axis instead of horizontally (see Figure 2.9).

Table 2.1 Direct Comparison of Extended Graphics for Computer-Aided Engineering Graphics (CIRCL)

Mainframe-FORTRAN	Mini-FORTRAN	Micro-BASIC
SUBROUTINE CIRCL(X,Y,THO,THF,RO,RF,DSHI)	SUBROUTINE CIRARC(X,Y,R,SANG,N,THETA)	4000 REM SUBROUTINE CIRCLE
C----CIRCLE MOVES THE PEN OF A PLOTTER OR	X=X-R	4005 READ #3; X,Y,R,S,N,T
C----THE BEAM OF A CRT IN A CIRCLE OR SPIRAL	SANG=(3.14/180.)*SANG	4010 LET X=X-R
C----ARC DEFINED BY THE STARTING POSITION (X,	XX=R*(1-COS(SANG))	4015 LET S=(3.14/180.)*S
C----Y) WHEN THE STARTING ANGLE (THO) AND THE	YY=R*(SIN(SANG))	4020 LET X3=R*(1-COS(S))
C----ENDING ANGLE (THF) HAVE BEEN STATED.	DX=X+XX	4025 LET Y3=R*SIN(S)
C----RO AND RF ARE THE SIZE OF THE STARTING	EY=Y+YY	4030 LET D2=X+X3
C----ENDING RADIUS, WHILE DSHI IS THE CODE	CALL PLOT(DX,EY,3)	4035 LET E2=Y+Y3
C----FOR SOLID OR DASHED DISPLAY 0.=SOLID &	THETA=(3.14/180.)*THETA	4040 PRINT USING 9901;D2,E2
C----.5=DASHED LINE DISPLAYS.	THETO=THETA	4045 LET T=(3.14/180.)*T
C	DO 2 I=1,N	4050 LET T1=T
	FEE=SANG+THETA	4055 FOR I=1 TO N
I5=4.51+DSHI	PX=R*(1-COS(FEE))	4060 LET F=S+T
I2=2	SY=R*(SIN(FEE))	4065 LET P2=R*(1-COS(F))
CALL PLOT(X,Y,3)	DX=X+PX	4070 LET S2=R*SIN(F)
CALL WHERE(DTH,DTH,FCTR)	EY=Y+SY	4075 LET D2=X+P2
TO=THO/57.2958	CALL PLOT(DX,EY,2)	4080 LET E2=Y+S2
TF=THF/57.2958	2 THETA=THETA+THETO	4085 PRINT USING 9902;D2,E2
C----FIND CENTER OF ARC IN X DIRECTION	RETURN	4090 LET T=T+T1
C=X-RO*COS(TO)	END	4095 NEXT I
TN=(TF-TO)/DTH		4100 RETURN
IF (TF-TO) 102,104,104		

```
102 TN=ABS(TN)
    DTH=-DTH
C——FIND CENTER OF ARC IN Y DIRECTION
104 B=Y-RO*SIN(TO)
    N=TN
    IF(N) 115,115,105
105 TN=(RF-RO)/TN
    RN=RO-TN
    DO 110 I=1,N
    TO=TO+DTH
    RN=RN+TN
    X=RN*COS(TO)+C
    Y=RN*SIN(TO)+B
    IF(KNT) 112,112,111
112 I2=I5-I2
    KNT=7.*FCTR
111 KNT=KNT-1
110 CALL PLOT(X,Y,I2)
115 X=RF*COS(TF)+C
    Y=RF*SIN(TF)+B
    RETURN
    END
```

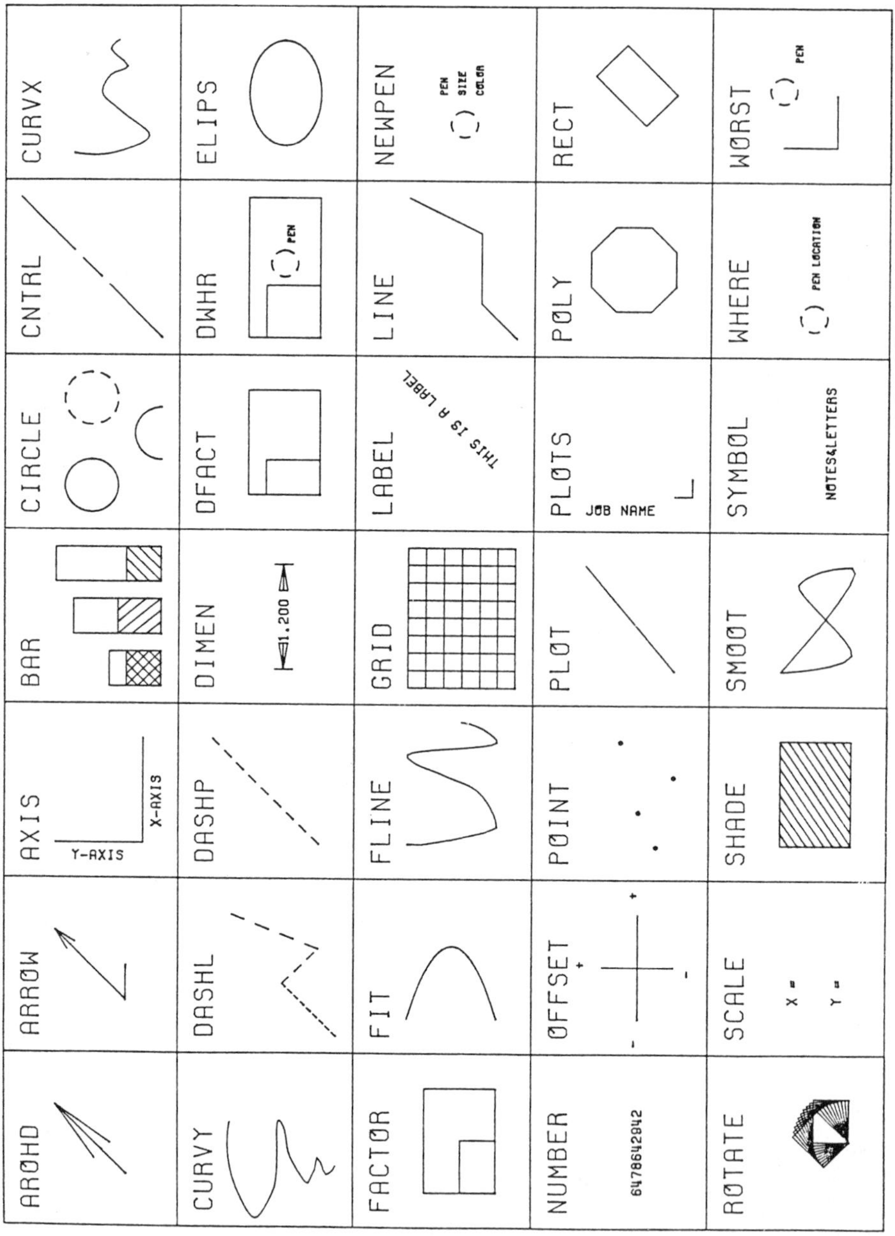

Figure 2.9 Complete graphic outputs from all geometric construction subroutines used on a CalComp device.

DASH(X,Y,DL)

This subroutine displays a dashed line to be used for hidden lines, phantom lines, breaks, or broken lines. It is used within a program as:

CALL DASH(X,Y,DL)

Two variations of this subroutine are offered, DASHP, as described above, and DASHL, which draws several line segments. Naturally an array of data points must be read into DASH for more than a single dashed line to be drawn. NPTS stands for the number of points to be connected, while INC is the increment between array elements. The arrays must be dimensioned with at least NPTS + two elements. DASHL does not provide for varying dash lengths. A dashed line with dashes approximately 0.1 inch long is drawn connecting sequential points in the array. Coding is optimized so that plotting may either begin at the first point and progress forward or begin at the last point and progress backward. If scaling is not required, the designer must place the appropriate minimum and delta values in the specified elements of the arrays. These values should be 0. and 1. and would appear as the last values in the delta arrays.

DASHL is so hard to use that most designers have resorted to the complete use of DASHP and enclosing it in a DO loop, which does the same graphic routines. Because of this the P has been dropped, and the hidden line routine has become DASH out of common usage. Table 2.2 illustrates the three uses of the subroutine.

DIMEN(X,Y,DIME,THETA,SCALE)

This subroutine will draw a complete dimension line including arrowheads and extension lines as shown in Figure 2.9. The dimension line may be rotated from 0 to 360 degrees counterclockwise from the X axis. This subroutine is used at every angle of THETA, as might be expected; therefore care should be taken in selecting X and Y when rotating. DIME is the size to be dimensional and SCALE is the scale of the drawing.

DFACT(XFACT,YFACT)

This subroutine may be used to expand a drawing in either the X or Y direction if XFACT or YFACT is greater than 1. If either variable is less than 1., the drawing is reduced. This is an important concept, as an ellipse can be plotted by changing one of the CIRCL dimensions. In addition, many display techniques on graphic CRTs use this technique for fitting larger data on a small screen size.

Table 2.2 Direct Comparison of Extended Graphics for Computer-Aided Engineering Graphics (DASH)

Mainframe-FORTRAN	Mini-FORTRAN	Micro-BASIC	
SUBROUTINE DASH(X,Y,DL)	SUBROUTINE DASH(X,Y,TL,DL,THETA)	5000	REM SUBROUTINE DASH
C----DASH MOVES THE PEN OF A PLOTTER OR	CALL PLOT(X,Y,3)	5005	READ #3;X,Y,P,D,T
C----THE BEAM OF A CRT IN A DASHED LINE	X1=X	5010	PRINT USING 9901;X,Y
C----DEFINED BY THE ENDING POINT OF THE	Y1=Y	5015	LET X1=X
C----LINE (X,Y) AND BY THE LENGTH OF	THETA=THETA*.017453	5020	LET Y1=Y
C----EACH OF THE DASHES (DL).	M=(TL/DL)/3.	5025	LET T=T*.017453
C	DO 100 I=1,M	5030	LET M=(P/D)/3.
		5035	FOR I=1 TO M
CALL WHERE(XT,YT,ST)	TCOS=DL*COS(THETA)	5040	LET TC=D*COS(T)
C----COMPUTE DELTA X AND Y	TSIN=DL*SIN(THETA)	5045	LET TS=D*SIN(T)
DX=X-XT	X1=TCOS+X1	5050	LET X1=TC+X1
DY=Y-YT	Y1=TSIN+Y1	5055	LET Y1=TS+Y1
DS=DL	CALL PLOT(X1,Y1,2)	5060	PRINT USING 9902; X1,Y1
IC=2	X1=TCOS+X1	5065	LET X1=TC+X1
C----COMPUTE LENGTH OF DASHED LINE	Y1=TSIN+Y1	5070	LET Y1=TS+Y1
S=SQRT(DX*DX+DY*DY)	CALL PLOT(X1,Y1,3)	5075	PRINT USING 9901;X1,Y1
IF(S-.02*ST) 6,10,6	X1=TCOS+X1		

```
10   DS=DS/S
C----TEST IF DASHED LINE LESS THAN DL
     IF(DS-.5) 2,2,7
7    DS=.5
2    DX=DX*DS
     DY=DY*DS
     S=DS
     ST=ABS(DX)-ABS(DY)
     IF(ST) 3,4,4
3    S=DY
4    ST=ABS(S/DS)-ABS(S)
     DS=ABS(S)
5    XT=XT+DX
     YT=YT+DY
     ST=ST-DS
     CALL PLOT(XT,YT,IC)
     IC=5-IC
     IF(ST) 6,6,5
6    CALL PLOT(X,Y,IC)
     RETURN
     END


     Y1=TSIN+Y1
100  CALL PLOT(X1,Y1,2)
     RETURN
     END


5080  LET X1=TC+X1
5085  LET Y1=TS+Y1
5090  PRINT USING 9902;X1,Y1
5095  NEXT I
5100  RETURN
```

DWHR(X,Y,XFACT,YFACT)

This routine is used after DFACT has changed the axis proportions to return the pen to locations X and Y. It does not break the ratios set for each axis, but after they are set, PLOT will function under DFACT instead of plotter coordinates. DFACT will affect all grpahic subroutines following it in the program. Therefore if a reduction of .5 has been called for DFACT, only another call of 2. will return the plotter to full size (see Figure 2.9).

ELIPS(X,Y,RMAJ,RMIN,THETA,SANG,EANG,IPEN)

The graphic subroutine ELIPS is similar to CIRCL in that an ellipse or an elliptical arc may be drawn. X and Y are the starting point locations on the major diameter of the ellipse. RMAJ and RMIN are the lengths of the major and minor radii of the elliptical arc. THETA allows an angle of rotation to be read into the subroutine. The angle of rotation is counterclockwise from the X axis. SANG and EANG are the angles, in degrees with respect to THETA, of the arc's starting and ending points. IPEN is a pen code and is considered like PLOT in that the integer 2 is pen down to the starting point X and Y; while integer 3 is pen up (see Figure 2.9).

FACTOR(SIZE)

This subroutine enables the designer to enlarge or reduce the size of the completed plot. Both the lettering and the plotted points are changed according to the factor SIZE. If SIZE is 1., no modification takes place. Less than 1. causes reduction, while greater than 1. will result in enlargements. Remember that all plotter subroutines following FACTOR will be affected. See DFACT for changes.

FIT(X1,Y1,X2,Y2,X3,Y3)

This subroutine generates a semihyperbolic fit using three given points. It was written to replace the manual method of sum of the squares and the use of a french curve. If the three points chosen are impossible to fit by this method, the routine draws straight-line segments.

FLINE(XARAY,YARAY,NPTS,INC,LINTYP,INTEQ)

This subroutine is used in the construction of engineering graphs and charts due mainly to its ability to plot data points from an array and annotate the points with centered symbols. XARAY and YARAY are the names of the arrays containing the data to be plotted as the abscissas and ordinates. NPTS is the number of data points to be plotted in the graph, and INC is the increment between elements in the array.

LINTYP stands for line type and is used with INTEQ, the integer equivalent, to annotate the graph. The following inputs may be used:

LINTYP = 0: A line is plotted between point.
LINTYP = 1: A line is plotted with a symbol at every data point.
LINTYP = 2: A line is plotted with a symbol at every second data point.
LINTYP =N: A line is plotted with a symbol according to N points.

INTEQ contains the designer's choice of symbols to be displayed on the graph line.

GRID(X,Y,DX,NXSP,NYSP)

The GRID routine draws a linear grid of any size. X and Y are the coordinates of the grids lower left corner. DX stands for delta X and is the size of each grid along the X axis of the engineering drawings. DY is similar for the Y direction. NXSP stands for the number of X spaces, while NYSP stands for the number of Y spaces. This determines the total area to be gridded.

LABEL(X,Y,X2,Y2,IBCD,NCHAR,HT,ISIDE,DSTFLN,FPN,NDEC)

This rather impressive subroutine is very useful for automatically centering notes on drawings. The size of the characters is adjusted to fit the space allowed. These two features set LABEL aside from SYMBOL and make it extremely useful. X and Y are the coordinates of the starting point, and X2 and Y2 are the coordinates of the ending point. IBCD is the string of characters to be plotted. NCHAR stands for the number of characters in the string, while HT stands for the height of the desired characters. Depending on the data values of X, Y and X2, Y2, a positioning code is needed for clockwise and counterclockwise reading; it is the integer 1 placed in ISIDE for clockwise and the integer 2 placed in ISIDE for counterclockwise reading. DSTFLN is the length from X, Y to X2, Y2. FPN stands for floating-point number and is used whenever numeric characters are to be plotted instead of alpha. NDEC is the number of places to the right of the decimal point in FPN.

LINE(XAR,YAR,X,Y,NPT)

A simple routine for connecting a number of points with a line is often needed in geometric construction work. This routine is much simpler than FLINE and is used more often in engineering drafting and graphics. XAR and YAR contain the data points to be connected, while X and Y allow the designer to place the construction anywhere she wants the graphics to appear. NPT is the total number of points to be displayed. Careful study of the subroutine listing will indicate that NPT is needed to create the DO loop for execution of the plotter pen.

NEWPEN(IPEN)

This subroutine is basic to every office and allows the designer to change pen sizes or colors during the execution of a drawing. It is important that the rules for proper presentation be followed for automated drafting sheets also. IPEN is an integer code that changes the pen. The coding varies widely from one operation to another, but usually a single integer code is worked out for ball-point pen or liquid ink and a change of colors from black to blue to red to green.

NUMBER(X,Y,SIZE,FLNUM,THETA,NDIGIT)

This subroutine is used to provide numerical annotation for the engineering drawing in a fashion similar to that of subroutine LABEL. The floating-point number is converted to its fixed-point decimal equivalent, and then the digits are individually plotted using the SYMBOL routine. X and Y are lower left-hand coordinates for the numbers to be plotted. The height of the number is placed in HT. FLNUM stands for the floating-point number to be plotted. ANGLE is the degree of rotation at which the numbers are to be drawn. NDIGIT stands for the number of digits to be plotted.

OFFSET(XOFF,XSCALE,YOFF,YSCALE)

This subroutine is used to set the offset and scaling factors to be used with other plotting routines. The coordinates for a particular point using this subroutine are computed as X=(X-XOFF)/XSCALE and Y=(YOFF)/YSCALE.

POINT(XARRAY,YARRAY)

This subroutine is identical to LINE except the pen up command is used between data points.

PLOT(X,Y,IPEN)

As indicated in Table 2.3, this subroutine is the most basic routine controlling the movement of the pen. It is used to reposition the pen, draw straight lines between two points, or to reset the plotter origin. X and Y are the coordinates to which the pen will move. IPEN determines whether the pen is up or down during the move and whether or not the origin is to be reset. A +2 argument value causes the pen to draw a line. A +3 will produce a move, while +12 and +13 move the pen

Table 2.3 Direct Comparison of Extended Graphics Routines for Computer-Aided Engineering Graphics (PLOT)

Mainframe-FORTRAN	Mini-FORTRAN	Micro-BASIC

SUBROUTINE PLOT(X,Y,IPEN)
C----PLOT MOVES THE PEN OF A PLOTTER OR
C----THE BEAM OF A CRT TO A NEW POSITION
C----WHICH DISPLAYS A LINE OR SPACE ON
C----THE OUTPUT DEVICE.
C
C----PARAMETER DESCRIPTIONS:
C---X THE X-COORDINATE OF THE FINAL
C---   DISPLAY POSITION.
C---Y THE Y-COORDINATE OF THE FINAL
C---   DISPLAY POSITION.
C
C----IPEN
C---   IF IABS(IPEN) .EQ. 2 A LINE IS
C---   DISPLAYED.
C---   IF IABS(IPEN) .EQ. 3 A SPACE IS
C---   DISPLAYED.
C---   IF IABS(IPEN) .EQ. 999 THE PLOT
C---   IS TERMINATED.
C---   A -IPEN DEFINES A NEW ORIGIN.
IF(IPEN.NE.999) GO TO 100
C----TERMINATE ALL PLOTTING
CALL DRAW(0,0,0,999)
RETURN
100 LINE=0
IF (IABS(IPEN).EQ.2) LINE = 9
C----SET KORG TO 1000 IF RE-ORIGIN REQUIRED
KORG=0
IF(IPEN.LT.0) KORG=1000
C----SET KORG TO 9000 IF END OF PLOT
IF (IPEN.EQ.999) KORG=9000
C----DRAW THE LINE
CALL DRAW(X,Y,1,KORG+LINE)
RETURN
END
	SUBROUTINE PLOT(X,Y,IPEN)
	C----THIS ROUTINE CONVERTS MAINFRAME PLOT
	C----COMMANDS INTO THE PLOT-10 FORMAT FOR
	C----DISPLAY ON THE TEKTRONIX 4010 DVST.
	IX=X*130.
	IY=Y*130.
	IF(IPEN.EQ.3) CALL MOVABS(IX,IY)
	IF(IPEN.EQ.2) CALL DRWABS(IX,IY)
	IF(IPEN.EQ.-3)CALL MOVREL(IX,IY)
	IF(IPEN.EQ.-2)CALL DRWREL(IX,IY)
	RETURN
	END
		2000 REM SUBROUTINE PLOT
		2005 READ #3:X,Y,P$
		2010 IF P$[1,1]="U" THEN 2025
		2015 PRINT USING 9902:X,Y
		2020 RETURN
		2025 PRINT USING 9901:X,Y
		2030 RETURN
		  : :
		  : :
		9901 REM PEN IS UP, BEAM OFF
		9902 REM PEN IS DOWN, BEAM ON

adjusting for the last call to OFFSET. The negative sequence, -2, -2, -12, -13, is the same as the positive, but a new origin is set at X, Y. If IPEN = 999, the plotter is turned off after move. This should be the last call for a program.

PLOTS

This subroutine is used to initialize all of the variables used by the several plotting subroutines and to return the pen to the HOME position. This subroutine should be the first called and should be called only once during a program's execution. All of the arguments are dummy arguments; they are included solely for compatibility with older series subroutines (see Table 2.3).

POLY(X,Y,SLEN,SN,THETA)

POLY is used to draw equilateral polygons. X and Y are the coordinates of the polygon's starting point. SLEN stands for side length and is the length of one of the polygon sides. SN is the number of sides of the polygon, while THETA is the angle, in degrees, of the first side of the polygon.

RECT(X,Y,HT,WD,THETA,IPEN)

Subroutine RECT has been written to draw rectangles at starting points X and Y. WD units wide and HT units tall. THETA allows the rectangle to be drawn at an angle on the drawing. This subroutine conforms to computer science use of (XPAGE, YPAGE, HEIGHT, WIDTH, ANGLE, IPEN) argument lists as shown in Table 2.4.

ROTATE(X,Y,Z)

This construction subroutine allows the designer to read in 3-dimensional data points and plot them as 2-dimensional plots. A simple rotation is projected by plotting X and Y.

SCALE(AR,AXL,NPT,INC)

This subroutine is used to scale the array of data points (AR) and determine the scaling factors necessary for the data points to be plotted. Two values are computed by this routine: (1) the beginning value to be plotted, and (2) the increment representing a unit change in the X and Y directions. The scaling factor is roughly computed as MAX VALUE-MIN VALUE/AXIS length. These two computed quantities are used by subroutines AXIS and LINE. AXL stands for axis length, while NPT is the number of points in AR. INC is the repeat cycle for the array of values. If INC = 1, all points are used. If INC is less than 0, the MIN value is the starting value, and if INC is greater than 0, the MAX value is used.

Table 2.4 Direct Comparison of Extended Graphics Routines for Computer-Aided Engineering Graphics (RECT)

Mainframe-FORTRAN	Mini-FORTRAN	Micro-BASIC
SUBROUTINE RECT(X,Y,H,W,TH,IV)	SUBROUTINE RECT(X,Y,W,H,TH)	3000 REM SUBROUTINE RECT
C----RECT MOVES THE PEN OF A PLOTTER OR	THETA=(3.14159/180.)*TH	3005 READ #3;X,Y,W,H,T
C----THE BEAM OF A CRT TO A NEW POSITION	A=X+COS(THETA)*WD	3010 LET T=(3.14159/180)*T
C----DEFINED BY THE ARGUMENTS (X&Y) AND	B=Y+SIN(THETA)*WD	3015 LET A=X+COS(T)*W
C----THEN DISPLAYS A RECTANGLE W UNITS	C=A-SIN(THETA)*HT	3020 LET B=Y+SIN(T)*W
C----WIDE AND H UNITS HIGH. THE IMAGE	D=B+COS(THETA)*HT	3025 LET C=A-SIN(T)*H
C----MAY BE ROTATED TH DEGREES, WHILE	E=C-COS(THETA)*WD	3030 LET D=B+COS(T)*H
C----IV CONTAINS THE IABS(IPEN) VALUE	F=D-SIN(THETA)*WD	3035 LET E=C-COS(T)*W
C----OF 2 OR 3.	C----DISPLAY THE RECTANGLE	3040 LET F=D-SIN(T)*W
C	CALL PLOT(X,Y,3)	3045 PRINT USING 9901;X,Y
THETA=TH/57.2958	CALL PLOT(A,B,2)	3050 PRINT USING 9902;A,B
XS=SIN(THETA)	CALL PLOT(C,D,2)	3055 PRINT USING 9902;C,D
XC=COS(THETA)	CALL PLOT(E,F,2)	3060 PRINT USING 9902;E,F
CALL PLOT(X,Y,IV)	CALL PLOT(X,Y,2)	3065 PRINT USING 9902;X,Y
X1=X-H*XS	RETURN	3070 RETURN
Y1=Y+H*XC	END	
C----DISPLAY BASE OF RECTANGLE		
CALL PLOT(X1,Y1,2)		
X2=X1+W*XC		
Y2=Y1+W*XS		
C----DISPLAY ROTATED SIDE OF RECT		
CALL PLOT(X2,Y2,2)		
X3=X+W*XC		
Y3=Y+W*XS		
C----DISPLAY TOP OF RECTANGLE		
CALL PLOT(X3,Y3,2)		
C----RETURN TO STARTING POSITION		
CALL PLOT(X,Y,2)		
RETURN		
END		

SHADE(X,Y,XARAY,YARAY,DLIN,THETA,NPTS,INC,NPTA,INCA)

This geometric construction technique draws section lines for any-shaped areas. X and Y are the lower data points of the area to be sectioned, while XARAY, YARAY are the upper points. TLEN is the length of the area along the X axis, while THT is the Y length of the area. DLIN stands for spacing between section lines. THETA is the angle of the section lines, NPTS is the number of data points in X, Y, and NPTA is the number on XARAY, YARAY. INC and INCA is the increment for X, Y and XARAY, YARAY.

SMOOT(X,Y,IPEN)

The SMOOT subroutine automates the use of a french curve. It will display a smooth curve through a set of data points. It does this by using a modified spline-fitting technique. The subroutine receives a single coordinate pair on each call and accumulates the pairs until it has received a minimum of three calls as:

CALL SMOOT(X,Y,IPEN) where IPEN = 0
CALL SMOOT(X,Y,IPEN) where IPEN = -2
CALL SMOOT(X,Y,IPEN) where IPEN = -24

No fewer than three calls are used. However, any number of IPEN = -2's may be used after IPEN = 0 and before IPEN = -24 as illustrated in Figure 2.10.

SYMBOL(X,Y,SIZE,MESAGE,THETA,NCHAR)

This construction technique is used to place notes on drawings. It may be used to write text such as titles and legends or to draw a single character centered at X and Y. The available characters are the same as LABEL. The height of the characters is stored in SIZE and is 1/1. This includes the space between letters. Therefore the length of a note used on a drawing can be found by NCHAR*SIZE. MESAGE is the desired character string to be plotted, and THETA allows the designer to rotate the plotted message at any desired angle. NCHAR stands for the number of characters contained in MESAGE.

WHERE(X,Y,FACTOR)

The designer often needs to return a pen location from a construction subroutine and reset a scale. This can be done with WHERE. The coordinates of the current pen position are returned to X and Y. The current scale factor as set by PLOTS or FACTOR is returned as FACTOR inside WHERE.

WOFST(XOFF,XSCALE,YOFF,YSCALE)

The last geometric construction subroutine used is similar to WHERE except that it returns the current values of the X and Y offset and scaling factors, XOFF =

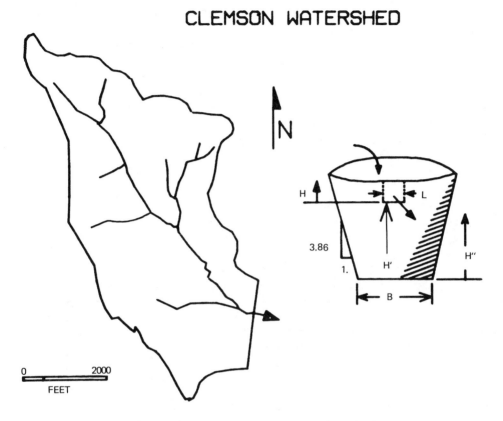

Figure 2.10 Example of CALL SMOOT used in a graphics display.

current offset value, XSCALE = X scaling factor, YOFF = current Y offset, and YSCALE = Y scaling factor.

SELECTING VIEWS

Now that the computer contains the instructions for geometric constructions, a procedure for developing the views of an engineering drawing may be employed.

This technique, called subpicturing, is one of the basic methods whereby a designer may select views for a drawing. All of the graphics conventions for the selection of working views still hold. The normal viewing surface is selected for the front view. One or more adjacent views are then selected. Depending on the complexity of the object to be drawn, two or three views are selected, the most common selection being the horizontal, frontal, and profile views. Designers use planning forms for ease of subpicturing. Figures 2.11 and 2.12 illustrate two types of planning sheets. A rough sketch is prepared on the coordinate grid provided. Many times the designer will sketch a line, stop and write the construction geometry call statement which will provide that line, and code it in the space provided. The sketch allows the designer to "play computer" or display the computer instruction for error sensing.

In general, the following is the suggested procedure for selecting views. Drawings and graphs, like computer listings, require some planning to achieve a pleasing and effective appearance.

1. The initial position of the pen when plotting operation begins is assumed to be the origin (X,Y=0.0). This location is set by CALL PLOTS or CALL BEGIN. A programmer can also select another location anywhere on the plotter surface (CALL PLOT(XLINE, YLINE, -3)). When selecting views for an engineering drawing, the obvious thing is to make sure that when summed the distances from plotter origin to drawing origin, the size of views, and the distance between views will fit the display device selected. In the case of a plotter containing a roll of drafting paper, the length of the paper roll determines the height of the drawing. The Y axis of the plotter is limited to the size of paper roll selected. If 18-inch paper is selected, only about 16 inches will be used for display purposes. The inch at the top and bottom is used by the plotter and is not available for plotting the drawing. The initialing CALL PLOTS sets the starting position; if the programmer called for a new origin, subtract this amount from the remaining space of 16 inches. Now add the height of the front view, the space between the front and top views, and the depth of the top view. Test this distance against the space available. A larger roll size may be needed, or the drawing may be scaled to fit the space.

2. The X axis is controlled by a rotating drum, the X direction of the flat bed, or the size of the CRT. In the case above the roll of paper provides for drawings up to 144 inches, or J size drawings. Most drawings will fit the X direction easier than they will in the Y axis.

3. Determine if a CALL FACTOR is needed. Remember this subroutine reduces both the X and Y dimensions. If the Y direction needs to be reduced to fit the roll and X is left full size, then CALL DFACT(1.,REDUCE) should be called after CALL PLOTS. REDUCE should be less than 1.

AUTOMATED DRAFTING PROGRAMMING RECORD

ENGINEERING GRAPHICS WORKSHEET

Tape No. _____

Prepared by _____

Checked by _____

Date _____

PLOT DESCRIPTION _____

PLOT NUMBER _____ SHEET NUMBER _____ OPERATION NUMBER _____

OPERATION DESCRIPTION _____

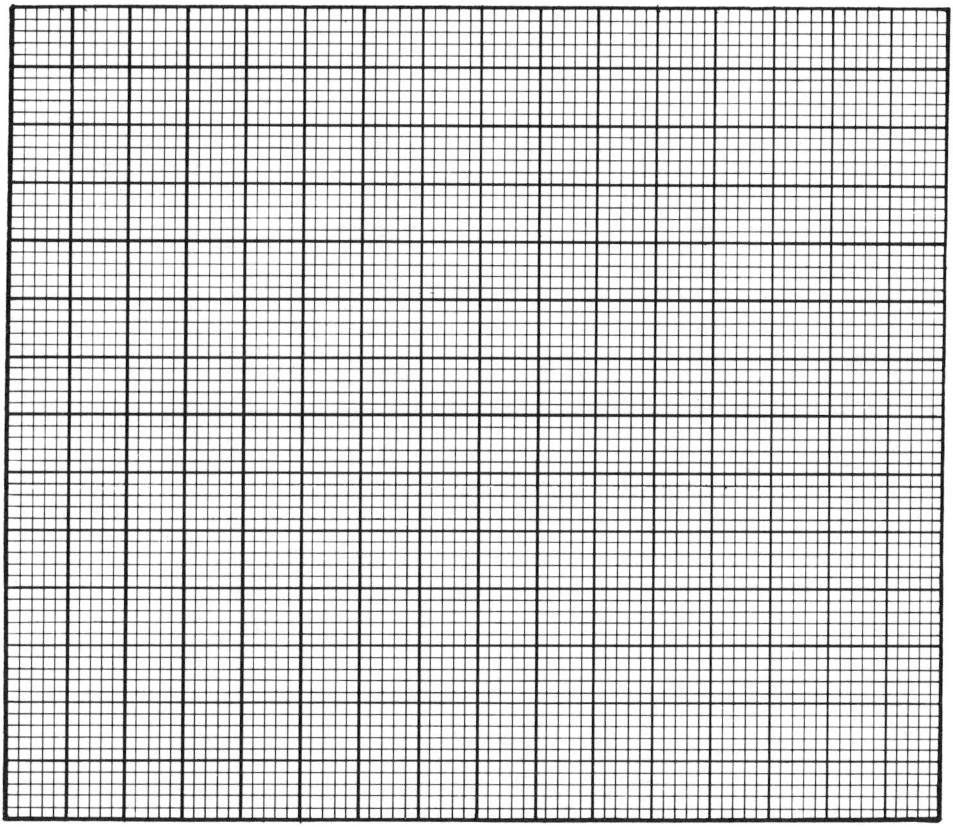

_____

_____

Figure 2.11 Size A coordinate worksheet used to digitize a pattern.

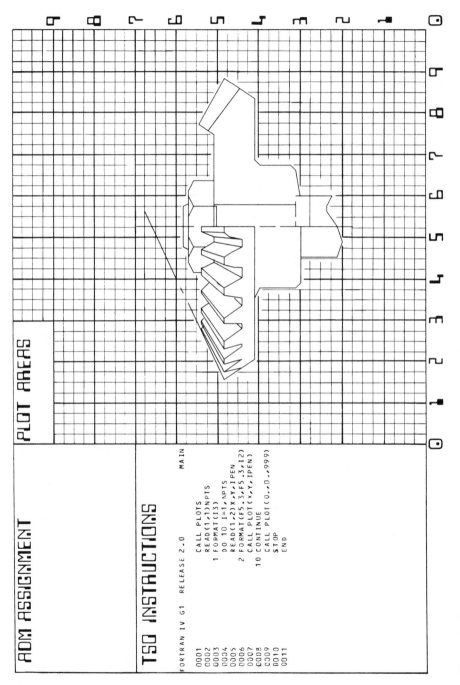

Figure 2.12 Size B worksheet allows coordination of digitizing and computer instructions.

NUMBER OF VIEWS AND SPACING

The alternative to subpicturing for the selection of orthographic views would be the use of an automatic view generator. This program would allow the designer to choose the views desired. The spacing between views would be variable so that different arrangements and spacings could be tried. This method of view selection requires that the drawing data be provided for the program. Remember that in the case of geometric construction for views only the starting points of figures need be known. The program method of view selection is very fast, but the geometry must be fairly simple, usually straight-line segments only. Figure 2.13 is an example of a program which reads digitized data to draw the frontal view and uses geometric construction subroutines to draw the horizontal.

Usually the two methods are not mixed. The drawing data are prepared as a series of points, each having X, Y, and Z coordinates. The number of these points to be plotted is read into the program first. The number of pen movements required to draw the object or connect the points is read next. The number of views to be drawn is specified along with the space provided for each view. The point coordinates are used by the program to draw the various views. A frontal view can be constructed by plotting the X and Y coordinates, while the horizontal view would require the X and Z coordinates. To plot a profile the Z and then Y coordinates are used. Figure 2.14 illustrates the typical type of input needed.

Figure 2.15 is a simple program to plot a three-view drawing. Note that the number of views is set, while the number of data points is variable up to 50. The space between views can be read into XTRANS and YTRANS.

SELECTING A SCALE

The geometric subroutine SCALE checks the entire list of commands and converts or scales the list to fit a particular unit size. You will note that the number of units called for in the subroutine SCALE was 10. In other words, the dimensions of the object to be represented in the engineering drawing could be any number of units but would be plotted a maximum of 10. Each dimension was scaled in proportion to a maximum of 10.

A unit may be set equal to an English inch or a convenient metric unit. Nearly 50 percent of all plotting is now being done on a metric scale. American manufacturers of automated drafting hardware are supplying either method of scaling. Scaling does not mean the conversion from English to metric measurement. Scaling means what it has always meant, the ability to represent large "real-world" sizes on a small piece of paper called an engineering drawing. The use of the computer has made scaling easier. The architect or engineer may think in full sizes which are related to the design and not have to worry if they will fit on the plotter.

```
C   ***************************************************************
C   *   THIS PROGRAM WILL DISPLAY A SET OF DIGITIZED POINTS ON A   *
C   *   PLOTTER OR A DVST.  THE OBJECT IS A FRONTAL VIEW OF A      *
C   *   BEVEL GEAR.  THE HORIZONTAL VIEW IS CONSTRUCTED FROM SUB-  *
C   *   ROUTINES MODIFIED FOR MAINFRAME, MINI, OR MICRO COMPUTER.  *
C   *                                                              *
C   ***************************************************************
C   ENTER PLOTS FOR PLOTTER OR INITT FOR DVST
        CALL PLOTS
        READ(1,*)NPTS
        DO 10 I=1,NPTS
          READ(1, *)X,Y,IPEN
   10 CALL PLOT(X,Y,IPEN)
C   END OF DIGITIZED POINTS, BEGINNING OF GEOMETRIC CONSTRUCTIONS
        CALL RECT(0.,.2,10.,16.,0.,3)
        CALL RECT(11.,.2,2.7,5.,0.,3)
        CALL SYMBOL(11.5,.5,.3,'POINT PLOTTING,0.,14)
        CALL PLOT(11.,1.1,3)
        CALL PLOT(16.,1.1,2)
        CALL CIRCL(9.625,6.2,0.,360.,3.75,3.75,.5)
        CALL CIRARC(5.875,6.2,2.25,0.,31,6.)
        CALL CIRARC(5.875,6.2,.5,0.,31,6.)
        CALL CIRARC(5.875,6.2,.61,0.,31,6.)
        CALL CIRARC(5.875,6.2,1.25,0.,31,6.)
        CALL PLOT(4.750,6.2,3)
        CALL PLOT(4.750,6.862,2)
        CALL PLOT(5.375,7.425,2)
        CALL PLOT(6.375,7.425,2)
        CALL PLOT(7.,6.862,2)
        CALL PLOT(7.,6.2,2)
        CALL PLOT(9.0,0.,999)
        STOP
        END
```

Figure 2.13 Computer program for accepting digitized points and plotting them as an orthographic view.

```
NUMBER OF POINTS TO BE PLOTTED = 17
NUMBER OF PEN MOVEMENTS REQ'D  = 36
NUMBER OF VIEWS TO BE DISPLAYED=  3

SPACE PROVIDED FOR EACH VIEW   = 6.
```

POINT COORDINATES

X	Y	Z
0.0	0.0	0.0
3.000	0.0	0.0
3.000	0.0	1.500
0.0	0.0	1.500
0.0	1.000	1.500
1.000	1.000	1.500
1.000	2.000	1.500
2.000	2.000	1.500
2.000	1.000	1.500
3.000	1.000	1.500
3.000	2.000	0.0
2.000	2.000	0.0
0.0	2.000	0.0
0.0	2.000	1.000
1.000	2.000	1.000
1.000	1.000	1.000
0.0	1.000	1.000

Figure 2.14 Typical computer format for the arrangement of input data for automatic spacing of views on the drawing sheet.

```
C     ****************************************************************
C     *                                                              *
C     *   AUTOMATIC VIEW GENERATOR FOR OUTPUT ON A DIRECT VIEW STORAGE *
C     *   TUBE OR ELECTROSTATIC PLOTTER.  CHANGE CALL INITT TO CALL    *
C         PLOTS IN THE PROGRAM FOR PLOTTER OUTPUT.                     *
C     *                                                              *
C     ****************************************************************
C     PROVIDE FOR FIFTY DATA POINTS TO BE STORED INSIDE PROGRAM MEMORY
          DIMENSION X(50),Y(50),Z(50),IPEN(50),XPLOT(50),YPLOT(50)
C     SELECT DVST OR PLOTTER COMMANDS
          CALL INITT(240)
C     SELECT READ STATEMENT FOR IBM HOST PROCESSOR
          READ(1,*) NDATA
C     NDATA IS THE NUMBER OF DATA POINTS TO BE STORED AND DISPLAYED
          READ(1,*) XTRANS,YTRANS
C     XTRANS,YTRANS ARE THE SPACES BETWEEN VIEWS -- NOW READ DATA POINTS
          DO 5 I=1,NDATA
        5 READ(1,*) X(I),Y(I),Z(I),IPEN(I)
C     MOVE TO POSITION OF FRONTAL VIEW
          CALL PLOT(.5,.5,-3)
C     NOW DISPLAY THE FRONT VIEW
          DO 10 J=1,NDATA
       10 CALL PLOT(X(J),Y(J),IPEN(J))
C     NOW DISPLAY THE TOP VIEW
          DO 20 K=1,NDATA
          Z(K)=Z(K)+YTRANS
       20 CALL PLOT(X(K),Z(K),IPEN(K))
C NOW DISPLAY THE SIDE VIEW
          DO 30 L=1,NDATA
          Z(L)=Z(I)-YTRANS+XTRANS
       30 CALL PLOT(Z(L),Y(L),IPEN(L))
          CALL FINITT(0,0)
          STOP
          END
```

Figure 2.15 Example of an automatic view generator for input data to display orthographic views on a direct view storage tube.

The scale is selected to match the physical limits of the display device. In the case of the interactive plotter a plotting area of 10 units by 10 units was set inside SCALE. It can easily be seen that other applications of scaling would require similar routines. Variations of SCALE have now been developed to determine scale factors of a data array. SCALG, for instance, is used for data on a logarithmic scale.

STANDARD TEMPLATE PARTS

One of the important features of many of the graphics systems available today is the ability to store standard template objects. In the electronics field schematic symbols are stored in memory and used as subpicture elements. Figure 2.16 illustrates the use of these to create a drawing. Much developmental work has been done in the electronics area. Mechanical work has included the standardization of

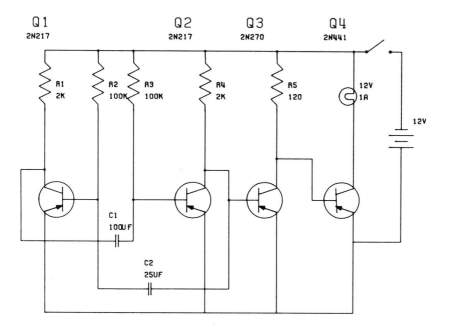

Figure 2.16 Example of an electronics schematic diagram displayed from template symbols.

piping symbols so that similar drawings can be done in the hydraulics and pneumatics areas. All the engineering documentations that require control devices can be preprogrammed and used in this manner. In addition to these obvious areas the following template parts have been developed:

Air traffic control
Aircraft cockpit design
Aircraft seating arrangement design
Architectural design
Automatic wiring lists
Biomedical symbology
Cabinet and panel layout
Calculation display of volumes
Chemical research molecular display
Circuit analysis and layout
Communications layout
Costume design
Display of radar maps
ECO (engineering change order)/
   reporting forms
Engineering schematics
Exploration of minerals
Flight simulation
Forecasting weather
Geophysics
Human engineering profiles
Industrial design
Integrated circuit
Laboratory and production charts

Management information graphs
Manufacturing diagrams
Mechanical and thermal networks
Monitoring of satellites
Music and voice patterns
N/C symbology
Nuclear modeling
Ore location mapping
Pattern recognition
PERT charts/CPM (critical path
   method) diagrams
Pharmacology
Power plant simulation
Printed circuits
Que/solar sampling
Sheet-metal layout
Spectrometer display
Stock market
Topographical mapping
Trajectory mapping
Underseas mapping
Visual and plastic arts modeling
Wind tunnel sampling

It is beyond the scope of this book to include the theory for all of these template symbols for special fields. The reader should be aware that they exist and should not be surprised when another area is added to the list. The concept of a template part that can be moved from location to location on the engineering drawing is important. This concept works just like the drafter using a plastic template which contains guides for making certain symbols. The template may be moved, rotated to an angle, and even flipped over. The computer has the same capability but can normally generate an entire drawing in the same time it takes the drafter to draw one symbol. When designing a template for use, the programmer considers ease of use by a draftsperson or designer.

To put a template system in the drawing room, we must find a way to translate the designer's ideas or sketch directly to a finished drawing. In a search for such a means, we must also not overlook human considerations. Drafters and designers are not computer operators or computer programmers and resist any attempt to translate their art to the computer field. A more satisfactory approach might therefore be to conceive a system with which the draftsperson could communicate directly without recourse to computer languages or data processing. This can be done by the selection of template parts.

A template system having two modes of operation is usually used. The first, an on-line method, is intended to be operated by a drafter. This does not require knowledge of computers, their operation, or their programming. Further, no off-line computer processing or subsequent operations are involved. No magnetic tapes, or disks need be handled. No photographic processes are used. No off-line symbol or aperture preparation is required. The output from this system is a completed master tracing ready for blueprinting, microfilming, or filing.

The second method of operation provides for off-line preparation of a batch program. The formats of these programs are identical to those used in on-line operation, except the computer will not prompt or ask questions of the user. The off-line programs are fed to the self-contained template drafting master program. The template system consists of a plotter controlled by a real-time computer based on mini- or microcontrol. For operation of this system magnetic memory is added to the configuration. Prestored are complete descriptions of each template symbol to be used. Many symbols may be stored, each containing lines, circles, and alphanumeric characters.

ARRANGING THE PARTS ON A SHEET LAYOUT

Input to the template system for preparation of a finished ink drawing is a crudely drawn sketch preferably, but not necessarily, on 10 squares to the inch grid paper. This sketch is translated by the system operator into a series of coded commands. These commands are typed directly into the system via the keyboard when operating on-line, or they are read from disk for later drawing when operating off-line.

Template symbols are located by means of X-Y coordinates visually taken from the grid background. For sketches on plain paper a film grid overlay is used. A simplified language system provides for rapid specification of the type and location of each template symbol. All symbols are initially sequentially numbered and referenced as to template type and location. All further reference to a symbol for locating interconnecting lines or text messages can now be made by simply calling the symbol number. The computer will look up its type and location.

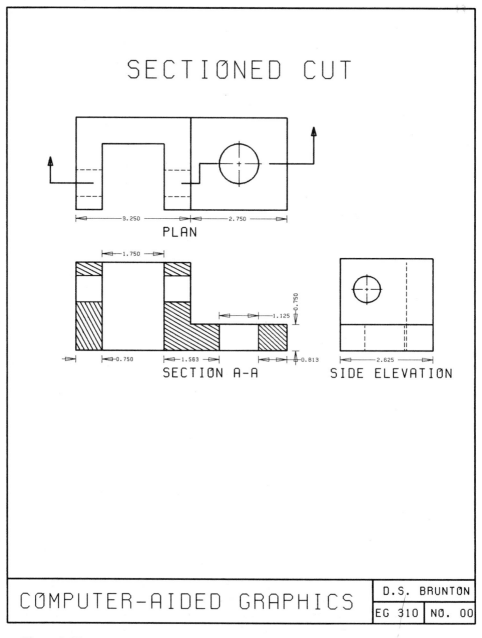

Figure 2.17 Use of template symbols, geometric constructions and automatic view generation techniques used throughout Chapter 2.

Upon completion of symbol entry the operator proceeds to enter all line data. Each line is quickly recorded and stored. Provision is included for lines to exactly butt on symbol terminals even though the template symbol was crudely drawn or inaccurately located. This is possible since the computer knows the exact location of each connection point of each symbol without regard to sketch accuracy. After the line work is completed, the operator starts on the last phase of the data preparation, text insertion. Text material includes symbol designation notes, dimensions, and any other alphanumeric data not previously included as part of a symbol. Text messages are entered via the keyboard at the drawing point indicated by a grid coordinate or by reference to a particular symbol point. Text may be called in a variety of sizes, and the message may be specified to be left, right, or centered on this position.

Plotting is begun as soon as data input is complete. Drawing time for an average B size drawing is about six seconds. The finished product will be a mechanically drawn vellum master with perfect symbology and with lettering quality superior to to LeRoy types, produced in a fraction of the time a skilled drafter would have required (see Figure 2.17).

THE COMPUTERIZED TITLE

With the knowledge of geometric constructions and computer subpicturing techniques a unique set of instructions for making a personalized title block can be stored in the computer. Title blocks are usually designed after a standard set by the user. There are military, government, company, and professional models to choose from. When designing a new company block a quick sketch is made on a coordinate work sheet. A storage label is chosen, usually TITLE, and the instructions are written for computer input. Figure 2.18 is a subroutine designed for student use. The student must provide the drawing number, the course number, the name of the student, and the title of the drawing.

The drawing number corresponds to the assignment number that the student is working on and must be changed each time the assignment is indexed. An assignment number is located below the name shown in Figure 2.19.

This technique is used to computerize the border line and title block for a size A drawing sheet. Size B sheets may be displayed by using the subroutine TITLEB shown in Figure 2.20.

The subroutine TITLEA or B is trial-run on the computer. A program must be written to call the subroutine:

```
CALL PLOTS
CALL TITLEA
CALL PLOT(0.,0.,999)
```

```
     STOP
     END
```

This simple program is placed before the subroutine and read into the computer. The computer interprets the program and sends the plotter the results, as shown in Figure 2.21.

```
C    ********************************************************************
C    *                                                                  *
C    *  SUBROUTINE FOR SIZE A FORMAT, STUDENT WORKSHEET TITLE BLOCK AND  *
C    *  NOTEBOOK PAGE LAYOUT.   THE STUDENT MUST SUPPLY NAME, COURSE NO. *
C    *  AND DRAWING NO. FROM THE DISPLAY PROGRAM WHICH CALLS THIS SUB-   *
C    *  ROUTINE.    CALL TITLEA                                          *
C    *                                                                  *
C    ********************************************************************
     SUBROUTINE TITLEA
     CALL RECT(.5,0.,10.5,8.5,0.,3)
     CALL PLOT(.5,.75,3)
     CALL PLOT(9.,.75,2)
     CALL PLOT(6.75,.75,3)
     CALL PLOT(6.75,0.,2)
     CALL PLOT(6.75,.375,3)
     CALL PLOT(9.,.375,2)
     CALL PLOT(7.625,.375,3)
     CALL PLOT(7.625,0.,2)
     CALL SYMBOL(.75,.25,.25,'COMPUTER-AIDED GRAPHICS',0.,23)
     RETURN
     END
```

Figure 2.18 Subroutine listing for computerized title block. The command CALL TITLEA, appears after the CALL PLOTS and automatically displays the border line and title block.

Figure 2.19 Display of CALL TITLEA for a size A drawing sheet.

```
C     ********************************************************************
C     *                                                                  *
C     *  SUBROUTINE FOR SIZE B FORMAT, STUDENT TITLE BLOCK AND POSTER    *
C     *  PAGE LAYOUT.  THE STUDENT MUST SUPPLY NAME, COURSE NUMBER, A     *
C     *  DRAWING SCALE, DATE, AND TITLE OF THE DRAWING.  CALL TITLEB      *
C     *                                                                  *
C     ********************************************************************
      SUBROUTINE TITLEB
      CALL RECT(0.,0.,10.5,17.,0.,3)
      CALL RECT(0.,0.,.75,1.,0.,3)
      CALL RECT(1.,0.,.75,3.5,0.,3)
      CALL RECT(4.5,0.,.375,2.5,0.,3)
      CALL RECT(4.5,.375,.375,2.5,0.,3)
      CALL RECT(7.0,0.,.375,3.5,0.,3)
      CALL RECT(7.0,.375,.375,3.5,0.,3)
      CALL RECT(10.5,0.,.75,5.25,0.,3)
      CALL RECT(15.75,0.,.75,1.25,0.,3)
      CALL SYMBOL(.1,.1,.08,'DRAWING NO.',0.,12)
      CALL SYMBOL(1.875,.5,.09,'ENGINEERING GRAPHICS',0.,21)
      CALL SYMBOL(1.625,.3125,.1,'COLLEGE OF ENGINEERING',0.,24)
C     CALL SYMBOL(1.750,.1,.12,'CLEMSON UNIVERSITY',0.,19)
      CALL SYMBOL(4.625,.12,.1,'SCALE',0.,5)
      CALL SYMBOL(4.625,.45,.1,'DATE:',0.,5)
      CALL SYMBOL(7.125,.12,.1,'COURSE',0.,6)
      CALL SYMBOL(7.125,.45,.1,'DR. BY:',0.,7)
      CALL SYMBOL(12.625,.1,.1,'TITLE OF DRAWING',0.,18)
      CALL SYMBOL(16.25,.1,.1,'GRADE',0.,5)
      RETURN
      END
```

Figure 2.20 Subroutine listing for size B title block and border line.

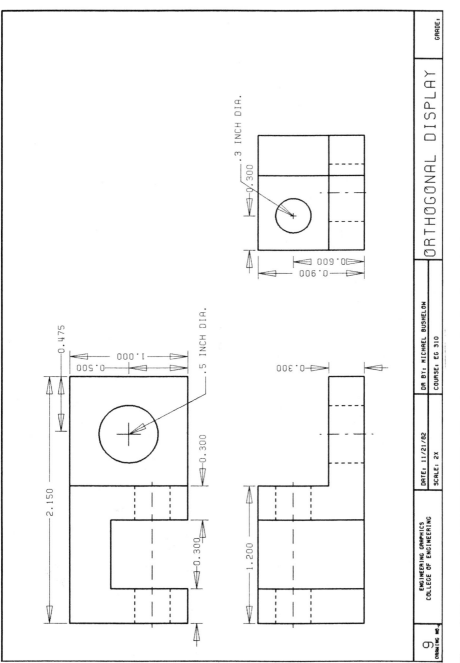

Figure 2.21 Example of CALL TITLEB with main program for drawing output.

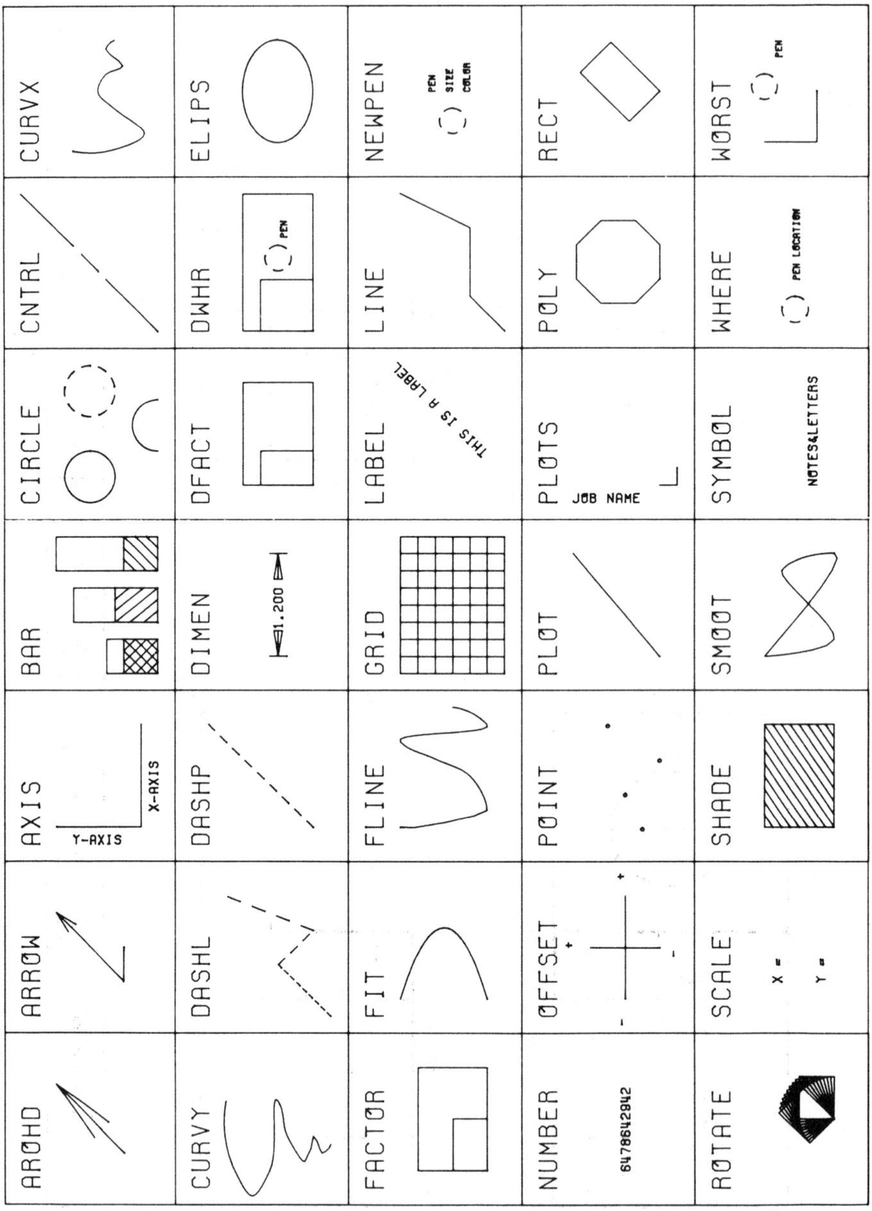
ARØHD
ARRØW
AXIS
Y-AXIS
X-AXIS
BAR
CIRCLE
CNTRL
CURVX
CURVY
DASHL
DASHP
DIMEN
1.200
DFACT
DWHR
PEN
ELIPS
FACTØR
FIT
FLINE
GRID
LABEL
THIS IS A LABEL
LINE
NEWPEN
PEN
SIZE
CØLØR
NUMBER
6478642842
ØFFSET
PØINT
PLØT
PLØTS
JØB NAME
PØLY
RECT
RØTATE
SCALE
X =
Y =
SHADE
SMØØT
SYMBØL
NØTES&LETTERS
WHERE
PEN LØCATIØN
WØRST
PEN

Exercise 1

EXERCISES

1. On a size A coordinate work sheet (shown in Figure 2.11), prepare a work-up for the geometric constructions shown on page 92.

2. Using the geometric constructions in exercise 1, prepare the instructions for the pattern shown below. This pattern is a combination of PLOT and CIRCL as described in the geometric constructions section of Chapter 2.

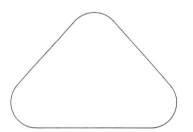

3. The pattern shown in exercise 2 is the outside of a plate cam that is to be mounted on a shaft. Show this shaft as indicated below.

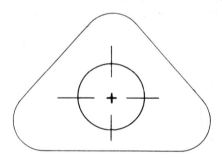

4. Design a reinforcement area for the shaft called a hub as shown below for exercise 3.

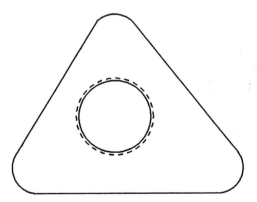

5. Display both the shaft and the hub with centerlines as shown below for exercise 4.

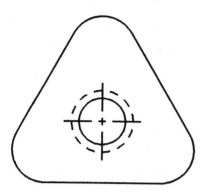

6. Complete the geometric construction shown below with a call fit. The finished graphics pattern should be balanced about a horizontal centerline.

7. Repeat exercise 3 for the pattern shown in exercise 6 as indicated below.

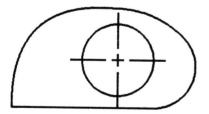

8. Output the geometric shape shown below on a DVST.

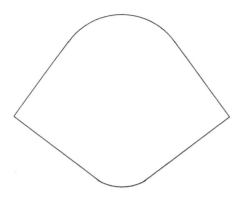

9. Repeat exercise 7 as shown below.

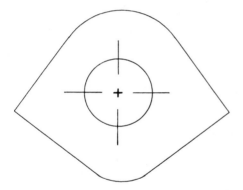

10. Repeat exercise 4 as shown below.

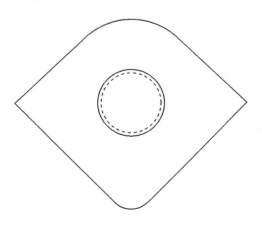

11. Prepare the construction shown below.

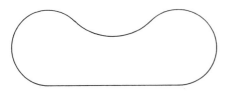

12. Repeat exercise 9 as shown below.

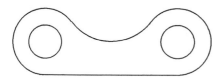

13. Repeat exercise 10 as shown below.

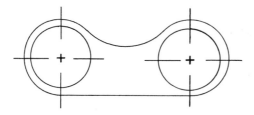

14. Prepare exercises 2, 6, 8, and 11 to be plotted inside a title block as shown on page 97.

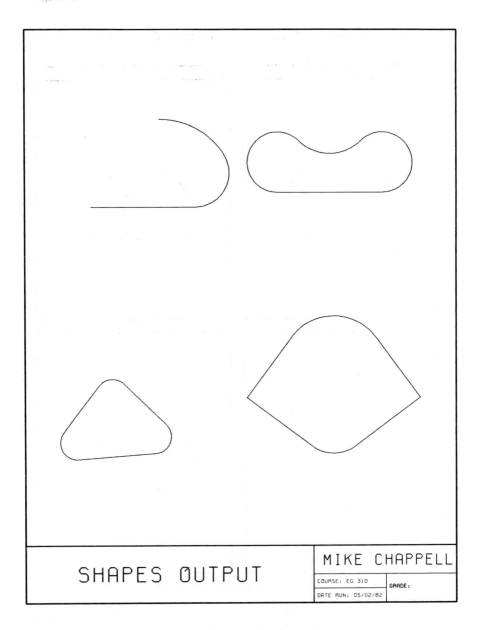

SHAPES OUTPUT

MIKE CHAPPELL

COURSE: EG 310

GRADE:

DATE RUN: 05/02/82

15. Prepare exercises 5, 7, 9, and 13 to be plotted as shown below.

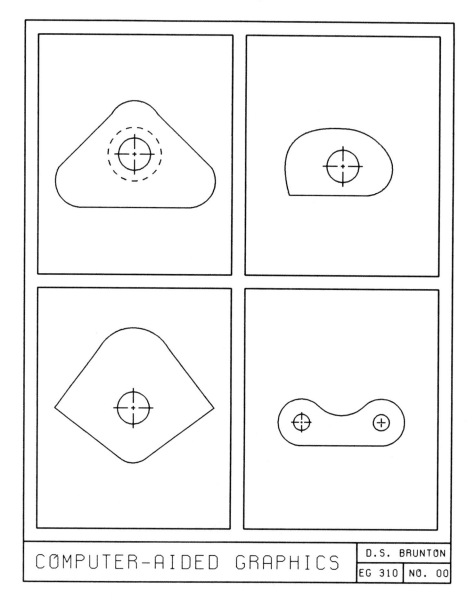

COMPUTER-AIDED GRAPHICS

D.S. BRUNTON	
EG 310	NO. 00

16. On a size B work sheet (shown in Figure 2.5), write a series of program
    statements that will use the geometric construction techniques to plot the
    logic diagram shown below. Use CALL SYMBOLs to prepare a partial truth
    table as follows:

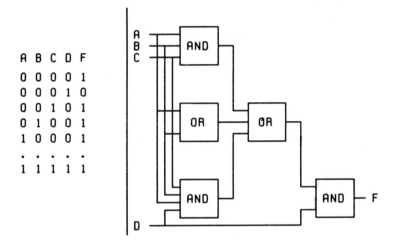

```
A  B  C  D  F

0  0  0  0  1
0  0  0  1  0
0  0  1  0  1
0  1  0  0  1
1  0  0  0  1
.  .  .  .  .
1  1  1  1  1
```

17. Enter the following program.

```
0001          DIMENSION AX(20),BY(20),CX(20),DY(20)
0002          DIMENSION ARAY1(50),ARAY2(50),ARAY3(50),ARAY4(50)
0003          DIMENSION ARAY5(50),ARAY6(50),ARAY7(50),ARAY8(50)
0004          CALL PLOTS
0005          CALL RECT(0.,0.,12.5,10.,0.,3)
0006          CALL FLOWER
0007          CALL PLOT(2.,5.,-3)
0008          CALL STAR
0009          CALL PLOT(6.,0.,-3)
0010          CALL FLOWRS
0011          CALL PLOT(-8.,-5.,-3)
0012          CALL GREEN
0013          CALL PLOT(0.,0.,999)
0014          STOP
0015          END
```

18. Attach the first subroutine.

```
0001                    SUBROUTINE FLOWER
0002                    CALL CIRCL(6.,9.,0.,360.,1.,1.,0.)
0003                    DO 10 I=1,36
0004                    RI=I
0005                    ANG=RI*10.
0006                    THETA=ANG*3.14159/180.
0007                    X=5.+2.*COS(THETA)
0008                    Y=9.+2.*SIN(THETA)
0009                    XXX=5.+2.5*COS(THETA)
0010                    YYY=9.+2.5*SIN(THETA)
0011                    CALL ELIPS(X,Y,.5,.25,ANG,0.,360.,3)
0012                    CALL ELIPS(XXX,YYY,.75,.35,ANG,0.,360.,3)
0013            10      CONTINUE
0014                    RETURN
0015                    END
```

19. Attach the second subroutine.

```
0001                    SUBROUTINE STAR
0002                    DO 20 I=1,36
0003                    RI=I
0004                    RI=RI*10.
0005                    THETA=RI*3.14159/180.
0006                    X1=1.*COS(THETA)
0007                    X2=1.3*COS(THETA)
0008                    Y1=1.*SIN(THETA)
0009                    Y2=1.3*SIN(THETA)
0010                    X3=1.8*SIN(THETA)
0011                    Y3=1.8*COS(THETA)
0012                    CALL PLOT(0.,0.,3)
0013                    CALL PLOT(X1,Y1,2)
0014                    CALL POLY(X2,Y2,0.1,-5.,66.)
0015            20      CALL AROHD(X3,Y3,X3,Y3+0.3,0.25,0.25,22)
0016                    RETURN
0017                    END
```

20. Attach the third subroutine.

```
0001                        SUBROUTINE FLOWRS
0002                        DIMENSION AX(20),BY(20),CX(20),DY(20)
0003                        DO 30 I=1,15
0004                        RI=I
                     C      ANG=RI*6.28318/15.+3.14159/2.
0005                        ANG=RI*6.28318/15.
0006                        IF (I .EQ. I/2*2) GO TO 40
0007                           AX(I)=2.*COS(ANG)
0008                           BY(I)=2.*SIN(ANG)
0009                           CX(I)=1.*COS(ANG)
0010                           DY(I)=1.*SIN(ANG)
0011                           GO TO 30
0012                40         AX(I)=1.*COS(ANG)
0013                           BY(I)=1.*SIN(ANG)
0014                           CX(I)=2.*COS(ANG)
0015                           DY(I)=2.*SIN(ANG)
0016                30      CONTINUE
0017                        AX(16)=CX(1)
0018                        BY(16)=DY(1)
0019                        CX(16)=AX(1)
0020                        DY(16)=BY(1)
0021                        AX(17)=0.
0022                        AX(18)=1.
0023                        BY(17)=0.
0024                        BY(18)=1.
0025                        CX(17)=0.
0026                        CX(18)=1.
0027                        DY(17)=0.
0028                        DY(18)=1.
0029                        CALL FLINE(AX,BY,-16,1,1,4)
0030                        CALL FLINE(CX,DY,-16,1,1,5)
0031                        RETURN
0032                        END
```

21. Attach the fourth subroutine.

```
0001      SUBROUTINE GREEN
0002      DIMENSION ARAY1(50),ARAY2(50),ARAY3(50),ARAY4(50)
0003      DIMENSION ARAY5(50),ARAY6(50),ARAY7(50),ARAY8(50)
0004      CALL RECT(5.5,2.,0.2,2.5,45.,3)
0005      CALL RECT(4.855,2.,0.2,2.5,135.,3)
0006      CALL ELIPS(2.5,3.0,0.75,.35,160.,0.,360.,3)
0007      CALL ELIPS(4.25,4.4,0.75,.35,80.,0.,360.,3)
0008      CALL ELIPS(6.5,3.0,0.75,.35,-200.,0.,360.,3)
0009      CALL ELIPS(6.4,4.45,0.75,.25,80.,0.,360.,3)
0010      CALL BAR(4.875,0.5,0.,6.,.5,6.,.3,10)
0011      CALL DFACT(1.,0.5)
0012      CALL CIRCLE(6.875,1.75,1.50,0.,30,12.,ARAY1,ARAY2,ARAY3,ARAY4)
0013      CALL SHADE(ARAY1,ARAY2,ARAY3,ARAY4,0.25,60.,15,1,15,1)
0014      CALL CIRCLE(3.375,1.75,1.50,0.,30,12.,ARAY5,ARAY6,ARAY7,ARAY8)
0015      CALL SHADE(ARAY5,ARAY6,ARAY7,ARAY8,0.25,60.,15,1,15,1)
0016      CALL DFACT(1.,1.)
0017      RETURN
0018      END
```

22. Attach the fifth subroutine.

```
0001                    SUBROUTINE CIRCLE(X,Y,R,SANG,N,THETA,ARAY1,ARAY2,ARAY3,ARAY4)
0002                    DIMENSION ARAY1(50),ARAY2(50),ARAY3(50),ARAY4(50)
0003                    X=X-R
0004                    SANG=(3.14/180.)*SANG
0005                    XX=R*(1-COS(SANG))
0006                    YY=R*(SIN(SANG))
0007                    DX=X+XX
0008                    EY=Y+YY
0009                    CALL PLOT(DX,EY,3)
0010                    THETA=(3.14/180.)*THETA
0011                    THETA1=THETA
0012                    DO 2 I=1,N
0013                    FEE=SANG+THETA
0014                    PX=R*(1-COS(FEE))
0015                    SY=R*(SIN(FEE))
0016                    DX=X+PX
0017                    EY=Y+SY
0018                    IF(I .LE. N/2)ARAY1(I)=DX
0019                    IF(I .LE. N/2)ARAY2(I)=EY
0020                    IF(I .GT. N/2)ARAY3(I-N/2)=DX
0021                    IF(I .GT. N/2)ARAY4(I-N/2)=EY
0022                    CALL PLOT(DX,EY,2)
0023           2        THETA=THETA+THETA1
0024                    ARAY1(N/2+1)=0.
0025                    ARAY1(N/2+2)=1.
0026                    ARAY2(N/2+1)=0.
0027                    ARAY2(N/2+2)=1.
0028                    ARAY3(N/2+1)=0.
0029                    ARAY3(N/2+2)=1.
0030                    ARAY4(N/2+1)=0.
0031                    ARAY4(N/2+2)=1.
0032                    RETURN
0033                    END
```

23. Output the graphic image provided from exercises 17, 18, 19, 20, 21, and 22.
24. Output exercise 23 on the CalComp plotter and use CALL NEWPEN to add color to the image.
25. Output exercise 23 on the DVST model 4027 or a color CRT and change shapes.

3

Computerizing the Design Process

The design language structure for a computer-aided design display is a series of commands which move the plotter pen, DVST beam, or tool path in such a manner that the end result is a properly drawn design, working drawing, or finished production part. This concept is basic to computer-aided design (CAD) and is illustrated in Figure 3.1. The design engineer prepares the design layout so that the computer can automatically generate parts lists, detail drawings, location and clearance fit checks, and assembly drawings. Automated graphics is not an end in itself; if it is properly done, it is a beginning of a sequence which includes graphics, design, and production or manufacture. The whole idea behind drafting is to communicate design intent. If the engineer is unaware of the method diagrammed in Figure 3.1, then automatic drafting is not possible. The CAD technique allows us to include all the information for design analysis (testing), prototype construction (experimentation), and manufacture of a product.

If we assume that the drafting automation discussed in the first two chapters is only one part of an automated network, then drafting is a function that can be automated and follows the automation of engineering design. Manufacturing planning, production control, tool design, and manufacturing operations follow. Notice in Figure 3.1 that a stream of information connects all of these functions: it is the data base for the entire network. While this book is particular in its treatment of the drafting function, the other functions cannot be ignored. All drafting personnel must understand how the network is organized so that they can get information from and put information into the data base. Figure 3.2 is a good illustration of the total data base for the network. Notice that is divided into 2-D, 3-D, and non-graphic (see Chapter 1). When Figures 3.1 and 3.2 are compared,

DESIGN/MANUFACTURING NETWORK

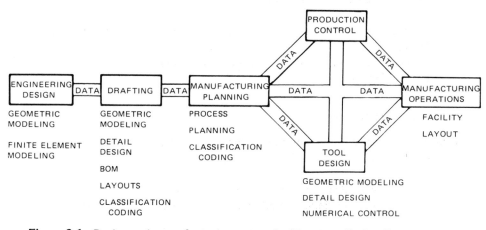

Figure 3.1 Design and manufacturing network. (Courtesy Gerber Systems Technology, Inc.)

an understanding of the function is clear. In Figure 3.1, starting at the left of the diagram, engineering design has two main data types:

1. Geometric modeling (input)
2. Finite element modeling (input/output)

Moving to the right, drafting has five main data types:

1. Geometric modeling (shared with engineering design and used as basic input for all drawing--output)
2. Detail design (output)
3. Bill of materials (input to manufacturing planning)
4. Layout drawings (input to production control and manufacturing operations
5. Classification coding (input to tool design and manufacturing operations)

Moving along the network, manufacturing planning has two main data types:

1. Process planning (input from drafting, output to production control and tool design)
2. Classification coding

The network branches into production control, tool design and manufacturing operations which have four main data types:

1. Geometric modeling (input from both drafting and engineering design)
2. Detail design
3. Numerical control (automated machine tool operation)
4. Facility layout

DATA BASE COMPONENTS

Figure 3.2 gives a good representation of the types of data bases and how they are used. The CORE representation is:

1. 2-D, schematic diagram representations of all types.
2. 3-D, geometric modeling, detail drafting, finite element modeling and numerical control.
3. Non-graphic, bills of materials and schedules of all types.

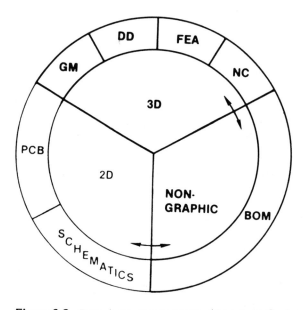

Figure 3.2 Data base components. (Courtesy Gerber Systems Technology, Inc.)

These data base components are used to produce the following items in the remainder of this chapter:

Parts
Patterns
Symbols
Output files (data sets)

PARTS OF THE SYSTEM

An operating system for the entire network is shown in Figure 3.3. This is known as the software architecture, and it is in two main parts. One part is the application control and the other support of these applications. The main functions listed earlier are manipulated through the graphic subroutine package described in the first nine chapters of this text. The subroutines become useful for each application through the skillful use of data base access routines. These routines are:

ARC	variation of XARC, YARC, ZARC
ANGLE	modification of rotation
ATANGL	display other that THETA
BEARG	bearing of a line
CENTER	indicates tool travel --CNTRL
CYLIND	circular cylinder tool form
DATAPT	space location in 3-D
DOT	tool point -solid object
GO	tool control
HOME	origin of tool position
IN	inside tolerance for tool
LINES	tool path -- displacement
OUT	outside tolerance for tool
PLANE	three or more DATAPT's
PT	2-D space location
R	radius of part feature
RTHETA	arc segments along radius
SLOPE	angle in degrees of feature
TANTO	tangent to
UNIT	display element size
VECTOR	magnitude and direction
XYPLAN	surface on a planning model
XZPLAN	surface on a planning model
YZPLAN	surface on a planning model

SOFTWARE ARCHITECTURE

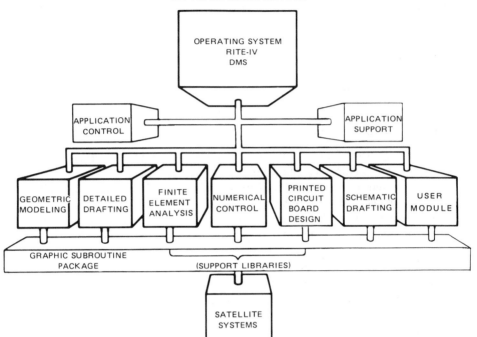

Figure 3.3 Parts of the software architecture. (Courtesy Gerber Systems Technology, Inc.)

The listing of data base access routines are used by the processing unit of each satellite system as shown in Figure 3.4. Notice that the communications controller keeps us in touch with the network described in Figure 3.1 and the various parts shown in Figure 3.3. The items shown in Figure 3.4 have been described in detail throughout the first two chapters, but now you can see how they fit into the overall network approach to design theory. The main concern here is to understand these access routines and the applications of these to network operations.

ARC

The ARC routine generates a pen path, CRT beam, or tool path which is composed of tangential slope lines to the desired or true arc. As indicated in Chapter 2, these lines cover minute distances which change very rapidly for drafting output, or tool control. When displaying arcs the center of arc radius must be given to the graphics routine. The I and J dimensions in Figure 3.5 provide the informa-

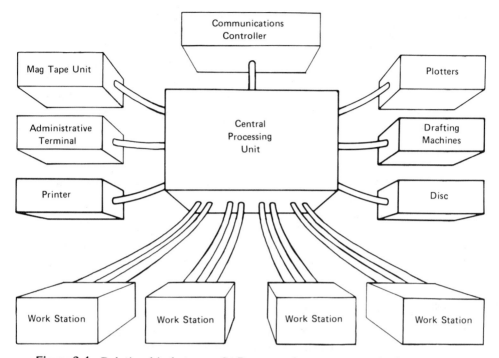

Figure 3.4 Relationship between CAD user and system network. (Courtesy Gerber Systems Technology, Inc.)

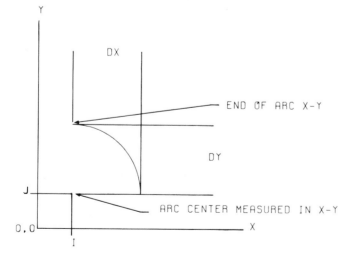

Figure 3.5 ARC access routine

109

tion for the arc center offset in 3-D along the Z axis. I represents the distance a-long the X axis between the beginning of the arc and the center of the arc. J, in turn, is the Y distance offset. The end point of the arc is given as DX and DY in notation and as X and Y distances in an access routine. This differs from the sub-routines shown in Chapter 2. Here the entire arc was always in the same plane. In access routines the starting and ending points do not have to be in the same plane. For example, an arc can be produced from a different display (Z axis) depth as shown in Figure 3.7.

ANGLE

This access routine is used to describe any engineering design angle less than 90 degrees that is measured from the intersection of two axes on a 2-dimensional plane surface within a 3-D model. Two examples are shown in Figure 3.7; X-Y plane and Y-Z plane. In Figure 3.6, a 2-D example of the intersection of the X and Y display axis is demonstrated. Using the ANGLE routine, an engineer can send a 3-D model of a machine part to a drafter's terminal for inspection and detail drawing development.

ATANGL

All engineering design angles greater than 90 degrees are accessed through ATANGL. Figure 3.9 demonstrates this concept which generates from the center of a circle by the rotation of the cutter. This then produces a tool path, direction of cut, depth of cut, and profile of the finished part. The plane of the cut may be at any convenient angle as shown in Figure 3.8. Atangl is used to describe the lo-

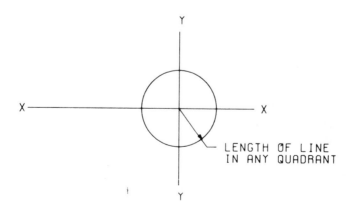

Figure 3.6 ANGLE access routine

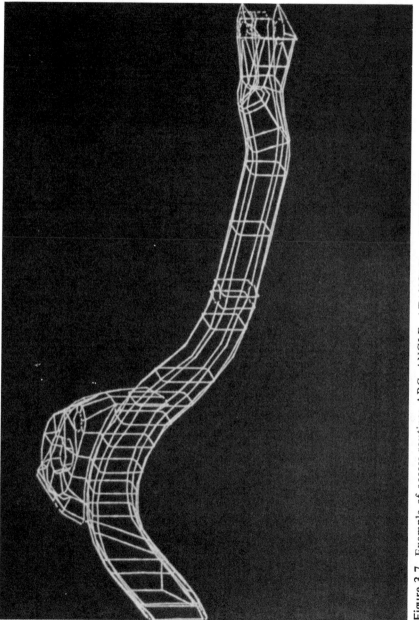

Figure 3.7 Example of access routines ARC, ANGLE, ATANGLE, and BEARING.

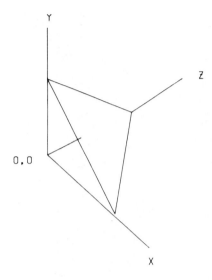

Figure 3.8 ATANGLE access routine

cation of a manufactured plane surface. It is referenced by the angle between the reference axes and the surface as shown in Figure 3.8. Examples of manufactured plane surfaces are shown in Figure 3.9 above. The plate mold is a flat surface plate before the cutting tool removes the material to form the geometric profiles.

BEARG

The flat piece part shown in Figure 3.9 is typical of the use for the access routine shown in Figure 3.10. A bearing angle is read from the horizontal viewport and helps in the specification of the tooling.

CENTER

Figure 3.11 clearly demonstrates that a CENTER location need not be in two dimensions with a Z-axis reading of zero. If the center of a circle which represents the diameter of a tool has coordinate readings of 4 in X, 3 in Y, and 5 in Z, the circle image would appear smaller than the actual size of a tool in two dimensions or could appear as an ellipse as shown in Figure 3.11. Of course this is an optical illusion but necessary if a draftsperson is to enter this into the data base so that manufacturing operations can produce the require part as shown in Figure 3.12. Compare the design intent shown in Figure 3.11 with the finished product shown in Figure 3.12. Another reference to Figure 3.1 shows the left to right

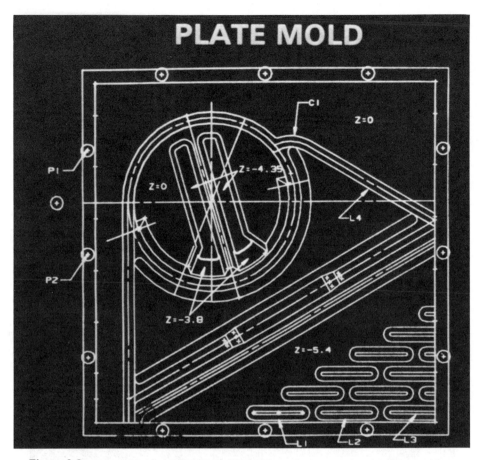

Figure 3.9 Example of ATANGLE, BEARG, and center access routines. (Courtesy Gerber Systems Technology, Inc.)

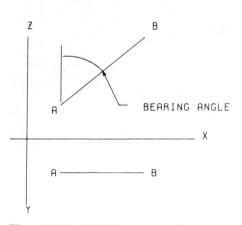

Figure 3.10 BEARG access routine

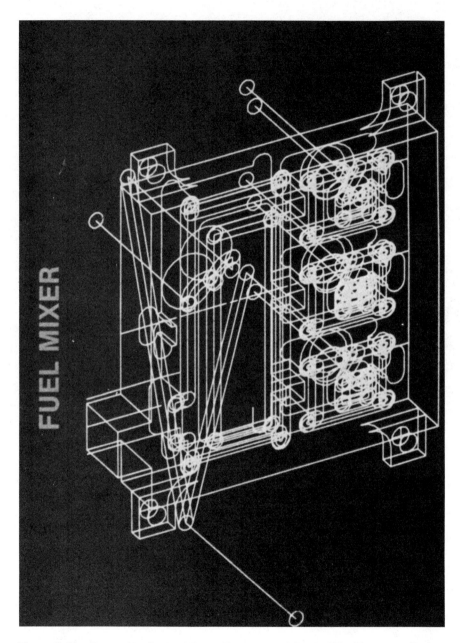

Figure 3.11 Example of CENTER, CYLIND, and DATAPT. (Courtesy Gerber Systems Technology, Inc.)

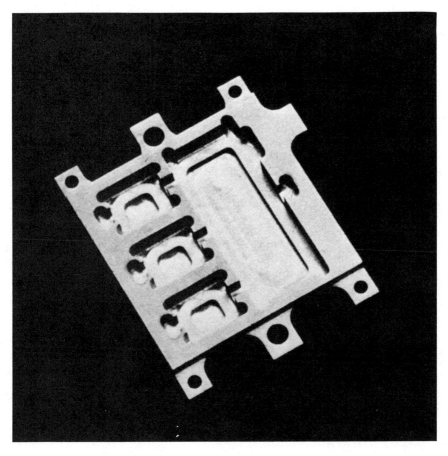

Figure 3.12 Finished part. (Courtesy Gerber Systems Technology, Inc.)

movement of design information called automated data base. Figure 3.3 indicates the flow of information from the access routines to the drafting phase and finally into the data base for the automated manufacture of the finished part. Drafting becomes the link between the engineer's idea and the machine tool operations necessary to control the final form of the product. Automated drafting now becomes more than the production of drawings.

CYLIND

A circular cylinder is produced by a generation of a plane surface, denoted as a circle in Figure 3.13, through space. Access routines like CYLIND are useful in displaying the many positions that a tool may take during a machining operation.

The finished part shown in Figure 3.12 is a result of the proper use of CYLIND in Figure 3.11. Of course CYLIND is used with other access routines to define the part outline, tool travel, material removal rates and depth of cuts used to machine a finished part. A CYLIND routine can be displayed with a top and bottom circle and centerline as shown in Figure 3.12 or a pair of tangent lines may be displayed by the use of TANTO as shown in Figure 3.13.

DATAPT

A data point is a 3-dimensional location for a point, expressed in display units and direction of travel. Data points are more easily used when stored in a computer on a space model as shown in Figure 3.15. Points are used to specify graphic location for other access routines as well, Figure 3.14 is a good example of this.

DOT

The access routine DOT is an example of a graphic shape that can be located by DATAPT as shown in Figure 3.14 above. A dot pattern is more common than the use of a single dot. The electronics fabrication industry makes excellent use of DOT.

GO

A GO access routine is used to indicate either pen motion or tool motion. It can be shown directly as the MOVE graphics command learned in earlier chapters or the

    CALL PLOT(XPAGE,YPAGE,3)

computer program statement.

HOME

A home access routine returns the pen to the origin or returns the tool to the starting position. The HOME position is clearly shown in Figure 3.11 and will appear again in many of the later diagrams (see Figure 3.16).

IN

When 3-dimensional objects are displayed in a 2-dimensional display area, two important concepts are used. They are inside and outside control boundaries. IN is used to control the boundary closest to HOME. Figure 3.17 illustrates the control necessary for manufacturing operations, while Figure 3.18 illustrates the concept for drafting output.

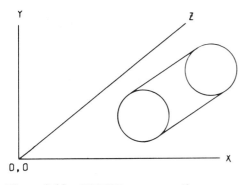

Figure 3.13 CYLIND access routine.

Figure 3.14 Example of DATAPT, DOT, and GO access routines. (Courtesy Gerber Systems Technology, Inc.)

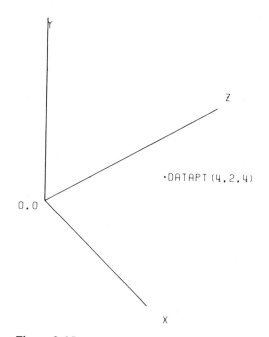

Figure 3.15 DATAPT access routine.

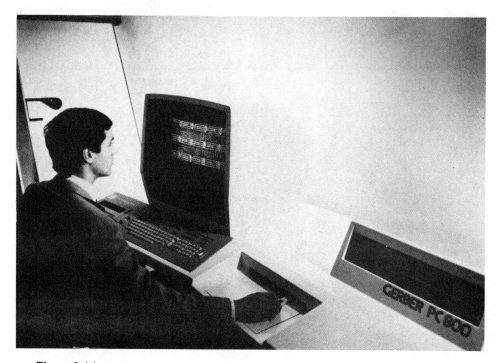

Figure 3.16 CAD operator uses access routines. (Courtesy Gerber Systems Technology, Inc.)

Figure 3.17 Control from IN and OUT routines. (Courtesy Gerber Systems Technology, Inc.)

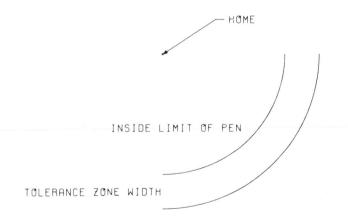

Figure 3.18 IN and OUT access routines.

LINES-VECTORS

The access routine **LINES** is probably the most used routine in the examples shown in this chapter (see Figure 3.19). It can be directly compared to **DRAW** in the graphics commands or

    CALL PLOT(XPAGE,YPAGE,2)

computer program statement.

OUT

This access routine controls the outside of the tool path farthest from **HOME**. Figures 3.17 and 18 demonstrated this.

PLANE

Shown in Figures 3.20 and 21, a **PLANE** has 3-dimensional data and at least three data points.

PT

Shown in Figure 3.10, a **PT** is a two-dimensional representation of **DATAPT**.

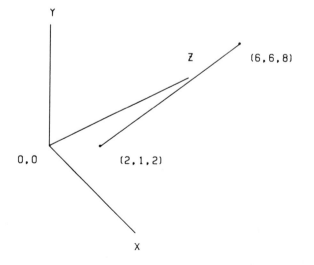

Figure 3.19 Lines access routine.

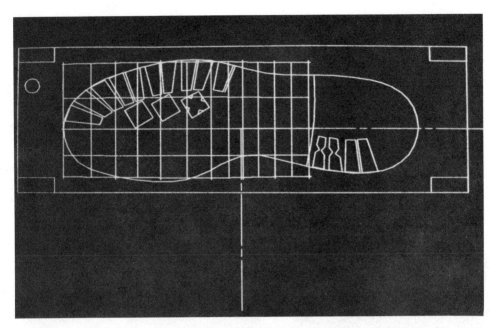

Figure 3.20 Examples of OUT, PLANE, PT, R, THETA, and TANTO. (Courtesy Gerber Systems Technology, Inc.)

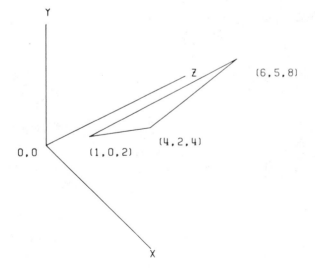

Figure 3.21 Plane access routine.

R

Without the R access routine the operations shown in Figure 3.22 could not be programmed. R is the notation or storage symbol for the radius of a circle or the arc of a surface.

RTHETA

This access routine describes the tool path taken in Figure 3.22. It is illustrated in Figure 3.23 and demonstrated for modeling purposes in Figure 3.24.

SLOPE

Any line that can not be read from a data base location must be calculated and then stored for later use. One form that a line can take is SLOPE.

Figure 3.22 Manufacturing operation from a data base supplied from Fig. 3.20. (Courtesy Gerber Systems Technology, Inc.)

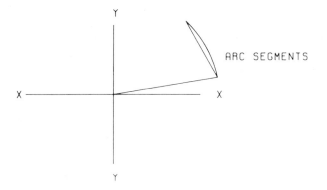

Figure 3.23 RTHETA access routine.

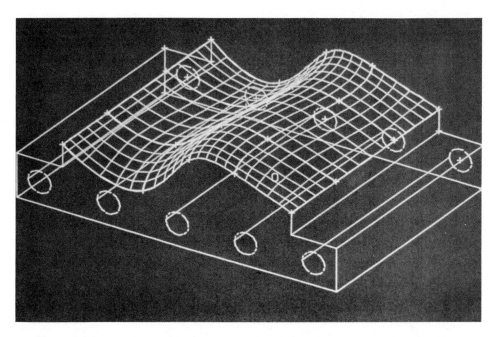

Figure 3.24 Example of RTHETA, SLOPE, TANTO, and PLANE. (Courtesy Gerber Systems Technology, Inc.)

TANTO-UNIT

Tangent to is a symbol for computer use and describes the exact point at which two graphic shapes are tangent. This enables the access routines to adjust to the grid units being used for display or manufacture.

XY,XZ,YZ PLAN

Shown in Figure 3.25 as XYPLAN it is composed of a grid matrix of units. This allows plane surface features to be added to a planning, detail, or manufacturing display as shown in Figure 3.26.

WRITING A CAD PROGRAM

In general the following is the suggested procedure for preparing a CAD program:

1. Code the design sketch.
2. Prepare a graphics work sheet to determine a sequence of operations and select the correct NEWPEN values.
3. Calculate the coordinate parts.
4. Write the program.

In the first step of program preparation, the CAD user lists and codes on the design sketch all geometry and operations which will be plotted. If special graph-

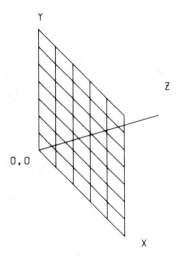

Figure 3.25 XYPLAN access routine.

ics routines are needed, a sketch will be prepared and sent for computer-aided translation at this time so that the loop can be started.

The graphics work sheet that is shown in Figure 3.27 has been used at Clemson University to assist beginning programmers to organize and tabulate all the necessary information for input. Most industries have a similar procedure, for it contains useful comments such as tool sequence, operation of CAD routines, and origin location. As was the case in template drafting in Chapter 2, it might be helpful if the programmer assumes that the tool moves and the table remains stationary (true for flat bed plotters only). Then tool movements to the right, up and away from the origin, all have positive increasing values. CADs vary from manufacturer to manufacturer, as pointed out in Chapter 1. Therefore the CAD user disregards relative motions of one form to another and thinks only in terms of tool motion, the calculation process becomes routine.

Tool Motion

Before beginning the use of mathematical expressions for the elements of motion it is important to describe these elements in the terminology associated with CAD:

1. The class of motion is either parallel, angular, or rotary.
2. The direction is right-left, up-down, in-out (tolerances).
3. The distance is the physical value (absolute or incremental).
4. NEWPEN is the diameter size, color, or type of tool image.

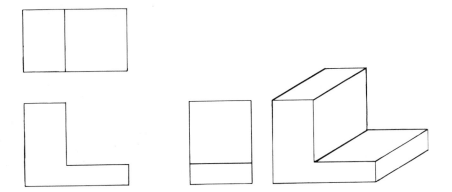

Figure 3.26 Pictorial illustration of 3-D dimensional points in space.

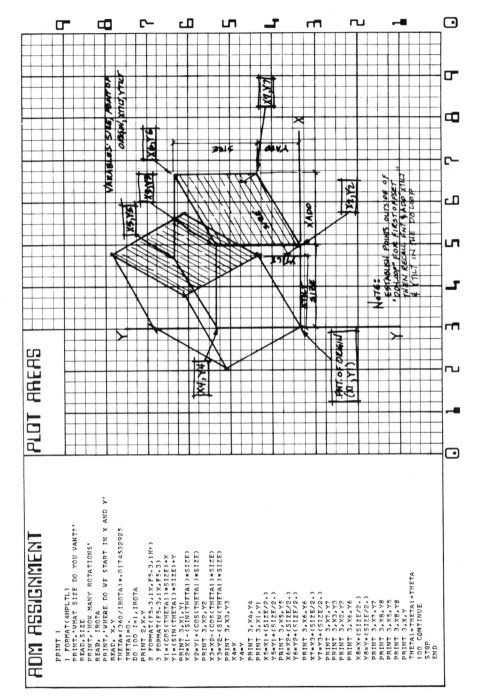

Figure 3.27 Geometry for relay rack.

It is not possible to separate one of these elements from another because tool motion is not a single thing in itself but the combination of the interaction of all of the above.

Control Datums

The cartesian coordinate system is made up of intersecting planes called axes. These three planes intersect as a common point (0, 0, 0), forming 90-degree angles with each other. It is from these planes or axes that tool movements are calculated and plotted. The DVST or plotter has only two axes in which to plot, but real-world objects contain all three. Therefore the graphics processor can translate three axes into a two-plane viewing surface and display the object for us as an orthographic drawing or a pictorial.

The X axis is the basic reference axis. Once it has been established, and the XYPLAN oriented with relation to the tool, the rest of the geometry naturally falls into place. As an example, the first motion of CAD and its X travel, normally seen as traveling from left to right. To this motion is assigned the basic reference of the Y axis. From this simple motion the CAD operator has established the XYPLAN of operation.

Axis Motion

As stated above, the axes X, Y, and Z intercept at a common point. This point becomes the reference location for both direction and relative motion such as rotation and is called absolute zero. At this point in the graphics processor all axes have a value of zero. To obtain various geometric relationships such as the frontal plane of an orthographic projection, the graphics processor displays the X and Y coordinate list. To obtain the profile view, the processor displays the Z and Y list. The horizontal view is obtained from the X and Z data list. To display pictorials the graphics processor rotates the absolute axes at a convenient viewing angle, oblique or isometric. Figure 3.33 is a series of points displayed in this manner.

Repetitive Routines

Much of the drawing or plotting done on direct view storage tube is repetitive in nature. In fact if the design to be automated does not contain some repetitive aspects, it probably will not be a cost savings to display in this manner. However, many of the machine parts designed today have graphic patterns which lend themselves to CAD control. In the architectural field, building elevations contain many straight, repetitive graphic routines and can be drawn economically on the CAD format. As an example, suppose a mechanical design called for a relay to be mounted in a channel section. The geometry is a pattern of holes in the Y axis and a rectangular opening 1 by 2 inches in length along the X axis. This in itself does not justify the use of the CAD. But suppose that forty relays were to be mounted 3 inches on center in a single length of channel? This, then, would be an excellent automated technique because the single relay geometry could be coded into the graphics processor with one command to move the proper amount for 3-inch centering. These commands could then be written in a DO loop so that the processor could provide for a channel display with relay mount geometry for forty or more sections. Working drawings produced like this can also be digitized so that numerically controlled machine tools can produce the finished parts directly from the design intent or drawing in this case.

The commands necessary for the relay rack described would begin with a statement for establishing the axes at a HOME position. Figure 3.28 was displayed on a DVST, so this command would be

CALL INITT

The second command given would be for the lower left-hand corner of the first rectangle to be drawn:

X=1

The third command is for the location of the first hole along the Y axis:

XPAGE=2.5

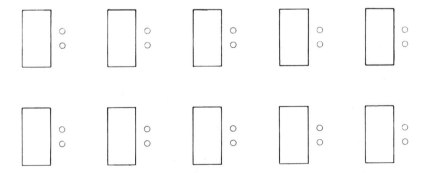

Figure 3.28   Design sketch for graphics program.

The fourth command is the starting of the DO loop for forty objects to be drawn:

DO 100 I=1,40

The fifth command establishes the Y location for the first hole:

YPAGE=1.75

The next command draws the first circle, which is the location of the first hole in the channel:

CALL CIRCL(XPAGE,YPAGE,0.,360.,.1,.1,0.)

The next command resets the Y location for the second hole:

YPAG=YPAGE+.5

The eighth command draws the second hole in its proper location:

CALL CIRCL(XPAGE,YPAG,0.,360.,.1,.1,0.)

The next command draws the rectangular opening in the channel:

CALL RECT(X,3.5,2.,1.,0.,3)

The next command moves the rectangle 3 inches in the X direction:

100 X=X+3

The command entered next is usually the last graphic command to the processor:

CALL FINITT(0,0)

Repetitive routines always involve a "looping" device. The DO statement is most often used; however, an IF and GOTO arrangement can be used. The next type of repetitive routine that is used quite often in writing a graphics program is the technique which groups like geometric construction together under a DIMENSION and DATA arrangement.

DIMENSION X(18),Y(18)

You will remember from Chapter 1 that this reserves space for eighteen sets of coordinate data to be stored in X and Y.

DATA X/3*3.9,3*11.7,3*19,5,3*27.3,3*35.1,3*42.9/

assigns eighteen values to X_1 through X_{18}. The next DATA statement assigns the values to Y_1 through Y_{18}. The CALL INITT statement is the first graphics statement in a program and needs to be used only once. The

```
    DO 9 I=1,18
 9  CALL CIRARC(X(I),Y(I),.375,0.,60,6.)
```

commands are the repetitive loop for drawing eighteen circles, each having a radius of 0.375 display units and sixty line segments of 6 degrees each.

Continuous Motion Statement

When repetitive routines are used correctly, the output to a plotter or DVST display device appears to be a continuous motion effect. In the case of architectural studies, the architect may choose to display the design space around the viewer. The effect is that the viewer is moved through the structure from room to room. This is a great design aid because changes can be made prior to construction, and several choices may be examined during the design. In the case of working drawings of elevations, a continuous motion statement to create a geometry matrix would have to be developed. Suppose that a building elevation contained 100 windows, that the geometry for these 100 windows fell into seven or eight general types, and that the location for each window was different, so different that a pattern was not possible. For this case the programmer would code the template geometry for a window which contains the seven or eight possibilities, make a graphics loop, and store the data in the processor. Next the programmer would describe the logic of the window matrix in the form of a DIMENSION and DATA repetitive loop and merge the two in the final graphics program.

No matter what the application, the total input to CAD systems contains all of the required software to produce a final drawing more accurately and faster than manual methods. The technique of continuous motion is also used in some rotation displays where the designer wishes to see all of the positions of the move through space. To do this a design sketch is needed so that the graphics programmer can code the geometry for input to a machine. Figure 3.28 might be such a sketch.

If the graphics programmer gets such a sketch, his job is reduced because the engineer understands automated graphics. Many times, however, the engineer is not aware of the automated techniques, and the technician must make sketches of his own to work from. A rather detailed description of this is contained in the exercises at the end of this chapter. The note at the bottom of the sketch calls for considerable knowledge of graphics programming. The programmer would draw a logic diagram of the entire problem before attempting to write the code.

When the CAD commands are complete, a trial run of the problem would be made. Errors in the coding can then be corrected, and an output medium, usually magnetic tape, can be produced for later use on the N/C machine tool. A CAD run is shown in Figures 3.29 through 3.41. Any errors found in the graphics should be corrected before the program is stored in computer files. The program is saved for other interactive users. The program can then be used over and over by designers working on a CAD network as shown in Figure 3.1.

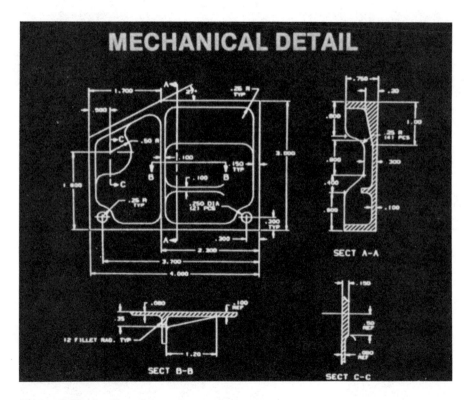

Figure 3.29 Problem 1 exercise.

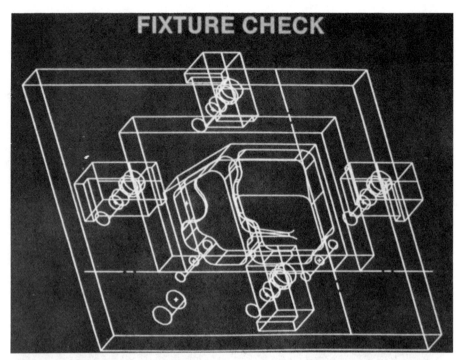

Figure 3.30 Problem 2 exercise.

Figure 3.31 Problem 2 (continued).

132

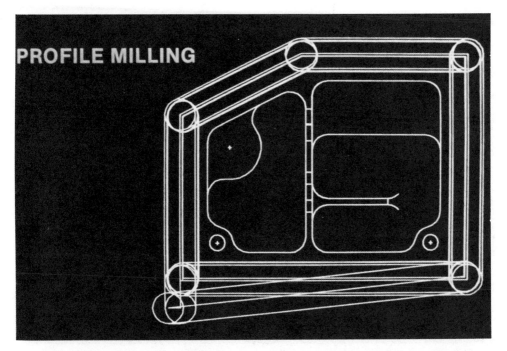

Figure 3.32 Problem 3 exercise.

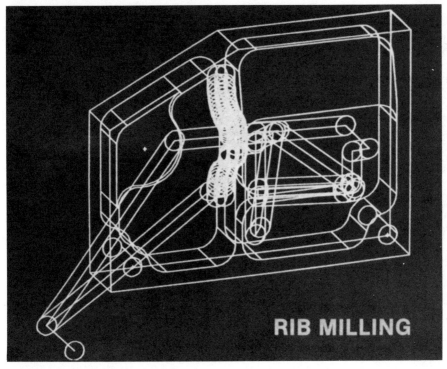

Figure 3.33 Problem 4 exercise.

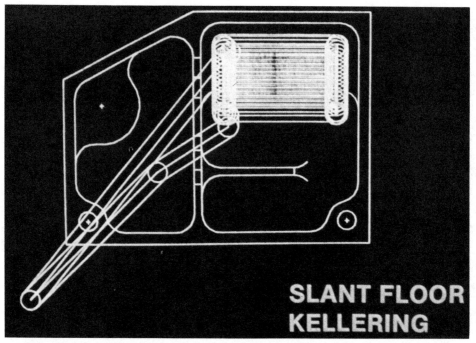

Figure 3.34 Problem 5 exercise.

Figure 3.35 Problem 6 exercise.

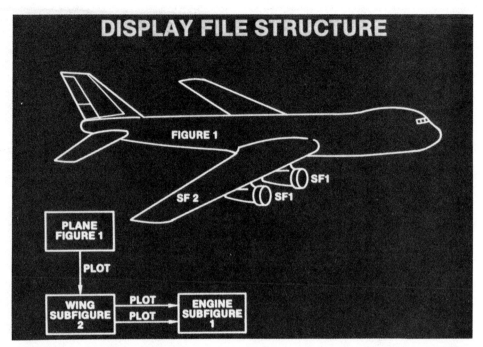

Figure 3.36 Problem 7 exercise.

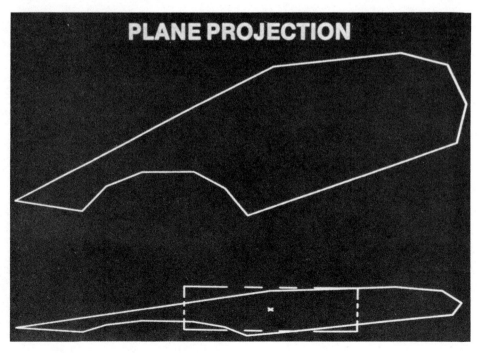

Figure 3.37 Problem 8 exercise.

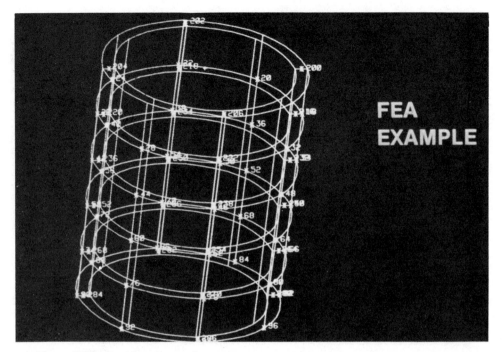

Figure 3.38 Problem 9 exercise.

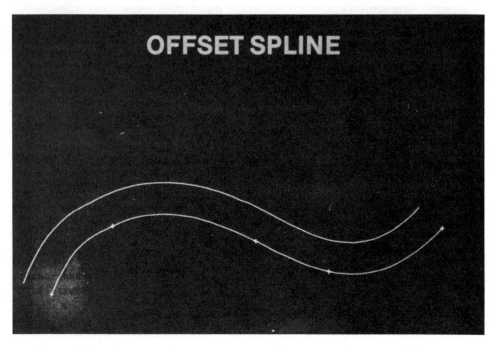

Figure 3.39 Problem 10 exercise.

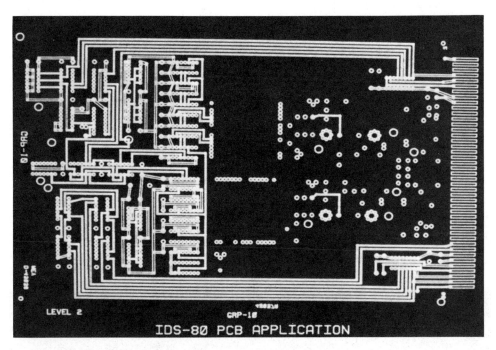

Figure 3.40 Problem 11 exercise.

CONVERTING THE THEORY TO PRACTICE

In the preceding sections of this chapter we have explained the theory of CAD and not the particular operation of one kind of system that is available today. The following exercises are presented as a method for operation of a CalComp plotter and the display of the drawing on DVST. Instructions are given to the plotter from a computer terminal called a CRT. Here a connection to a host computer is made for processing CAD programs. The exercises contain a procedure for previewing a set of instructions for the plotter. Here a separate facility has been provided for hands-on experience of computer operation. The student leaves the environment of the graphics laboratory and enters a CAD environment.

EXERCISES

The following 12 exercises are keyed to Figures 3.29 through 3.41. These figures do not have captions, but represent a typical output that each problem requires.

1. Prepare a detailed drawing as it might come from the DRAFTING function shown in Figure 3.1. A typical output is shown in Figure 3.29.

2. Prepare a geometric model of this part that looks like Figure 3.30 so that MANUFACTURING PLANNING can design a holding fixture shown in Figure 3.31.
3. Prepare a geometric model for profile milling of the part as shown in Figure 3.32.
4. Next provide a tool path display for the rib milling required for this part as shown in Figure 3.33.
5. Provide a production control display as shown in Figure 3.34.
6. Prepare manufacturing data base to produce the part shown in Figure 3.35.
7. Produce the display file structure shown in Figure 3.36.
8. Use this file structure to display a plane projection as shown in Figure 3.37.
9. Output the FEA model shown in Figure 3.38 that is contained in the ENGINEERING DESIGN.
10. Use the TANTO access routine to display Figure 3.39.
11. Use the DOT and LINES access routines to display Figure 3.40.
12. Use access routines to display Figure 3.41.

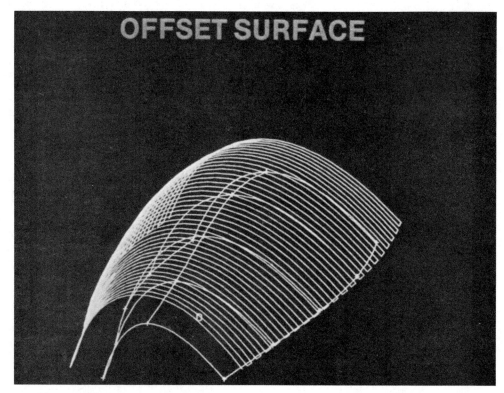

Figure 3.41   Problem 12 exercise.

4

Graphics Systems and Programming

Computer graphics for drafting applications is generally thought of as being either passive or active in nature. When drafting is done in a computer mode rather than manual documentation, the graphics can be done with the aid of the computer or with computer memory modules. The latter is referred to as computer-assisted rather than computer-aided. The two terms aided and assisted do not carry the same meaning. Computer-aided is an "active" process because it appears that the computer has the ability to solve graphic problems without prior input by humans. Types of hardware in this class are referred to as "smart." A smart terminal has a microprocessor built into it for computer-aided instruction of graphics. See Chapter 3.

Computer-assisted graphics systems are referred to as "passive." Passive graphic solutions are also done by a computer but are referred to as "off-line." An example of this type of graphic display was shown in Chapter 2. There may or may not be a time delay when passive systems are used; however, in an active system the answer is immediate and is referred to as "real-time" graphics. In the last few years real-time graphics for drafting have been used in connection with an interactive graphics system (IGS). The IGS is manufactured especially for active graphics problems falling into one of four major application lines: drafting, mapping, image processing, or business analysis.

The standard product of a drafting IGS is an electrical (Figure 4.1), mechanical (Figure 4.2), architectural (Figure 4.3), or organizational drawing (Figure 4.4). These IGSs generate more accurate drawings and patterns at a lower cost and in less time. The IGS processor or computer handles the repetitive aspects of drafting, freeing the operator to focus on the creative side of the work.

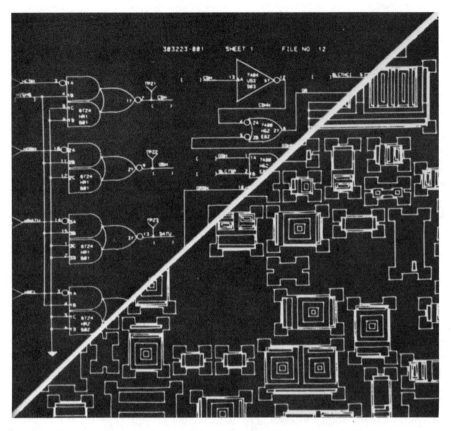

Figure 4.1 Electrical system design. (Courtesy Adage, Inc.)

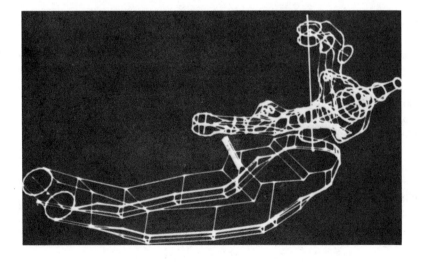

Figure 4.2 Automobile design. (Courtesy Adage, Inc.)

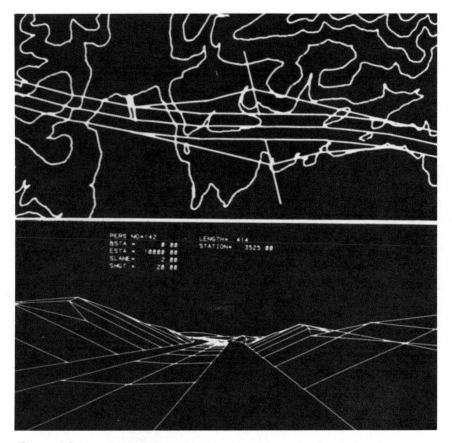

Figure 4.3   Land development. (Courtesy Adage, Inc.)

The drafting problem will be given in most cases but has to be identified as IGS possible or not. The term "computer valuable" or IGS possible means that the designer will make a decision about whether the extent and complexity of the design warrants the time and expense of the IGS process. If the answer is yes, then a model of the problem is constructed to determine if this particular design is unique or if it fits into a larger or more universal design problem. Whenever possible the designer writes the program so that not only the problem at hand can be solved but also any other of that type. The ability to correctly formulate the problem is the key to the success or failure of an IGS in a design office.

The model of the problem can be studied to check the computability of the problem. The conversion of a specific problem to a universal solution is done in this step. For example, an office has many cases where digitized test data are giv-

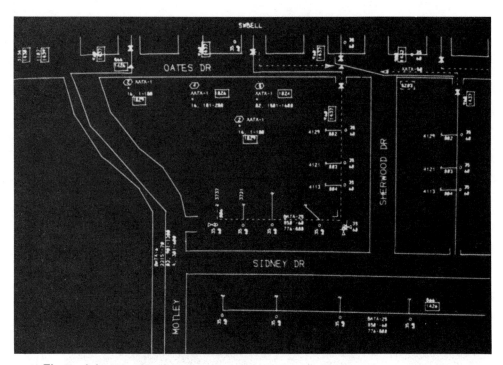

Figure 4.4   Database maintenance. (Courtesy Adage, Inc.)

en as X, Y, and Z values for force vectors. It is required that a program be written to accept these data and give us the true length (in digits) and then plot or display the true length vector. A graphical model or picture as shown in Figure 4.5 is studied to determine the mathematical solution. Here the true length = $(X^2+Y^2+Z^2)**.5$; the plotting of this true length vector, however, depends on the location of PT1 (point 1) and whether the true length vector is to appear in the top or front views. Once this is known the IGS subroutine PLOT can be used to move the pen to PT1 and then draw the new vector from PT1 to PT2.

The coding program for this problem will be designed to compute the true length of any values of PT1 and PT2 and therefore makes it useful for every vector problem of this nature that your office has. A graphical model often involves the use of one or more axes to denote motion or placement of data. A data point (DATAPT) was defined in Chapter 3 as a unique location measured by cartesian coordinates X, Y, and Z. A point (PT) is the coordinate for X and Y only.

The use of graphical models can be helpful in the formulation of mathematical solutions used in drafting programs. The mathematical solution is in the form of an expression. An expression is any desired combination of DATAPTs called variables, constants, and operation signs describing a series of operations,

Figure 4.5 Vectors displayed on IGS CRT screen. (Courtesy Imlac, Inc.)

X+Y**2-5.*(DATAA+DATAB)/Y, for example. A mathematical model consists of a variable name followed by an equal sign and then an expression:

    X=A+B
    X=2.0
    TL=(X**2+Y**2+Z**2)**.5

Certain rules for writing statements like this should be followed:

1. Only one variable name is permitted to the left of the equal sign:
   A+B=X is not permitted
   X=A+B is correct
2. "=" means "replaced by;" remember the destructive feature explained in Chapter 1.

Variable names must begin with an alpha character, while alphanumeric variables can be used such as X1, A2, AXIS8, and ROW1. Only the first six characters of a variable name will be remembered by the IGS, so most items are limited to a combination of six letters or numbers. Variable names are divided into two main groups, those beginning with I, J, K, L, M, and N and those beginning with the rest of the alphabet. I through N are used for storage of whole numbers without decimal parts, and the remaining letters are used for numbers containing decimals. The IGS operates as though it has many mailboxes in memory. Each variable has its own mailbox, and every mailbox has a name. For variables, the name of the mailbox (say IX) is different from what is contained in the mailbox. For example, the name of the mailbox is IX and can be

IX=JHT+3

The name of the mailbox is on the left-hand side of the equals sign, whereas the IGS goes to another mailbox called JHT, looks inside, and writes down the numerical value currently contained in JHT but does not disturb JHT. It does the same for the constant 3. The IGS then adds JHT and 3 and replaces what used to be in the IX mailbox by the sum JHT+3. Therefore JHT and 3 are not changed, but what used to be in the IX mailbox is lost.

The program is compiled automatically by the IGS into machine language plot commands. Preparing a graphics program is thus a two-step process. The machine language is used to draw the desired results (engineering drawing). Machine control languages differ from manufacturer to manufacturer, but the higher-level programming language (FORTRAN or BASIC) is universal and once learned can be used on any IGS. Examples of FORTRAN77 and BASIC coding called subroutines and subprograms, respectively, appeared in Chapter 2. They should be studied again for logic structures and design.

DETAIL DRAWINGS

Before plunging into a detailed description of the many types of detail drawings that an IGS can produce, it seems fitting to devote some explanation to how the digital computer is programmed for a drafting and design environment. Programming for IGS design stations falls into two logical groups. The first is the draftsperson or designer who knows very little about computers or how high-level languages are used to create subroutines or subprograms. This kind of user wants to be able to draw standard parts, as described in Chapter 2, and is therefore concerned with learning how to use a programmer's set of instructions in order to plot a detailed drawing.

The second interest in programming is from the designer who wishes to go farther than the computer programmer or the draftsperson and link the input (picture-type information) with the output such that each input is immediately fed back to an operator via a display. This combination best uses the interactive part of the IGS. This type of operation requires more knowledge of programming than either the casual user or the computer programmer. It is true that the IGS was unheard of several years ago. When we consider what the computer is and how it has helped in the design field of engineering, it was only natural that gradually the computer would be used to document as well as design. The computer of then, and the IGS of now, was and still is an extremely fast and accurate slide rule, sorter, data processor, simulated rememberer (if there is such a word), logic organizer, comparer, evaluator, electronic drafting machine, and specification writer. The IGS will do whatever a human directs it to do more accurately and faster than any human alive. The real danger of such a wonder machine is that we tend to use the IGS as a crutch. We must continue to think; the IGS will handle the long manual routine items such as listing data points or drawing lines.

How, then, can the IGS be put to immediate use in the classroom or engineering office to do detail drawing? First, do not fear the machine; study how it works and how to communicate with the particular model that you have chosen from Table 1.3 in Chapter 1. Second, consider how much of your daily routine is taken up with detailing or highly repetitive nonthinking drafting tasks. If this is more than one-third, these types of tasks can be done by the computer and release over 30 percent of the work force to do design tasks. Thirty percent will return the cost of the IGS in 1 year for a large office.

If a small office is involved, maybe a time share renting technique will work effectively. Three, begin by automating the simplest tasks first to gain understanding and confidence in IGS usage. If possible, choose a reoccurring problem that must be solved by a different set of data each time and requires 1 or more hours to solve by a draftsperson. Chances are the time required to computerize the problem will take a couple of hours also, but the program can be used over and over again by inserting different data and solving the problem in milliseconds after that. Once a task has been set up and stored, the time required to repeat it is 1/100,000 of manual. Naturally one-time jobs are not done on an IGS.

A detail drawing is usually a type of production drawing. In the case of the machine drawing for mechanical engineers it is the working drawing containing all necessary shop information for the production of individual pieces of the machine. A detail drawing should give complete information for the construction of the design intent. In the case of an architect or civil engineer the detail drawing may be a wall section or stair detail. Detail drawings almost always involve sectional views to fully explain the construction, manufacture, or assembly of an object or circuit. Electrical engineers make excellent use of detail drawings, not only for connection diagrams but also for construction detail of electronic hardware.

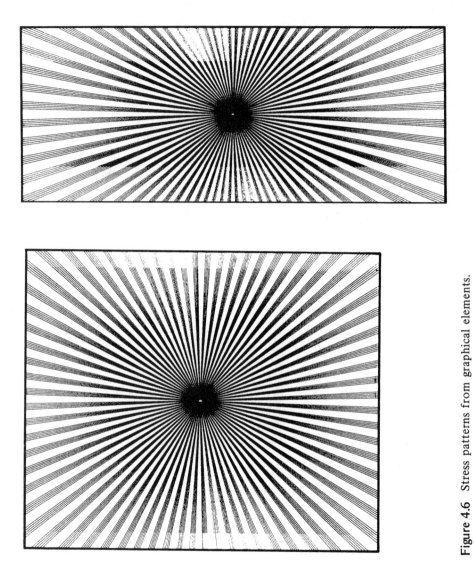

Figure 4.6   Stress patterns from graphical elements.

The IGS is used in all fields of engineering documentation for detailing the design layout. The designer has input the overall design intent, analyzed the design parameters, and tested the validity of the design. Figure 4.6 illustrates an output from a graphical finite analysis program which the design engineer has used to show stress patterns in the finished part. A set of detailed drawings can now be made from the design data stored in the memory of the IGS. To run a finite element analysis program the machine part must be described by a series of data points. These points form a network of small patches over the entire surface of the part. Parts with curved surfaces, holes, slots, raised surfaces, and other odd characteristics are not a problem because the size of the grid patchwork can be made to any size. The smaller the size of the patchwork, the more complex the shape that may be described. Figure 4.7 is an output of a grid patchwork for a curved surface.

With the design patchwork as a guide, the procedure for making a detailed drawing is as follows:

1. Select the views, remembering that in Chapter 3 the front view is described by plotting the X and Y array from the DATAPT list. The other views are plotted by selecting the X and Z array from the DATAPT list for the horizontal view and the Z and Y array for the profile view. Figure 2.15 is a program listing for plotting all three views of an object. In addition to the three primary views there may be sectional views or auxiliary views of surfaces not fully described by the three principle views.
2. Choose a drawing scale, by calling factor, which will allow an arrangement of the views and the location of needed dimensions, notes, and part labels.
3. Call out the location for centerlines of features such as holes, slots, or machined sections and block in all fillets and rounds.
4. Add dimensions by CALL DIMEN, remembering that this subroutine contains extension lines, dimension lines, arrowheads, and annotation for placement and specifications of dimensions.
5. Select the proper notes by the use of CALL LABEL and fill in the automated title block and related notes necessary to the drawing.
6. Check the output by previewing on the DVST, make any corrections in computer memory, and output on the digital plotter.

Figures 4.8 through 4.15 illustrate several detailed drawings made in this fashion. Detail drawings are made quickly and easily using this method. Automated drafting is truly the generation of working drawings from the design database used by the engineer in Chapter 3.

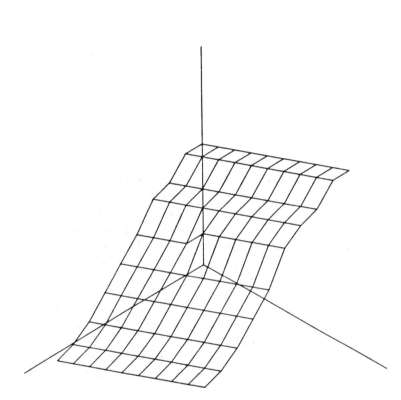

Figure 4.7 Surface described as a grid patch network.

```
C     ***************************************************************
C     *                                                             *
C     *  DISPLAY PROGRAM FOR EITHER THE ELECTROSTATIC PLOTTER OR    *
C     *  THE DVST TO DEMONSTRATE A DETAILED DRAWING OF A MACHINE    *
C     *  PART.  RUNS FROM THE IBM 370/3081 OR THE VAX 11/780.       *
C     *                                                             *
C     ***************************************************************
C     SELECT OUTPUT DEVICE WITH PLOTS OR INITT
      CALL INITT(240)
C     SELECT INPUT STATEMENT FOR IBM OR VAX
      READ(1,*) NPTS
      DO 30 I=1,NPTS
      READ(1,*)X,Y,IPEN
   30 CALL PLOT(X,Y,IPEN)
      CALL DASHP(3.75,2.75,.15)
      CALL CIRCL(4.125,8.25,90.,270.,.375,.375,0.)
      CALL CIRCL(5.25,7.,270.,360.,.25,.25,0.)
      CALL CIRCL(5.5,8.5,0.,90.,.25,.25,0.)
      READ(1,*)NPTS2
      DO 40 J=1,NPTS2
      READ(1,*)X,Y,DIME,ANGLE
   40 CALL DIMEN(X,Y,DIME,ANGLE,1.)
      READ(1,*) NPTS3
      DO 50 K=1,NPTS3
      READ(1,*)X,Y,TLEN,THETH,ALINE
   50 CALL CENTER(X,Y,TLEN,THETH,.125,.03125,ALINE)
      CALL FINITT(0,0)
      STOP
      END
      SUBROUTINE CENTER(X,Y,TLEN,THETA,DASH,SPACE,ALINE)
      THETA=3.14/180.*THETA
      TOTAL=DASH+SPACE+SPACE+ALINE
      NUM=TLEN/2./TOTAL
      CALL PLOT(X,Y,3)
      X1=X
      Y1=Y
      DO 31 I=1,NUM
      X1=X1-DASH/2.*COS(THETA)
      Y1=Y1-DASH/2.*SIN(THETA)
      CALL PLOT(X1,Y1,2)
      X1=X1-SPACE*COS(THETA)
      Y1=Y1-SPACE*SIN(THETA)
      CALL PLOT(X1,Y1,3)
      X1=X1-ALINE*COS(THETA)
      Y1=Y1-ALINE*SIN(THETA)
      CALL PLOT(X1,Y1,2)
      X1=X1-SPACE*COS(THETA)
      Y1=Y1-SPACE*SIN(THETA)
      CALL PLOT(X1,Y1,3)
      X1=X1-DASH/2.*COS(THETA)
      Y1=Y1-DASH/2.*SIN(THETA)
```

Figure 4.8 Source program for detailed display of machine part.

```
31 CALL PLOT(X1,Y1,2)
   X1=X
   Y1=Y
   CALL PLOT(X,Y,3)
   DO 41 J=1,NUM
   X1=X1+DASH/2.*COS(THETA)
   Y1=Y1+DASH/2.*SIN(THETA)
   CALL PLOT(X1,Y1,2)
   X1=X1+SPACE*COS(THETA)
   Y1=Y1+SPACE*SIN(THETA)
   CALL PLOT(X1,Y1,3)
   X1=X1+ALINE*COS(THETA)
   Y1=Y1+ALINE*SIN(THETA)
   CALL PLOT(X1,Y1,2)
   X1=X1+SPACE*COS(THEAT)
   Y1=Y1+SPACE*SIN(THETA)
   CALL PLOT(X1,Y1,3)
   X1=X1+DASH/2.*COS(THETA)
   Y1=Y1+DASH/2.*SIN(THETA)
41 CALL PLOT(X1,Y1,2)
   X1=X1*COS(THETA)+X
   Y1=Y1*SIN(THETA)+Y
   RETURN
   END
//G.SYSIN DD *
64
2. 2. 3          10.5 2. 2        5.5625 8.25 3      4.125 7.875 1.125 90. .375
5.5 2. 2         10.5 3.5 2       6.125 8.25 2       4.125 7.875 1.125 0. .375
5.5 2.75 2       9.5 3.5 2        5.375 8.75 3       5.25 7.25 .75 90. .1875
2.75 2.75 2      9.5 3. 2         5.875 8.75 2       5.25 7.25 .75 0. .1875
2.75 3.5 2       8.75 3. 2        5.25 8.875 3       5.25 8.5 .75 90. .1875
2. 3.5 2         8.75 2. 2        5.25 9.875 2       5.25 8.5 .75 0. .1875
2. 2. 2          8.75 2.75 3      5.5 8.625 3        4.125 2.375 1.125 90. .375
2. 3. 3          10.5 2.75 2      5.5 9.875 2        9.625 2.375 1.125 90. .375
2.75 3. 2        9.25 2.75 3      8.6875 2. 3        /*
2. 7. 3          9.25 2. 2        8.0625 2. 2        //
5.25 7. 2        10. 2. 3         8.6875 3. 3
5.5 7.25 3       10. 2.75 2       8.0625 3. 2
5.5 7.5 2        2. 3.5625 3      3.75 2. 3
4.125 7.5 2      2. 3.875 2       11
4.125 8.25 3     5.5 2.8125 3     2. 3.6875 .75 0.
5.5 8.25 2       5.5 3.875 2      2. 3.9375 3.5 0.
5.5 8.5 2        8.75 3.0625 3    1.8125 2. 1.5 90.
5.25 8.75 3      8.75 3.875 2     5.6875 2. .75 90.
2. 8.75 2        10.5 3.5625 3    8.0625 2. 1. 90.
2. 7. 2          10.5 3.875 2     8.75 3.6875 .75 0.
2. 7.75 3        4.125 7.3125 3   8.75 3.9375 1.75 0.
2.75, 7.75 2     4.125 6.8125 2   4.125 6.8125 1.375 0.
2.75 7. 3        5.5 7.125 3      5.25 9.8125 .25 0.
2.75 8.75 2      5.5 6.8125 2     5.9375 8.25 L5 90.
8.75 2. 3        5.5625 7.5 3     6.1875 7.5 .75 90.
                 6.125 7.5 2      8
```

Figure 4.8 *(continued)*

```
5. 5 3 .875 2
8.75 3.0625 3
8.75 3.875 2
10.5 3.5625 3
10.5 3.875 2
4.125 7.3125 3
4.125 6.8125 2
5. 5 7.125 3
5. 5 6.8125 2
5.5625 7.5 3
6.125 7.5 2
5.5625 8.25 2
6.125 8.25 3
5.375 8.75 2
5.875 8.75 3
5.25 8.875 3
5.25 9.875 2
5. 5 8.625 3
5. 5 9.875 2
8.6875 2. 3
8.0625 2. 2
8.6875 3. 3
8.0625 3. 2
3.75 2. 3
11
2. 3.6875 .75 0.
2. 3.9375 3.5 0.
4.8125 2. 4.5 90.
5.6875 2. .75 90.
8.0625 2. 1. 90.
8.75 3.6875 .75 0.
8.75 3.9375 1.75 0.
4.125 6.6125 1.375 0.
5.25 9.8125 .25 0.
5.9375 8.25 .5 90.
6.1875 7.5 .75 90.
8
4.125 7.875 1.125 90. .375
4.125 7.875 1.125 0. .375
5.25 7.25 .75 90. .1875
5.25 7.25 .75 0. .1875
5.25 8.5 .75 90. .1875
5.25 8.5 .75 0. .1875
4.125 2.375 1.125 90. .375
9.625 2.375 1.125 90. .375
```

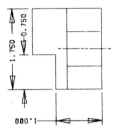

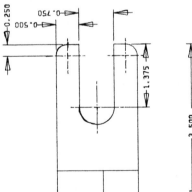

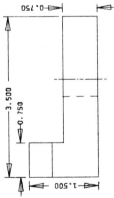

Figure 4.8 (continued)

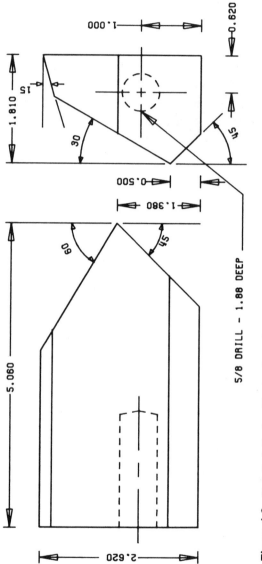

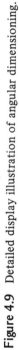

Figure 4.9 Detailed display illustration of angular dimensioning.

```
C     **************************************************************
C     *                                                            *
C     *  DISPLAY PROGRAM FOR EITHER THE ELECTROSTATIC PLOTTER OR    *
C     *  THE DVST TO DEMONSTRATE A DETAILED DRAWING OF A MACHINE    *
C     *  PART.  RUNS FROM THE IBM 370/3081 OR THE VAX 11/780.       *
C     *                                                            *
C     **************************************************************
C     SELECT OUTPUT DEVICE WITH PLOTS OR INITT
      CALL PLOTS
      DIMENSION X(100),Y(100),IPEN(100)
      DATA X/4.25,2*5.,5.,3.5,2*2.,2*4.25,7.,2*9.,2*8.5,2*7.75,2*7.
     +,2*8.,9.,8.,7.,3.5,4.25,2*5.5,3.5/
      DATA Y/2*2.,2.5,2*3.5,2*2.,3.125,2*2.,2*3.5,2*3.25,2*3.5,2*3.
     +5,2*2.,3*2.5,3.25,2*5.,6.,2*7./
      DATA IPEN/3,7*2,3,13*2,3,4*2/
      DO 1 I=1,27
    1 CALL PLOT(X(I),Y(I),IPEN(I))
      CALL RECT(2.5,5.,.75,1.5,0.,3)
      CALL RECT(2.,6.5,.5,1.5,0.,3)
      CALL RECT(2.,5.,.75,2.25,0.,3)
      CALL PLOT(2.,3.25,3)
      CALL DASHP(4.,3.25,.133)
      CALL PLOT(7.,3.,3)
      CALL DASHP(9.,3.,.133)
      CALL PLOT(7.,2.5,3)
      CALL DASHP(9.,2.5,.133)
      CALL PLOT(2.5,5.,3)
      CALL DASHP(2.5,7.,.133)
      CALL PLOT(3.,5.,3)
      CALL DASHP(3.,7.,.133)
      CALL CIRCL(3.,2.75,0.,360.,.25,.25,0.)
      CALL DIMEN(2.0,7.25,3.5,0.,1.)
      CALL DIMEN(2.,4.75,2.25,0.,1.)
      CALL DIMEN(2.,3.75,1.5,0.,1.)
      CALL DIMEN(4.25,1.75,1.25,0.,1.)
      CALL DIMEN(7.,4.,.75,0.,1.)
      CALL DIMEN(8.5,3.75,.5,0.,1.)
      CALL DIMEN(1.75,2.,1.5,90.,1.)
      CALL DIMEN(1.75,5.,2.,90.,1.)
      CALL DIMEN(5.75,5.,1.,90.,1.)
      CALL DIMEN(5.75,2.,.5,90.,1.)
      CALL CENTER(2.75,2.75,2.,90.,.175,.175,.475)
      CALL CENTER(2.75,2.75,2.,0.,.175,.175,.475)
      CALL PLOT(7.,4.,3)
      CALL PLOT(7.,3.75,2)
      CALL PLOT(7.75,4.,3)
      CALL PLOT(7.75,3.75,2)
      CALL PLOT(0.,0.,999)
      STOP
      END
```

Figure 4.10 Computer program.

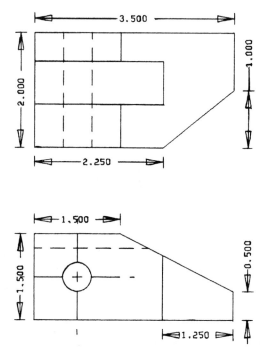

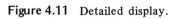

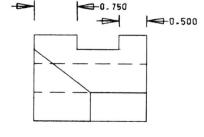

Figure 4.11 Detailed display.

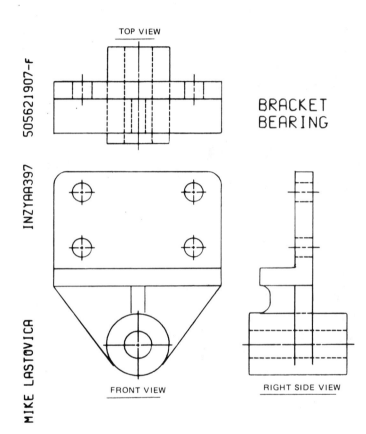

Figure 4.12 Detailed drawings.

508523654

INZYAA453

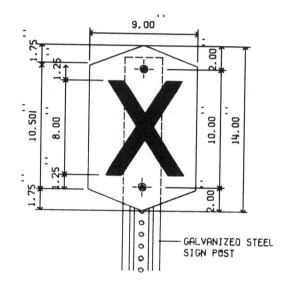

R.R. WHISTLE POST

WHISTLE POST IS TO BE USED
IN ADVANCE OF ALL PUBLIC
ROAD CROSSINGS AND IN ADVANCE
OF CERTAIN HEAVILY USED
PRIVATE ROAD CROSSINGS WHERE
WHISTLE WARNING IS CONSIDERED
NECESSARY.

NICK MRAZ

Figure 4.13 Sample display.

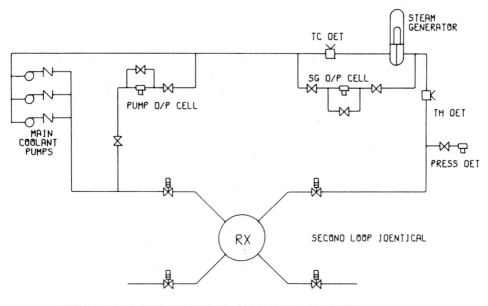

BASIC NUCLEAR REACTOR PRIMARY SYSTEM
(PRESSURIZING SYSTEM OMITED)

Figure 4.14 Typical diagram.

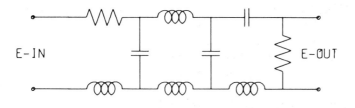

LADDER-TYPE FILTER CIRCUIT

Figure 4.15 Ladder-type filter circuit.

SECTIONAL VIEWS

The invisible surfaces or features of a simple object are easily shown by the use of a hidden line. Hidden lines are equally easy to place on a computer-generated drawing by the use of DASHP or DASHL. The IGS operator can place as many as required. When the IGS memory is required to place hidden lines from three different arrays of X, Y, and Z data lists it is a different matter. The result is a perplexing mass of hidden lines for the interior of a machine part. Whenever this happens the IGS operator usually makes one or more of the views in section. A view in section is obtained by imagining the object to be separated by a cutting plane. This cutting plane is described to the computer as a bounded area. The area bounded is the solid section of the interior of the machine part. These solid sections can then be crosshatched for ease of reading by calling SHADE. See Figure 2.17.

When the bounded area cuts a machine part lengthwise, the section obtained is called a longitudinal section; a crosswise cut is a cross section. If the bounded area cuts entirely across the machine part, it is known as a full section. Other arrangements of bounded surfaces will produce the traditional half sections, broken sections, revolved sections, removed sections, and phantom sections (Figure 4.16).

The SHADE subroutine draws section lines in any shaped area formed by two lines defined by two sets of points. SHADE assumes that an imaginary line connects the first points of the two lines and that another line connects the last points of the two lines. Sectioning is done in the bounded area enclosed by the defined lines and the imaginary lines.

The calling sequence is

CALL SHADE(XARRAY1,YARRAY1,XARRAY2,YARRAY2,DLIN,
    ANGLE,NPTS1,INC1,NPTS2,INC2)

XARRAY1 and YARRAY1 are the names of the arrays containing the X and
    Y coordinates of the data points to be plotted for line 1.
XARRAY2 and YARRAY2 are the names of the arrays containing the X and
    Y coordinates of the data points to be plotted for line 2.
DLIN is the distance between shading lines.
ANGLE is the shading line inclination angle, in degrees.
NPTS1 is the number of data points forming line 1.
INC1 is the increment between elements of the arrays forming line 1.
NPTS2 is the number of data points forming line 2.
INC2 is the increment between elements of the arrays forming line 2.

The arrays must be dimensioned with at least NPTS + 2 elements. The adjusted minimum value and the adjusted delta value, normally provided by the SCALE subroutine, must be stored following the data array. If scaling is not required, the user must place the appropriate minimum and delta values in the specified elements of the arrays. For a full scale, these values should be 0.0 (minimum) and 1.0 (delta).

Most software subroutines for sectioning provide for one type of section line, which is the general material type. If, for instance, a material such as concrete is sectioned and the operator needs to show the sectioned area in its true material representation, he will probably section the object with open shading and stipple a representative portion by hand. In the case of Figure 4.17 a soil section was desired. In this case a general section line was used with a varying spacing technique; next the operator hand-stippled the rocks and stones; seeing that the computer would produce perfectly round stones and not ones with ragged edges.

The combination of computer output and manual clarification is a common tool employed in many offices. All notation and graphing were output from the

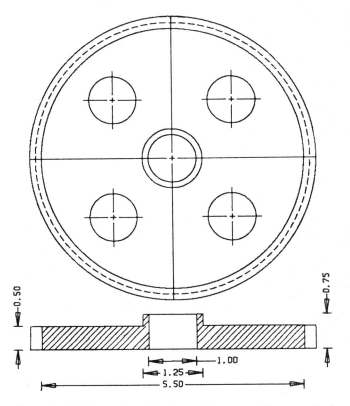

Figure 4.16 Example of shade used in a machine part display.

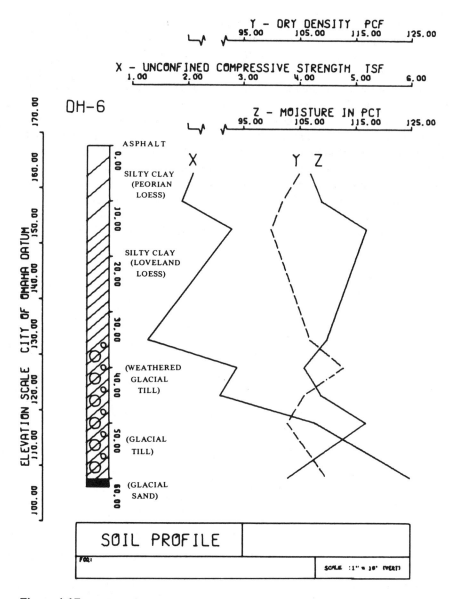

Figure 4.17   Soil profile display.

computer. Section techniques were used in Figures 4.16 and 4.17. The user can note that the drawings all look quite natural.

DIMENSIONING AND NOTATION

Earlier in this chapter we discussed detail drawings; in addition to giving the shape of a production part, information such as the space between surfaces, locations of features, type of material, numbers required, and kind of finish must be included. The technique for including this information on a detail drawing is called dimensioning and notation. When a detailer dimensions an object such as a machine part or building, she exercises engineering judgment and indicates a thorough knowledge of machine tools or construction practices.

The techniques of automated drafting for dimensioning and notation do not differ from conventional methods. The part still has to be described systematically by dividing it into simple geometric shapes. The rules learned in earlier engineering drawing classes hold true also. The dimensioning of an object is accomplished by specifying each elemental form to indicate its size and relationship relative to a centerline, baseline, or finished surface.

The procedure for using automated dimensions and notes are outlined in the following steps:

1. Divide the object to be dimensioned into mental geometric shapes and decide which are size and which are location dimensions.
2. Call DIMEN for placement of the size dimensions on each geometric shape.
3. Select the locating centerlines and call CNTRL for the proper placement.
4. Call DIMEN for the plotting of the location dimensions.
5. Add the final overall dimensions by CALL PLOT and CALL DIMEN in combination.
6. Call LABEL for adding notes that must be centered in a title space or follow a CALL LEADER; CALL SYMBOL may be used for block notes.
7. All leaders, bars, boxes for metric sizes, and CALL NUMBER for computer calculations to be placed inside notes.

The subroutine DIMEN was described in detail in Chapter 2 and should be referred to in order to place dimensions where they will be most easily understood. The extension, dimension lines, and arrowheads are done at the same time. The actual length of the dimension line is the product of DIME (the labeled length) and SCALER. If the actual length is 1.2 inches or longer, the annotation is printed in the middle of the dimension line. If the dimension line is between 0.8 and 1.2 inches long, the annotation is placed after the line. If the line is less than 0.8 inch long, the arrowheads are placed outside, along with the annotation (see Figure 4.21).

```
C  ***************************************************************
C  *   THIS PROGRAM ILLUSTRATES THE USE OF THE FOLLOWING GRAPHIC   *
C  *   SUBROUTINES FOR AUTOMATED GRAPHICS                          *
C  *                                                               *
C  *        PLOT                                                   *
C  *        SYMBOL                                                 *
C  *        DIMEN                                                  *
C  *        DASHP                                                  *
C  *        CIRCLE                                                 *
C  *        AROHD                                                  *
C  ***************************************************************
       CALL PLOTS
       CALL SYMBOL(11.,6.5,.2,'WEDGE',0.,5)
       CALL SYMBOL(11.,6.,.2,'BLOCK',0.,5)
       DIMENSION XLINE (50), YLINE (50),IPEN (50)
       DATA XLINE/5.38,10.,10.,8.8,7.6,7.6,5.3,5.38,6.,6.,8.8,8.8
      +,5.3,7.68,6.,6.,8.8,8.8,7.68,10.,10.,5.38,5.38,7.7,8.,8.1,
      +8.28,8.38,9.,8.18,11*8.8/
       DATA YLINE/2.,2.,2.3,3.74,2.,3.14,4.,2.,3.78,4.2,4.2,2.,2.
      +74,5.,5.,5.64,5.64,6.64,6.64,5.64,5.64,5.64,7.26,7.26,5.,5
      +*3.58,3.1,3.38,3.48,3.68,3.78,4.4,5.3,5.8,5.9,6.1,6.2,6.8/
       DATA IPEN/3,3*2,3,3*2,3,3*2,3,6*2,3,4*2,3,2,3,2,3,2,3,2,3,
      +2,3,2,3,2,3,2,3,2/
       DO 1 I=1,42
     1 CALL PLOT(XLINE(I),YLINE(I),IPEN(I))
       CALL PLOT(8.8,2/74,3)
       CALL DASHP(7.68,3.14,.1)
       CALL PLOT(7.68,3.14,3)
       CALL DASHP(7.93,6.64,.08)
       CALL PLOT(8.43,6.64,3)
       CALL DASHP(8.43,6.64,.08)
       CALL DIMEN(5.38,4.85,2.3,0.,1.)
       CALL DIMEN(8.18,5.56,.62,0.,1.)
       CALL DIMEN(8.95,3.58,.62,90.,1.)
       CALL DIMEN(10.35,2.,2.2,90.,1.)
       CALL DIMEN(5.23,2.,2.,90.,1.)
       CALL PLOT(9.05,4.2,3)
       CALL PLOT(10.25,4.2,2)
       CALL DIMEN(5.38,4.85,2.3,0.,1.)
       CALL DIMEN(5.23,5.,2.26,90.,1.)
       CALL DIMEN(5.38,7.41,.62,0.,1.)
       CALL DIMEN(6.,7.51,2.8,0.,1.)
       CALL DIMEN(10.15,5.64,1.,90.,1.)
       CALL DIMEN(10.35,6.64,.62,90.,1.)
       CALL AROHD(7.,4.5,7.98,3.723,.3,.1,12)
       CALL PLOT(6.5,4.5,3)
       CALL PLOT(7.,4.5,2)
       CALL SYMBOL(5.85,4.45,.1,'.50 DIA',0.,7)
       CALL CIRCLE(8.18,3.58, .25,0.,36,10.)
       CALL PLOT(18.,0.,999)
       STOP
       END
```

Figure 4.18 Example of dimensioning program.
162

Figures 4.18 and 4.20 illustrate an automated method of organizing a system of lines, symbols, figures, and notes to indicate size and locations. Output drawings are shown in Figures 4.29 and 4.21. Figure 4.22 is an example of the use of notes to describe and dimension an architectural detail. Remember that few details are drawn full size, so the use of SCALER will provide the automatic reduction of the dimensioning package and leave the notation sizes full.

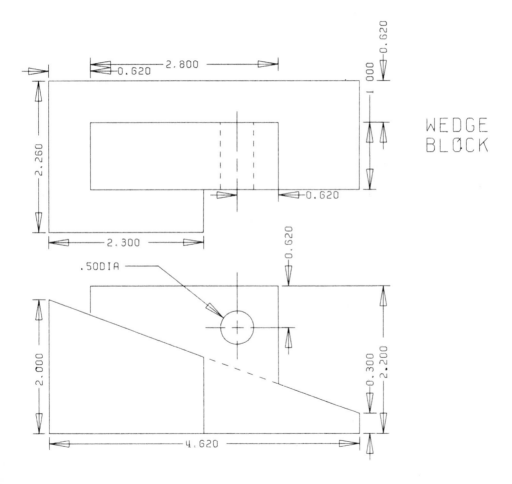

Figure 4.19 Example of dimensioning program display output.

```
 CALL PLOTS
 DIMENSION X(50),Y(50),IPEN(50),THETA(50),SCA(50),DIM(50),DASH(50)
+,SPACE(50),ALINE(50),TL(50),TLEN(50),X1(50),Y1(50),IPEN1(50),DL(5
+0)
 DATA X/2*3.,2.,5.,5.2,8.,2.,2*5.2,2*8.,2*2.,3.,2*5.,3.8,4.6,5.8,6
+.6,5.2,3*4.2,3*6.2,2*2.,5.2,2.,4.2,1.8,1.6,1.8,2*8.2,8.4,8.2/
 DATA Y/2.,4.25,5.4,2.,6.,2.6,2*9.,7.7,8.6,2*10.,2*7.,7.6,6*9.,2*5
+.2,2*9.5,2*2.8,10.2,6.8,5.2,2*1.8,2*2.,7.,2.8,5.2,2.6,9./
 DATA IPEN/3,2,3,2,3,2,3,*2/
 DATA TL/16*0.,4*1.05,2.85/
 DATA DL/16*0.,5*.1/
 DATA THETA/16*0.,4*90.,2*0.,4*90.,6*0.,7*90./
 DATA TLEN/21*0.,6*1.3/
 DATA DASH/21*0.,6*.1/
 DATA SPACE/21*0.,6*.1/
 DATA ALINE/21*0.,6*.3/
 DATA DIM/27*0.,6.,1.,2.8,2.2,2.,3.4,4.,3.,2.4,.8,3.4,1./
 DATA SCA/27*0.,12*1./
 DATA X1/16*0.,3.8,4.6,5.8,6.6,7.95/
 DATA Y1/16*0.,4*9.95,9./
 DATA IPEN1/16*3,5*2/
 CALL RECT(2.,2.,4.,6.,0.,3)
 CALL CIRCLE(6.2,2.8,.4,0.,180.,2.)
 CALL CIRCLE(4.2,5.2,.4,0.,180.,2.)
 DO 1 I=1,16
1 CALL PLOT(X(I),Y(I),IPEN(I))
 DO 1 J=1,16
 CALL PLOT(X1(J),Y1(J),IPEN1(J))
2 CALL DASHP(X(J),Y(J),DL(J))
 DO 3 K=22,27
3 CALL CENTER(X(K),Y(K),TLEN(K),THETA(K),DASH(K),SPACE(K),ALINE(K))
 DO 4 L=28,39
4 CALL DIMEN(X(L),Y(L),DIM(L),THETA(L),SCA(L))
 CALL SYMBOL(2.8,8.,.4,'B',0.,1)
 CALL SYMBOL(6.4,8.4,.4,'A',0.,1)
 CALL SYMBOL(4.6,3.,.4,'B',0.,1)
 CALL SYMBOL(6.7,3.2,.4,'A',0.,1)
 CALL SYMBOL(8.8,10.4,.1,'SURFACES A & B PARALLEL',0.,23)
 CALL SYMBOL(8.4,1.,.1,'DRILL 2 HOLES',0.,13)
 CALL SYMBOL(8.25,7.55,.1,'O.4',0.,4)
 CALL SYMBOL(7.95,1.15,.1,'9/16',0.,4)
 CALL AROHD(8.2,8.,8.2,8.6,.3,.1,12)
 CALL PLOT(1.7,6.,3)
 CALL PLOT(1.9,6.,2)
 CALL PLOT(8.1,2.6,3)
 CALL PLOT(8.3,2.6,2)
 CALL PLOT(8.1,8.6,3)
 CALL PLOT(8.3,8.6,2)
 CALL LEADER(7.9,1.2,7.4,1.2,6.5,2.5)
 CALL TITLE
 CALL PLOT(18.0,0.0,999)
 STOP
 END
```

Figure 4.20 Display program.

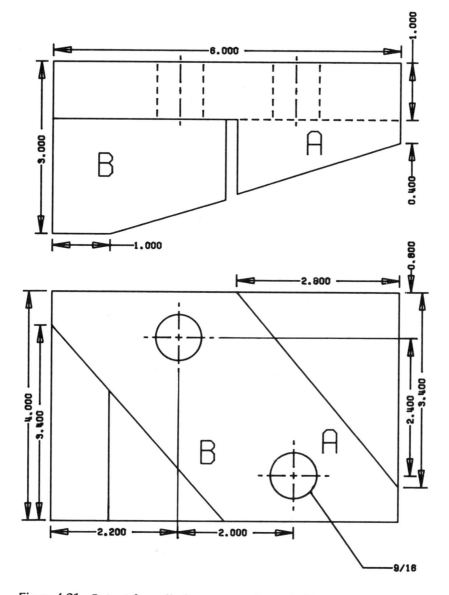

Figure 4.21 Output from display program shown in Fig. 20.

The use of fractional dimensioning such as 1/2, 1/4, and the like have mostly been dropped from mechanical details but are still used in architectural details. The decimal system is used with the subroutine DIMEN. United States industry has adopted a dual system of English and metric for the time being. The English annotation is placed inside the dimension line for mechanical drawings, with the metric size placed directly below this in a rectangular box. A note is placed on the drawing stating

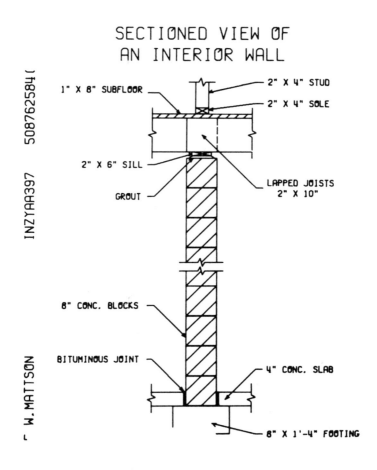

Figure 4.22 Architectural example of notes.

NOTE: ALL DIMENSIONS ARE GIVEN IN ENGLISH INCHES WITH METRIC SIZES PLACED DIRECTLY BELOW AND OUTLINED BY A SOLID BOX. ALL METRIC SIZES ARE IN MILLIMETERS UNLESS OTHERWISE NOTED.

It is not our purpose of this section to repeat a detailed treatise of dimensioning practices, geometric positioning and tolerancing, designation of surface finishes, or classes of fits. It is enough to say that many excellent books, ANSI (American National Standards Institute) standards, and handbooks exist on this subject. Having the computer do the sizing and dimensioning of parts does not give the designer license to avoid using the fifty or so rules set forth in any excellent engineering graphics text. The operator of an automated graphics system uses either of two recognized methods, aligned or unidirectional. She does not invent a new system. She may write a few system subroutines for drawing true-position symbols or the like but uses them as they have always been used.

Limits are calculated by the computer and placed automatically for the operator after the proper input of nominal size, basic size, allowance, tolerance, limits of size, and type of fit has been placed in the computer program designed to do this. There is no magic involved in the use of an automatic drafting machine. Everything must be preprogrammed for ease of operation later.

THREADS AND FASTENERS

The ability to represent screw threads is based on a clear understanding of automated dimensioning practices, just discussed, and the ability to see an application for their use such as piping. Nearly one-half of the documentation of threads and fasteners is related to dimensioning. For example, the following note may be used on a threaded hole:

$\dfrac{5}{16}$ DRILL -.94 to 1.00 DEEP

90° C'SK TO .40 - .42 DIA

$\dfrac{3}{8}$ -24 UNF - 2B

.62 MIN DEPTH OF FULL THRD.

The threaded hole was produced by a few simple statements written in the form of a subroutine, as shown on the next page:

```
C  ****************************************************************
C  *                                                              *
C  *   SUBROUTINE FOR THE DISPLAY OF A THREADED HOLE LOCATION IN  *
C  *   PLAN VIEW.  ARGUMENTS ARE: XPAGE,YPAGE, DMAJ & DMIN        *
C  *                                                              *
C  ****************************************************************
       SUBROUTINE THOLE(XPAGE,YPAGE,DMAJ,DMIN)
       X=XPAGE+DMAJ/2.
       CALL CIRCL(X,YPAGE,0.,360.,DMAJ/2.,MAJ/2.,.5)
       X1=XPAGE+DMIN/2.
       CALL CIRCL(X1,YPAGE,0.,360.,DMIN/2.,DMIN/2.,0.)
       RETURN
       END
```

The program statement used to plot the 0.375-diameter threaded hole on the drawing would be

CALL THOLE(2.625,4.500,.375,.291)

This statement in a graphics program would cause a 3/8-inch-diameter threaded hole representation to appear at X=2.625 and Y=4.500 for the center of the hole in plan view. THOLE did not exist until the user wrote it and placed it in memory. Once stored, the subroutine can be used over and over again for representation of a threaded hole.

An elevation view of this threaded section would require another subpicture to be stored in computer memory, to be recalled at the will of the draftsperson or designer. An example of a subroutine for plotting elevation views of the threaded hole follows:

```
C  ****************************************************************
C  *                                                              *
C  *   THIS SUBROUTINE DISPLAYS AN ELEVATION OF A THREADED HOLE   *
C  *                                                              *
C  ****************************************************************
       SUBROUTINE THOLER(XP,YP,DM,DIN,DEPTH)
       X=XP+DM/2.
       CALL PLOT(X,YP,3)
       Y=YP-DEPTH
       CALL DASHP(X,Y,.05)
       X2=X-DM
       CALL PLOT(X2,Y,3)
       CALL DASHP(X2,YP,.05)
       XM=X2+(XP+DIN/2.)
       CALL PLOT(XM,XP,3)
       CALL DASHP(XM,Y.05)
       YY=Y-DM/10.
       CALL DASHP(XP,YY,.05)
       XXM=XP-DIN/2.
       CALL DASHP(XXM,YP,.05)
       RETURN
       END
```

The remaining half of the documentation of automated threads and fasteners rests with the ability to write template figures as described in Chapter 2. These template parts should contain the branching necessary to plot simplified, schematic, or detailed thread representation. This is usually one argument variable which allows the user to select the type of representation desired.

Threads in section may be handled with the combination of techniques described under "Sectional Views" in this chapter and the subroutines listed earlier. A separate set of software is available for pictoral representation of conventional ANSI thread symbols as well as

1. Square threads
2. Acme and stubb acme threads
3. Buttress threads
4. ISO (International Standards Organization for Metric Screw Threads) metric screw threads
5. ANSI-OMFS metric screw threads

Techniques for pictorial representation are presented in Chapter 5.

Template Figures for Fasteners

Subroutines for the representation of bolts and fasteners should conform to ANSI B18.2-1965. ANSI has approved three series of bolts and nuts: regular series, heavy series, and light series. To automatically plot these template parts, the user must select from the following types:

1. Studs
2. Cap screws
3. Machine screws
4. Set screws
5. Keys
6. Taper pins
7. Lock washers or plain
8. Rivets
9. Springs
10. Miscellaneous devices covered by annotation and solid object

Commercially Available Software Packages

Preprogrammed software is available from IGS manufacturers or consulting engineering firms who specialize in developmental software. It is beyond the scope of this text to spend more time on the *creation* of programming software (see Chapter 2). The emphasis is on the *use* of available software to create an engineering drawing or diagram. See exercises 8 through 13 for practice in use of software routines.

PIPING DETAILS

Piping, piping systems, and the many components that make up piping diagrams are of interest to a great many engineers and technicians. This area of engineering graphics is largely ignored in conventional textbooks. It is of primary concern in a large number of industries due to the lack of qualified detailers and is one of the easiest areas to computer-automate. Although each engineering group is specialized, all are directly concerned with various forms of piping, hose, tubing, and the fittings that connect these components into workable systems.

This section is about piping systems. The term piping system means a complete network of pipes, valves, and other parts designed to do a specific job in a plant. In this section we shall introduce the reader to piping systems and how to detail them. Plant operations are so tied in to the piping systems that a piping or valve breakdown in one part of a plant can bring operations in another section to an almost immediate halt.

Piping carries fluids from one part of the plant to another. In addition to carrying liquids such as hydraulic fluids and oils, piping systems carry gas and compressed air, which are considered to be fluids because they flow. Fluids travel through a system at various temperatures, pressures, and speeds.

Before looking at a more involved network of pipes, consider a typical section of a system. Figure 4.23 shows a common arrangement of pipes, valves, and fit-

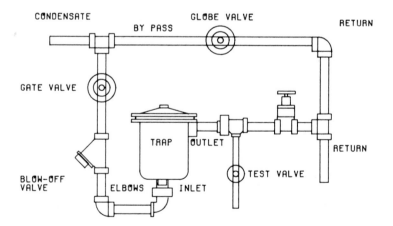

Figure 4.23 Piping example.

tings in a low-pressure line. The valves control the flow of fluid through the piping. The fittings connect the sections of pipe. In an actual installation, the length of piping between valves is much greater, depending on the application and its requirements. The purpose of this section of the system is to send the fluid through the trap, which bleeds the impurities out of the system so that only the fluid is carried through the piping. The impurities collected by the trap are produced when, for any number of reasons, fluid in the piping condenses. That is, the fluid cools enough so that some of it becomes liquid again. The trap is so constructed that the liquid is caught, but the fluid remains in the system.

To trace the line, begin at the upper left corner of Figure 4.23 where a fitting connects three pipes. This is where the fluid and condensate enter this section of the system. The fluid passes through the open gas valve and past the blowoff valve. When the blowoff valve is opened, the pressure in the line blows any debris in the line out of the system. With the valve closed, the fluid continues through the line to the trap.

To permit the pipeline to make a turn, a fitting called an elbow is drawn. This is done by a subroutine called ELBOW. Note that another elbow connects the pipe to the end of the fixture at the bottom of the trap. The fluid passes through the trap, leaving any condensate behind, and then it passes through the outlet. Another fitting is drawn by calling TEE, because it resembles the letter T. When it is necessary to test the fluid for any reason, the gate valve is closed, and the test valve is opened, and the fluid passes through the test valve for sampling. When no testing is being done, the fluid passes straight through the open gate valve and returns to the line. Gate valves are drawn by the computer through the use of call GATE. The subroutine ELBOW is a routine that the author has used to display this fitting and would appear as the following lines of FORTRAN:

```
C  ******************************************************************
C  *                                                                *
C  *   THIS DISPLAY ROUTINE ALLOWS FOUR LOCATIONS FOR ELBOW JOINTS*
C  *   IF THE POSITIONS ARE:                                        *
C  *                        1 = 0 DEGREES                           *
C  *                        2 = 90 DEGREES                          *
C  *                        3 = 180 DEGREES                         *
C  *                        4 = 270 DEGREES                         *
C  ******************************************************************
       SUBROUTINE ELBOW(XXX,YYY,SIZE,POS)
       CALL PLOT(XXX,YYY,3)
       XL=SIZE*7
       YY=YYY-SIZE
       XC=XXX+SIZE*6
       R=SIZE*6
       Y=YYY+SIZE
       IF(POS.EQ.1)GOTO 1
       IF(POS.EQ.2)GOTO 2
       IF(POS.EQ.3)GOTO 3
       IF(POS.EQ.4)GOTO 4
```

```
1 CALL RECT(XXX,YY,SIZE,XL,0.,3)
  CALL RECT(XXX,YYY,SIZE,XL,90.,3)
  CALL CIRCL(XC,YYY,0.,90.,R,R,0.)
  GOTO 10
2 CALL RECT(XXX,YYY,SIZE,XL,180.,3)
  XOFF=XXX+SIZE
  CALL RECT(XOFF,YYY,SIZE,XL,90.,3)
  YR=YYY+SIZE*6
  CALL CIRCL(XXX,YR,90.,180.,R,R,0.)
  GOTO 10
3 CALL RECT(XXX,YYY,SIZE,XL,270.,3)
  CALL RECT(XXX,Y,SIZE,XL,180.,3)
  XR=XXX-SIZE*6
  CALL CIRCL(XR,YYY,180.,270.,R,R,0.)
  GOTO 10
4 CALL RECT(XXX,YYY,SIZE,XL,0.,3)
  X=XXX-SIZE
  CALL RECT(X,YYY,SIZE,XL,270.,3)
  YR=YYY-SIZE*6
  CALL CIRCL(XXX,YR,270.,360.,R,R,0.)
10 RETURN
  END
```

Pipe fittings (like elbows) are preprogrammed as template symbols and are the parts used to connect sections of pipe, sections of hoses, and tubing. Those shown in Figure 4.23 are threaded fittings. When the system is first set up, the pipe symbols are located by a grid placement technique explained in Chapter 2, "Standard Template Parts." Next call plots are used to connect the fittings, and call symbols are added to label each section of the system.

This piping example illustrates the fact that a piping diagram and the actual system perform a particular job. The sole purpose of the piping in the diagram leading to and from the trap is to collect the condensate, which is undesirable. Regardless of how complicated the system may seem to be, the diagram is simply a network of components which carry a liquid or gas from one point to another. With the introduction of an automatic method of drawing the diagram, the engineer who is knowledgeable in piping assembly can now produce excellent diagrams for documentation and later installation. Actually, it is not that piping diagrams are more complicated than other forms of drafting; it is just that it may have many elements in it in order to accomplish its function.

The components represented by symbols have two purposes: (1) to help keep the fluid moving freely and smoothly through the system and (2) to help keep the system and fluid in good condition. The trap is an example, and filters are another. Because piping needs protection, piping diagrams include traps, strainers, and filters. Such symbols are especially important because the fluids carried through a system may be damaging to the piping, valves, and fittings. Steam under pressure, acids, various types of waste products, and paint are all good examples of such fluids. The filters and strainers keep these fluids free from sludge and sediment to protect both the equipment that the system serves and the piping itself. Well-designed piping diagrams have various features to minimize maintenance and wear and tear. One such protective feature is the blowoff valve which was used in Figure 4.23. The valve can be opened to blow out any foreign material in the line.

Piping diagrams are also illustrated with cleanout plugs, inserted in the line at intervals. A cleanout plug is a thick, threaded, round unit screwed into the side of the pipe. With the plur removed, access to the inside of the pipe is made possible.

Valve and Fitting Subroutines

Piping diagrams have many components, all related to the single function of moving fluids from one point to another for a particular purpose. The ways in which such components are designed and drawn depend on the fluids themselves and the pressures and the temperatures to be expected in the system.

Remember that the purpose of the trap shown in Figure 4.23 was to collect condensed liquid while keeping the fluid in the system. Other components include devices to regulate pressure. Some are protective devices such as valves that automatically open to vent fluid out of the pipe when the pressure in the lines gets too high. In lines carrying liquids the diagram calls for relief valves, preset to open at a given pressure. When they open, liquid flows through the valve and specially provided piping relieves the pressure in the main line. The gate valves illustrated in Figure 4.23 are operated by hand. That is the difference between protective valves and control valves.

To keep fluids clean and free from impurities, piping systems use many different types of filters and strainers. Common types include oil bath or fine-mesh screens. Oil bath and water sprayers can be used to remove dust and dirt particles from compressed air lines. If such particles are not removed, they can cause damage and excessive wear to air-driven tools and motors.

Figure 4.24 illustrates a schematic piping diagram rather than a picture-type diagram. This is an example of commercial filters and strainers for removal of water, an impurity from natural gas, by dehydration piping. Figure 4.25 is an example of process piping used in a gas pumping station. The engineer or technician responsible for the layout of the piping diagram shown in Figure 4.25 will select the order and template type from a software group of piping symbols called a piping library.

Pipe Hangers and Support Subroutines

Piping must be supported to keep the line straight and to prevent sagging. A rigid pipe that sags excessively will strain its connections. A pipeline may be designed to run at a slight angle and will be supported at suitable intervals. To some extent, rigid piping is self-supporting because it has a certain amount of mechanical

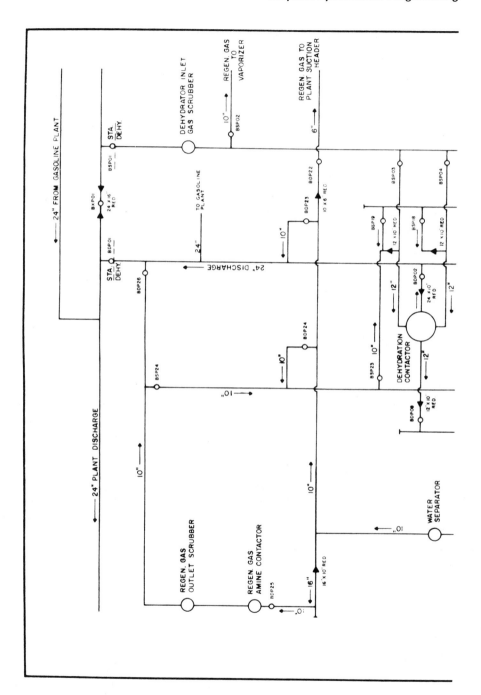

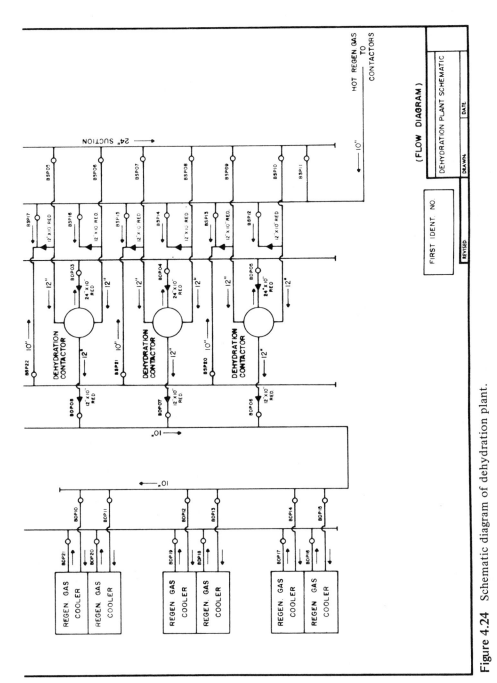

Figure 4.24 Schematic diagram of dehydration plant.

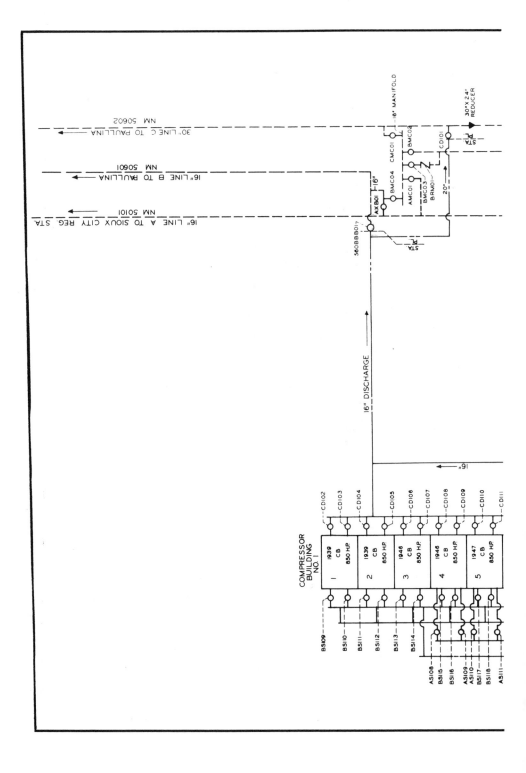

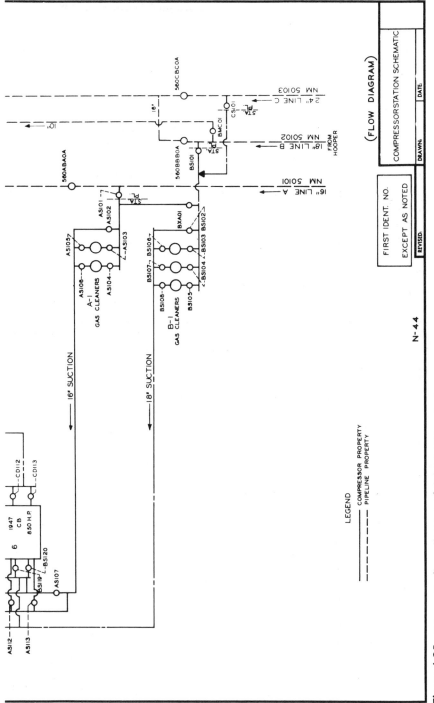

Figure 4.25 Schematic flow diagram of dehydration plant.

strength. Yet it must be supported by being fastened to the walls, ceiling, or floor. Subroutines used in the section on "Threads and Fasteners" in this chapter to design spring hangers to absorb vibration roll types permit expansion and contraction.

Nearly all materials, and metals in particular, expand as the temperature increases and contract or become smaller in size as the temperature decreases. To allow for this expansion and contraction in piping systems, expansion joints must be included in the piping diagram between sections of rigid pipe. As these sections expand or contract, the expansion joint compresses or expands accordingly. The design of a pipe hanger or support device must take into account the pipe size.

Pipe sizes are standardized and are usually expressed in terms of the outside diameter (OD) or inside diameter (ID), wall thickness, and length. Another consideration is weight per foot, which varies according to the pipe's wall thickness and material.

As a rule, pipe sizes are designated by diameter. Commercial sizes 12 inches and less are usually known by their nominal or approximate inside diameters. Above 12 inches, a pipe is ordinarily designated by its outside diameter. The actual OD of smaller-diameter pipes is greater than the nominal ID. At one time, piping was designated as standard, extra-strong, and double extra-strong. That method allowed no variation for wall thickness, and as pipe requirements became more numerous, greater variation was needed. As a result, piping today is classified according to schedule, the most common schedule members being 40, 80, 120, and 160. In diameters from 1/8 to 10 inches, the dimensions of standard pipe correspond to forty sizes. From 12 through 24 inches, the wall thickness is 0.375 inch for 40 schedule pipe.

The dimensions of extra-strong pipe are the same as schedule 80 sizes for piping ranging from 1/8 through 8 inches in diameter. From 10 through 24 inches, extra-strong pipe has a wall thickness of 0.500 inch. The double-strong pipe has no exact equivalent schedule number.

Schedule numbers range from 10 to 160, the difference being the wall thickness. Schedule 40, 3-inch diameter pipe, whose actual OD is 3.500 inches, has a wall thickness of 0.216 inch. The same pipe in schedule 80 would have a wall thickness of 0.300 inch. When the wall thickness of any given size of pipe is increased, the ID will increase.

Piping Applications

Piping applications fall into either of two main categories: process lines and utility or service lines. Process lines carry the fluids used in a manufacturing process. For example, one of the first operations in a paper mill is the reduction of incoming logs to chips of wood. The chips are often "cooked" in a unit called a digester, which contains a chemical solution of sodium sulfide and caustic soda pumped through pipes. Because it is a processing operation, these pipes are called process lines.

Utility or service lines include pipes that carry steam, gas, water, compressed air, and air-conditioning liquids. Ordinarily, determination can be made as to what type of line is used because the pipes are clearly marked on the diagram to show what kind of fluid they carry. Table 4.1 gives the identification code of piping. A uniform code for identifying piping contents has been established. Fire protection materials and dangerous materials are clear. Safe materials are those that offer little or no danger to life or equipment.

Information about specific piping for various materials is available from pipe manufacturers. Welded or seamless steel pipe is used for plumbing, heating, water, gas, and air lines. For high-temperature applications, and when pipe must be bent or shaped to allow interpipe connections, seamless carbon-steel pipe is used. Special steel-welded pipe is used for gas, liquid, and vapors. Welded wrought iron pipe is used for the condensate return of steam systems. Heavy-wall alloy steel pipe is also used for high-temperature applications.

Table 4.1 Pipe Identification Code[a]

Classification	Predominant color of system	Color of letters for legends
F, fire protection	Red	White
D, dangerous materials	Yellow (orange)	Black
S, safe materials	Green	Black
P, protective materials	Bright blue	White

Size of color bands and lettering		
Outside diameter	Width of band (inches)	Height of letters
3/4 to 1-1/4	8	1/2
1-1/2 to 2	8	3/4
2-1/2 to 6	12	1-1/4
8 to 10	24	2-1/2
Over 10	32	3-1/2

[a]Courtesy of Northern Natural Gas Company, Omaha, Nebraska.

Isometric Plumbing Diagrams

The majority of piping diagrams used in the architectural/construction field are called riser diagrams. Figures 4.26 and 4.27 illustrate the kind of diagram used in this field. As in the case with most architectural applications, the use of notes can be seen throughout. The isometric relationship of the diagram makes it easier to visualize inside a building space. Both illustrations have been sent to the CalComp plotter after previewing on an interactive graphics terminal.

With three major types of diagrams used:

1. Dual-line pictorial
2. Single-line schematic
3. Isometric riser

the designer has a choice of how to represent the piping system.

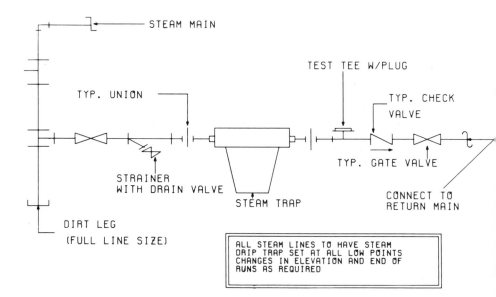

Figure 4.26 Architectural riser diagram.

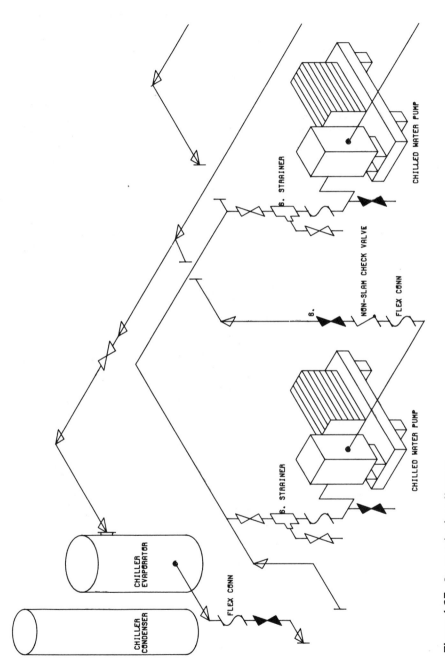

Figure 4.27 Isometric riser diagram.

AUTOMATED DRAFTING PROGRAMMING RECORD

ENGINEERING GRAPHICS WORKSHEET

Tape No. 310
Prepared by D L RYAN
Checked by C W MALSTROM
Date 5/28/79

PLOT DESCRIPTION Use Template Symbols

PLOT NUMBER 1812   SHEET NUMBER 310-5   OPERATION NUMBER 110

OPERATION DESCRIPTION RUN SYSIN SOURCE FTGICLG, PLOT = 1812

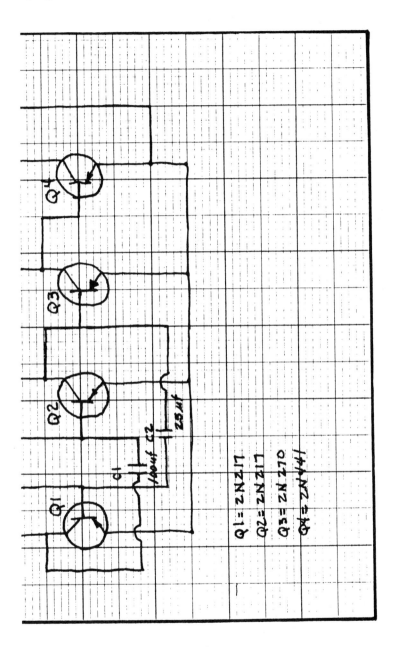

Figure 4.28 Freehand sketch of a typical circuit.

ELECTRONIC SCHEMATICS

The automated elementary diagram, often referred to as the schematic diagram, is one of the many types of diagrams used in the electronics industry. It was chosen for illustration here because it makes use of preprogrammed template symbols. This type of diagram shows the function and relation of the component devices of a circuit by means of a computer-stored symbol. Schematics do not show the physical relationship of components, however.

This type of automated output makes it possible for a person familiar with electronics to trace a circuit with ease. For this reason schematics are used for design and analysis of circuits. To give the graphics user a "feel" for the automation of schematic diagrams, several figures showing popular formats now in use are presented. The problems of automating such a diagram is discussed with each figure. A student without a background in electronics may not be able to understand all the author's comments about the logic of the circuits presented, but he should be able to grasp the technique for using template symbols stored in a computer memory.

Automating a Schematic Diagram

Figure 4.28 shows a freehand sketch of a typical circuit. This is the type of sketch that might be made by a design engineer or technician. The sketch is placed on a planning form as shown in Chapter 2. The purpose of the form is to furnish all the information necessary to make a finished output of this circuit.

As an operator of an ADM, you should produce a well-balanced plotter output that is standard in appearance. To do this, a slight change in configuration (reorientation of some symbols and lines) may be made, but the logic of the circuit must be maintained. A comparison of Figures 4.26 and 2.16 reveals that the transistors have been aligned, crossovers have been standardized, and components have reference numbers.

Figure 2.16 is the finished computer/plotter output of the schematic diagram. Standard ANSI referencing has been used. Transistor identification has been placed at the top of the diagram with larger-than-normal lettering. The author has selected this arrangement based on examples in various electronics engineering handbooks and reference texts. No claim of originality is taken for the symmetrical and fairly uniform density of the appearance.

There are certain basic arrangements of schematic symbols which are usually repeated in circuit diagrams; this makes the use of template logic beneficial. With template shapes and some types of interstage coupling, certain patterns are often discernible—usually early in the design, when the engineer starts to plan the schematic. Designation, or labeling of each component part of a circuit, is important. Standard CALL SYMBOL routines containing the abbreviations and prefixes are used for this purpose. Sufficient space must be allowed near each component for referencing. Conventional treatment is sometimes employed to eliminate the drawing of certain lines in order not to clutter the output. At the same time, additional material such as general notes and data on waveforms is often added to a schematic diagram.

Selected Examples

Electronic schematics, like piping diagrams, are extremely easy to automate if the basic symbols are provided as template parts. The recommended procedure for electronic diagrams is exactly the same as a piping single-line diagram. Several examples will be worked to illustrate the techniques of subpictures. Refer first to Figure 4.29; note that in this diagram all symbols are designed on a grid

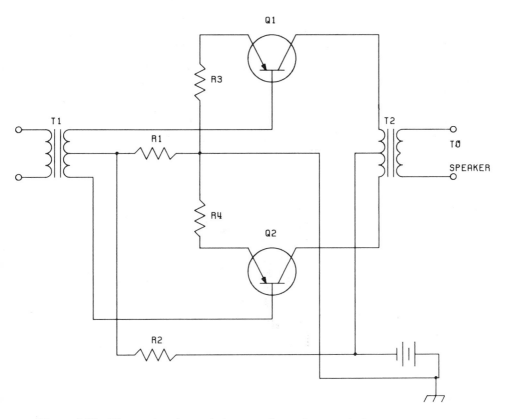

Figure 4.29 Electronic schematic by use of template symbols.

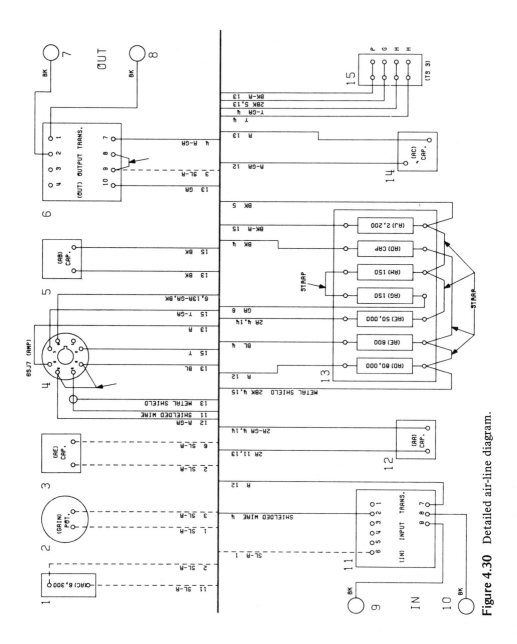

Figure 4.30 Detailed air-line diagram.

matrix as outlined in Chapter 3. The symbols are preprogrammed on an eight by eight grid background. If SIZE is 0.125, then the electronic symbol will be 1 inch in length. The symbols are located by overlaying a clear plastic grid directly on the engineer's sketch. XPAGE and YPAGE can be easily located. Each symbol is called by this method; now the lines representing wiring can be butted, directly aligned to each symbol.

Figure 4.30 is an example of how detailed a drawing can become by the use of template parts and a grid matrix design. Here the wires are routed by a DO loop and CALL PLOTS. The user makes good programming sense, as the logic is divided into basic construction steps. Figure 4.31 shows how even the annotation can be placed in a database memory module and recalled through the use of REAL MESSAGE and the use of a DO loop. Most electronic diagrams contain a large amount of annotation, and this user has done an excellent job of database management.

Figure 4.31 uses the mirror image technique of reversing the X and Y data base by the simple use of

CALL PLOT(Y,X,IPEN)

In this example, the data stored in the X array are plotted as Y pen controls, and the Y data are plotted as X pen controls.

Of course not all electronic engineering drawings are schematic diagrams; Figure 4.32 illustrates a point-to-point diagram plotted the same way a user might approach a schematic diagram. The important thing to remember is that the *use* of template figures is extreme at this point. The creation was discussed in Chapter 2; in the case of both piping and electronic diagrams preprogrammed software is available from manufacturers or consulting engineers. There is probably more software available for electronic drafting systems or integrated circuit design systems than all other forms of engineering drawing combined, because the history of development has been in industries which have invested heavily in the automation of this task. Table 4.2 compares the percentage of use in the areas of electronics design, mechanical design, mapping, and architectural/construction. You will note that nearly half of the present use in the United States is for the electronics field. Table 4.3 makes a prediction of percentage of use in 1989; here the author feels that mechanical, mapping, and architecture will become more balanced with electronics usage. Note that there will be less electronics applications, but the mechanical field will explode with the advent of computer-aided design (CAD) and computer-aided manufacturing (CAM). When CAD and CAM become of age, it will only be natural that computer-generated drawings will be used more and more by mechanical engineers.

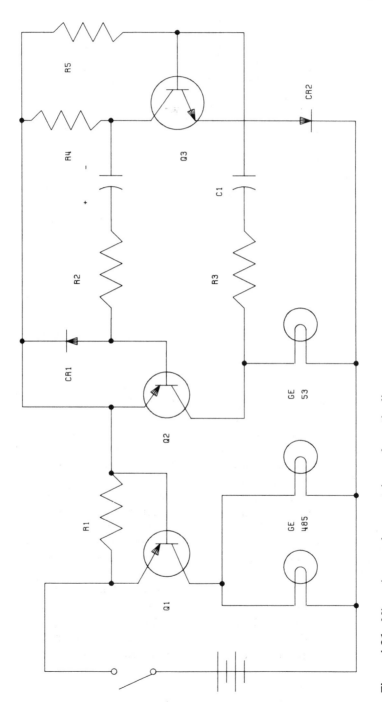

Figure 4.31 Mirror image placement in a schematic diagram.

Table 4.2 Interactive Systems by End Use[a]

Field of application	Description of use	Percent
Electronics	Principally printed circuit schematics and integrated circuit design (estimated to be 70% PC and 30% IC)	49
Mechanical	Drafting/piping/documentation	22
Mapping	Cartography	9
Architecture	Construction	20
		100

[a]Survey respondents of the Automated Drafting and Computer Graphics Seminar at Clemson University, South Carolina, November 1982.

Table 4.3 Projection of Table 4.2 Through 1989[a]

Field of application	Description of use	Percent
Electronics	Circuit design, PC, IC, CAM diagrams and working drawings	33
Mechanical	Piping/CAD/CAM/product development	28
Mapping	Remote image processing of cartography and lad use studies	28
Architecture	Construction detailing and and space analysis of building designs	11
		100

[a]William Taylor, SME Executive Vice President, *Reprographics*, Fall 1977.

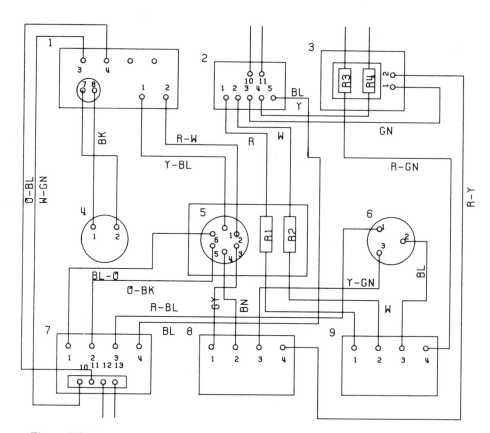

Figure 4.32 Point-to-point connection diagram.

EXERCISES

1. Prepare a graphical model for input to an IGS. The model should solve the following problem: A user has several sizes of pulleys and "v" belts which can be selected depending on the distance between pulley shafts. If the range of pulley shafts is from 11 to 22 units, spaced at even unit intervals, and pulley sizes may range from 4 to 12 units in diameter, what are the possible combinations? A graphical model for displaying the pulleys and selected belt can be prepared. Write a program which will interact with the designer, allowing her to select the variables. The program should then display the mechanical system as a picture for the user to study, adopt, or discard.

2. Select an electrical, mechanical, architectural, or organizational drawing from flat file storage. Place it on the graphics tablet of the IGS. Digitize the overall geometry by use of the tracking pen, mouse, or joy stick. Enter the X and Y locations under a drawing name. Now recall the drawing name and display the stored image. Make changes to the digitized drawing and store the new image under another drawing name.

3. Select a drawing with multiple symbols or repetitive patterns. Place it on the graphics tablet. Trace the symbol or pattern in incremental mode. Store the symbol under a subprogram name. Now write a program which CALLs the stored subprogram several times at different locations.

4. Prepare a library of special-purpose symbols for electrical, mechanical, or architectural use. Select a suitable ANSI standard and digitize the table of symbology on the IGS. Now prepare a sample drawing by calling the subpicture symbology at their proper locations.

5. Display the views shown below on the IGS working area. Build the profile of the object by displaying the ZARRAY and YARRAY of the data base. Choose a drawing scale by calling FACTOR, which will allow all three views and the placement of needed dimensions, notes, and part labels. Call out the location of centerlines of all features such as holes, slots, or machined sections. Add dimensions by CALL DIMEN, remembering that this subroutine contains extension lines, dimension lines, arrowheads, and annotation for placement and specification of dimensions. Select and prepare the notes by the use of CALL LABEL and CALL the automated title block and related notes necessary to the drawing. Check the output by previewing on the CRT, make any corrections in computer memory, and output on the digital plotter.

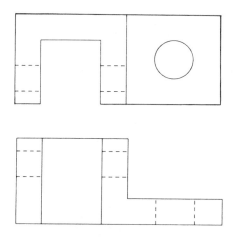

```
0001        CALL    PLOTS                          00000040
0002        CALL    HXHD(2.,6.,1.)                 00000050
0003        CALL    TAPHD(4.,6.,1.)                00000060
0004        CALL    SETHD(6.,6.,1.)                00000070
0005        CALL    ANGHD(8.,6.,1.)                00000080
0006        CALL    RHEAD(10.,6.,1.)               00000090
0007        CALL    HEX(1.,1.,1.)                  00000100
0008        CALL    SQHOLE(3.,1.,1.)               00000110
0009        CALL    HOLE(6.,2.,.5)                 00000120
0010        CALL    SEAT(3.,3.,.5)                 00000130
0011        CALL    TAPBOD(6.5,2.,1.)              00000140
0012        CALL    SQBOD(4.,4.,1.)                00000150
0013        CALL    ANGL(2.,8.,1.,15.)             00000160
0014        CALL    ANGL(4.5,8.,1.,45.)            00000170
0015        CALL    ANGL(7.,8.,1.,5.)              00000180
0016        CALL    ANGL(9.5,8.,1.,85.)            00000190
0017        CALL    STHRD(14.,4.,1.,1)             00000200
0018        CALL    STHRD(14.,8.,1.,5)             00000205
0019        CALL    THRD(10.,4.,1.,.5)             00000210
0020        CALL    TITLE(1.)                      00000220
0021        CALL    PLOT(0.,0.,999)                00000230
0022        STOP                                   00000240
0023        END                                    00000250
```

Exercise 8

6. Display the views shown with exercise 5 on the working area of the IGS. Prepare a sectional view of the object by CALL SHADE; this may be a profile or auxiliary view, depending on the type of section chosen. Choose a drawing scale and "window" the object for ease of operation. Place the cutting plane line and save the coordinates in a separate subpicture location in memory. Dimension this location with at least NPTS + 2 locations with 0.0 and 1.0 entered in the last two places of the cutting plane array. Use general section lines and display the drawing as in exercise 5.

7. Design the threaded fasteners for exercises 5 and 6. A simple procedure would be the digitizing of the ANSI B18.2-1965 template with a graphics tablet and pen. Place the plastic template on the tablet face. Trace the template openings in incremental mode. Save each shape in a subpicture file. Threaded fasteners can now be built by recalling the predefined geometry in its proper position on the drawing. The procedure is just like using a manual template except you are working at the speed of light to display the graphical image on the detailed drawing. Select a hex bolt that will fit the holes in exercise 5 and prepare a small detail file to be combined with either exercise 5 or 6 in IGS memory. Display the new file, check for errors on the CRT, and output on the digital plotter.

8. An alternate method to display threads and fasteners is to use established software. Enter the following testing program for threads and fasteners. (see page 192)

9. Attach the following list of subroutines and display.

```
FORTRAN IV G1   RELEASE 2.0            HXHD              DATE = 80342          16/38/13

       0001            SUBROUTINE HXHD(XP,YP,SIZE)                                         00000760
       0002            CALL PLOT(XP,YP,3)                                                  00000770
       0003            CALL PLOT((XP+.14)*SIZE,YP,2)                                       00000780
       0004            CALL PLOT((XP+.86)*SIZE,YP,3)                                       00000790
       0005            CALL PLOT((XP+1.)*SIZE,YP,2)                                        00000800
       0006            CALL PLOT((XP+1.)*SIZE,(YP+.3)*SIZE,2)                              00000810
       0007            CALL CIRCL((XP+1.)*SIZE,(YP+.3)*SIZE,90.,125.,.15*SIZE,.15*SIZE,    00000820
                      @0.)                                                                 00000830
       0008            CALL CIRCL(XP,(YP+.3)*SIZE,90.,55.,.15*SIZE,.15*SIZE,0.)            00000840
       0009            CALL CIRCL((XP+.9)*SIZE,(YP+.28)*SIZE,77.11,105.11,1.7*SIZE,        00000850
                      @1.7*SIZE,0.)                                                        00000860
       0010            CALL PLOT(XP,(YP+.3)*SIZE,3)                                        00000870
       0011            CALL PLOT(XP,YP,2)                                                  00000880
       0012            RETURN                                                              00000890
       0013            END                                                                00000900


FORTRAN IV G1   RELEASE 2.0            TAPHD             DATE = 80342          16/38/13

       0001            SUBROUTINE TAPHD(XP,YP,SIZE)                                        00001110
       0002            CALL PLOT(XP,YP,3)                                                  00001120
       0003            CALL PLOT((XP+.1)*SIZE,YP,2)                                        00001130
       0004            CALL PLOT((XP+.9)*SIZE,YP,2)                                        00001140
       0005            CALL PLOT((XP+1.)*SIZE,YP,2)                                        00001150
       0006            CALL PLOT((XP+1.)*SIZE,(YP+.8)*SIZE,2)                              00001160
       0007            CALL PLOT((XP+.9)*SIZE,(YP+.9)*SIZE,2)                              00001170
       0008            CALL PLOT((XP+.1)*SIZE,(YP+.9)*SIZE,2)                              00001180
       0009            CALL PLOT(XP,(YP+.8)*SIZE,2)                                        00001190
       0010            CALL PLOT(XP,YP,2)                                                  00001200
       0011            RETURN                                                              00001210
       0012            END                                                                00001220
```

```
FORTRAN IV G1  RELEASE 2.0              SETHD            DATE = 80342      16/38/13

0001                 SUBROUTINE SETHD(XP,YP,SIZE)                                    00001230
0002                 CALL PLOT(XP,YP,3)                                              00001240
0003                 CALL PLOT((XP+.2)*SIZE,YP,2)                                    00001250
0004                 CALL PLOT((XP+.8)*SIZE,YP,3)                                    00001260
0005                 CALL PLOT((XP+1.)*SIZE,YP,2)                                    00001270
0006                 CALL PLOT((XP+1.)*SIZE,(YP+.6)*SIZE,2)                          00001280
0007                 CALL CIRCLE((XP+.5)*SIZE,(YP-.6)*SIZE,1.3*SIZE,67.38,50,.905)   00001290
0008                 CALL PLOT(XP,(YP+.6)*SIZE,3)                                    00001300
0009                 CALL PLOT(XP,YP,2)                                              00001310
0010                 RETURN                                                          00001320
0011                 END                                                             00001330


FORTRAN IV G1  RELEASE 2.0              ANGHD            DATE = 80342      16/38/13

0001                 SUBROUTINE ANGHD(XP,YP,SIZE)                                    00001340
0002                 CALL PLOT(XP,YP,3)                                              00001350
0003                 CALL PLOT((XP-.3)*SIZE,(YP+.4)*SIZE,2)                          00001360
0004                 CALL PLOT((XP+1.)*SIZE,(YP+.4)*SIZE,2)                          00001370
0005                 CALL PLOT((XP+.7)*SIZE,YP,2)                                    00001380
0006                 RETURN                                                          00001390
0007                 END                                                             00001400


FORTRAN IV G1  RELEASE 2.0              RHEAD            DATE = 80342      16/38/13

0001                 SUBROUTINE RHEAD(XP,YP,SIZE)                                    00001500
0002                 CALL PLOT(XP,YP,3)                                              00001510
0003                 CALL PLOT((XP+1.)*SIZE,YP,2)                                    00001520
0004                 CALL CIRCLE((XP+.5)*SIZE,YP,.5*SIZE,0.,60,3.)                   00001530
0005                 RETURN                                                          00001540
0006                 END                                                             00001550


FORTRAN IV G1  RELEASE 2.0              HEX              DATE = 80342      16/38/13

0001                 SUBROUTINE HEX(XPAGE,YPAGE,SIZE)                                00000260
0002                 CALL POLY(XPAGE,YPAGE,SIZE,6.,0.)                               00000270
0003                 RETURN                                                          00000280
0004                 END                                                             00000290


FORTRAN IV G1  RELEASE 2.0              SQHOLE           DATE = 80342      16/38/13

0001                 SUBROUTINE SQHOLE(XP,YP,SIZE)                                   00000300
0002                 CALL RECT(XP,YP,SIZE,SIZE,0.,3)                                 00000310
0003                 RETURN                                                          00000320
0004                 END                                                             00000330


FORTRAN IV G1  RELEASE 2.0              HOLE             DATE = 80342      16/38/13

0001                 SUBROUTINE HOLE(XPAGE,YPAGE,RSIZE)                              00000340
0002                 CALL CIRCL(XPAGE,YPAGE,0.,360.,RSIZE,RSIZE,0.)                  00000350
0003                 RETURN                                                          00000360
0004                 END                                                             00000370


FORTRAN IV G1  RELEASE 2.0              SEAT             DATE = 80342      16/38/13

0001                 SUBROUTINE SEAT(XP,YP,XORSIZ)                                   00000420
0002                 XIRSIZ=XORSIZ-.1                                                00000430
0003                 CALL CIRCL(XP,YP,0.,360.,XORSIZ,XORSIZ,.5)                      00000440
0004                 CALL CIRCL(XP-.1,YP,0.,360.,XIRSIZ,XIRSIZ,0.)                   00000450
0005                 RETURN                                                          00000460
0006                 END                                                             00000470


FORTRAN IV G1  RELEASE 2.0              TAPBOD           DATE = 80342      16/38/13

0001                 SUBROUTINE TAPBOD(XP,YP,SIZE)                                   00001410
0002                 CALL PLOT(XP,YP,3)                                              00001420
0003                 CALL PLOT(XP,(YP-.9)*SIZE,2)                                    00001430
0004                 CALL PLOT((XP+.1)*SIZE,(YP-1.)*SIZE,2)                          00001440
0005                 CALL PLOT((XP+.5)*SIZE,(YP-1.)*SIZE,2)                          00001450
0006                 CALL PLOT((XP+.6)*SIZE,(YP-.9)*SIZE,2)                          00001460
0007                 CALL PLOT((XP+.6)*SIZE,YP,2)                                    00001470
0008                 RETURN                                                          00001480
0009                 END                                                             00001490
```

```
FORTRAN IV G1  RELEASE 2.0              SQBOD           DATE = 80342      16/38/13

0001                    SUBROUTINE SQBOD(XP,YP,SIZE)                          00000380
0002                    CALL RECT(XP,YP,SIZE*1.5,SIZE,0.,3)                   00000390
0003                    RETURN                                                00000400
0004                    END                                                   00000410


FORTRAN IV G1  RELEASE 2.0              ANGL            DATE = 80342      16/38/13

0001                    SUBROUTINE ANGL(XP,YP,SIZE,ANGN)                      00001780
0002                    CALL PLOT(XP,YP,3)                                    00001790
0003                    XP2=(XP+COS(ANGN*3.14159/180.))*SIZE                  00001800
0004                    YP2=(YP-SIN(ANGN*3.14159/180.))*SIZE                  00001810
0005                    CALL PLOT(XP2,YP2,2)                                  00001820
0006                    XP3=(XP2+COS(ANGN*3.14159/180.))*SIZE                 00001825
0007                    CALL PLOT(XP3,YP,2)                                   00001830
0008                    RETURN                                                00001840
0009                    END                                                   00001850


FORTRAN IV G1  RELEASE 2.0              STHRD           DATE = 80342      16/38/13

0001                    SUBROUTINE STHRD(XP,YP,SIZE,NUMT)                     00001670
0002                    CALL PLOT(XP,YP,3)                                    00001680
0003                    A=0.                                                  00001690
0004                    DO 10 I=1 ,NUMT                                       00001700
0005                    CALL PLOT((XP+.1+A)*SIZE,(YP+.2)*SIZE,2)              00001710
0006                    CALL PLOT((XP+.15+A)*SIZE,(YP+.2)*SIZE,2)             00001720
0007                    CALL PLOT((XP+.25+A)*SIZE,YP,2)                       00001730
0008                    CALL PLOT((XP+.3+A)*SIZE,YP,2)                        00001740
0009              10    A=A+(.3*SIZE)                                         00001750
0010                    RETURN                                                00001760
0011                    END                                                   00001770



FORTRAN IV G1  RELEASE 2.0              THRD            DATE = 80342      16/38/13

0001                    SUBROUTINE THRD(XP,YP,SIZE)                           00001560
0002                    CALL RECT(XP,(YP+.1)*SIZE,.2*SIZE,1.*SIZE,0.,3)       00001570
0003                    CALL RECT(XP,(YP+.3)*SIZE,.2*SIZE,1.*SIZE,0.,3)       00001580
0004                    CALL RECT(XP,(YP+.5)*SIZE,.2*SIZE,1.*SIZE,0.,3)       00001590
0005                    CALL RECT(XP,(YP+.7)*SIZE,.2*SIZE,1.*SIZE,0.,3)       00001600
0006                    CALL RECT(XP,(YP+.9)*SIZE,.2*SIZE,1.*SIZE,0.,3)       00001610
0007                    CALL RECT(XP,YP,.1*SIZE,1.*SIZE,0.,3)                 00001620
0008                    CALL PLOT((XP+.2)*SIZE,(YP+.2)*SIZE,3)                00001630
0009                    CALL PLOT((XP+.8)*SIZE,(YP+.2)*SIZE,2)                00001640
0010                    CALL PLOT((XP+.2)*SIZE,(YP+.4)*SIZE,3)                00001641
0011                    CALL PLOT((XP+.8)*SIZE,(YP+.4)*SIZE,2)                00001642
0012                    CALL PLOT((XP+.2)*SIZE,(YP+.6)*SIZE,3)                00001643
0013                    CALL PLOT((XP+.8)*SIZE,(YP+.6)*SIZE,2)                00001644
0014                    CALL PLOT((XP+.2)*SIZE,(YP+.8)*SIZE,3)                00001645
0015                    CALL PLOT((XP+.8)*SIZE,(YP+.8)*SIZE,2)                00001646
0016                    CALL PLOT((XP+.2)*SIZE,(YP+1.)*SIZE,3)                00001647
0017                    CALL PLOT((XP+.8)*SIZE,(YP+1.)*SIZE,2)                00001648
0018                    RETURN                                                00001650
0019                    END                                                   00001660
```

10. Practice the use of process piping software by entering the following testing program.

```
                  C     THIS PROGRAM DRAWS SEVERAL DIFFERENT ANSI SYMBOLS FOR    00000040
                  C     PROCESS PIPING.                                          00000050
0001                    CALL PLOTS                                              00000060
0002                    CALL FACTOR(1.)                                        00000070
                  C     THIS SUBROUTINE DRAWS A PUMP.                           00000080
0003                    XP=1.                                                  00000090
0004                    YP=1.                                                  00000100
0005                    FP=1.                                                  00000110
0006                    CALL PUMP(XP,YP,FP)                                    00000120
                  C     THIS SUBROUTINE DRAWS A GLOBE VALVE.                    00000130
0007                    XH=3.                                                  00000140
0008                    YH=1.                                                  00000150
0009                    FH=1.                                                  00000160
0010                    CALL HVALVE(XH,YH,FH)                                  00000170
```

```
          C     THIS SUBROUTINE DRAWS A INLINE PUMP          00000180
0011            XIP=5.                                       00000190
0012            YIP=1.                                       00000200
0013            FIP=1.                                       00000210
0014            CALL ILP(XIP,YIP,FIP)                        00000220
          C     THIS SUBROUTINE DRAWS A STOPPER.             00000230
0015            XS=7.                                        00000240
0016            YS=.75                                       00000250
0017            FS=1.                                        00000260
0018            CALL STOP(XS,YS,FS)                          00000270
          C     DRAWS A RIGHT TANK.                          00000280
0019            XR=1.                                        00000290
0020            YR=2.5                                       00000300
0021            FR=1.                                        00000310
0022            CALL RTANK(XR,YR,FR)                         00000320
          C     DRAWS A LEFT TANK                            00000330
0023            XL=4.                                        00000340
0024            YL=2.5                                       00000350
0025            FL=1.                                        00000360
0026            CALL LTANK(XL,YL,FL)                         00000370
          C     DRAWS A CHECK VALVE                          00000380
0027            XVC=6.                                       00000390
0028            YVC=2.5                                      00000400
0029            FVC=1.                                       00000410
0030            CALL VCV(XVC,YVC,FVC)                        00000420
          C     DRAWS A RISING CHECK VALVE.                  00000430
0031            XC=8.                                        00000440
0032            YC=2.5                                       00000450
0033            FC=1.                                        00000460
0034            CALL CVALVE(XC,YC,FC)                        00000470
          C     DRAWS A SCREWED CAP.                         00000480
0035            XT=10.                                       00000490
0036            YT=2.5                                       00000500
0037            FT=1.                                        00000510
0038            CALL SCAP(XT,YT,FT)                          00000520
          C     DRAWS A DRAIN PIPE.                          00000530
0039            XHP=11.                                      00000540
0040            YHP=2.5                                      00000550
0041            FHP=1.                                       00000560
0042            CALL HPIPE(XHP,YHP,FHP)                      00000570
          C     DRAWS A GATE VALVE.                          00000580
0043            XG=13.                                       00000590
0044            YG=2.5                                       00000600
0045            FG=1.                                        00000610
0046            CALL GVALVE(XG,YG,FG)                        00000620
          C     DRAWS A BALL VALVE                           00000630
0047            XVG=15.                                      00000640
0048            YVG=2.5                                      00000650
0049            FVG=1.                                       00000660
0050            CALL VGV(XVG,YVG,FVG)                        00000670
          C     DRAWS A BAFFLE.                              00000680
0051            XF=1.                                        00000690
0052            YF=4.                                        00000700
0053            FF=1.                                        00000710
0054            CALL BAFF(XF,YF,FF)                          00000720
          C     DRAWS A NOZZLE.                              00000730
0055            XHA=2.5                                      00000740
0056            YHA=4.                                       00000750
0057            FHA=1.                                       00000760
0058            CALL HAT(XHA,YHA,FHA)                        00000770
          C     DRAWS A PRESSURE NOZZLE.                     00000780
0059            XVA=4.                                       00000790
0060            YVA=4.                                       00000800
0061            FVA=1.                                       00000810
0062            CALL VAT(XVA,YVA,FVA)                        00000820
          C     DRAWS A DIAPHRAM VALVE.                      00000830
0063            XGL=7.                                       00000840
0064            YGL=4.                                       00000850
0065            FGL=1.                                       00000860
0066            CALL GLOBE(XGL,YGL,FGL)                      00000870
          C     DRAWS A SEGMENT OF HORIZONTAL PIPE.          00000880
0067            XWP=10.                                      00000890
0068            YWP=4.                                       00000900
0069            FWP=1.                                       00000910
0070            CALL WPIPE(XWP,YWP,FWP)                       00000920
          C     DRAWS A RIGHT REDUCER                        00000930
0071            XRP=1.                                       00000940
0072            YRP=6.                                       00000950
0073            FRP=1.                                       00000960
0074            CALL RPLUG(XRP,YRP,FRP)                      00000970
          C     DRAWS A LEFT REDUCER.                        00000980
0075            XLP=4.                                       00000990
0076            YLP=6.                                       00001000
0077            FLP=1.                                       00001010
0078            CALL LPLUG (XLP,YLP,FLP)                     00001020
```

```
              C     DRAWS A WELDED CAP.                                  00001030
0079                XLG=7.                                               00001040
0080                YLG=6.                                               00001050
0081                FLG=1.                                               00001060
0082                CALL WCAP(XLG,YLG,FLG)                               00001070
              C     DRAWS A CYLINDER                                     00001080
0083                XCL=8.                                               00001090
0084                YCL=6.                                               00001100
0085                FCL=1.                                               00001110
0086                CALL CYLIND(XCL,YCL,FCL)                             00001120
              C     DRAWS A RIGHT 90 ELBOW                               00001130
0087                XRE=1.                                               00001140
0088                YRE=9.                                               00001150
0089                FRE=1.                                               00001160
0090                CALL RELBOW(XRE,YRE,FRE)                             00001170
              C     DRAWS A LEFT 90 ELBOW.                               00001180
0091                XLE=2.                                               00001190
0092                YLE=9.                                               00001200
0093                FLE=1.                                               00001210
0094                CALL LELBOW(XLE,YLE,FLE)                             00001220
              C     DRAWS A SEGMENT OF VERTICAL PIPE.                    00001230
0095                XVP=3.                                               00001240
0096                YVP=8.5                                              00001250
0097                FVP=1.                                               00001260
0098                CALL VPIPE(XVP,YVP,FVP)                              00001270
0099                STOP                                                 00001280
0100                END                                                  00001290
```

11.   Attach the following process piping subroutines and display.

```
FORTRAN IV G1  RELEASE 2.0          PUMP           DATE = 80343      14/34/44              PAGE

0001                SUBROUTINE PUMP(XP,YP,FP)                            00001300
0002                CALL FACTOR(FP)                                      00001310
0003                CALL PLOT(XP,YP,-3)                                  00001320
0004                CALL PLOT(.5,0.,2)                                   00001330
0005                CALL CIRCL(.5,0.,180.,540.,.0625,.0625,0.)           00001340
0006                CALL PLOT(1.25,-.125,3)                              00001350
0007                CALL CIRCL(1.25,-.125,0.,-300.,.375,.375,0.)         00001360
0008                CALL PLOT(1.25,-.125,3)                              00001370
0009                CALL PLOT(1.25,.25,2)                                00001380
0010                CALL PLOT(1.125,.25,2)                               00001390
0011                CALL FIT(1.25,.25,1.12,.3125,1.0625,.312)            00001400
0012                CALL PLOT(-XP,-YP,-3)                                00001410
0013                RETURN                                               00001420
0014                END                                                  00001430


FORTRAN IV G1  RELEASE 2.0          HVALVE         DATE = 80343      14/34/44              PAGE

0001                SUBROUTINE HVALVE(XH,YH,FH)                          00001440
0002                CALL FACTOR(FH)                                      00001450
0003                CALL PLOT(XH,YH,-3)                                  00001460
0004                CALL PLOT(.25,0.,2)                                  00001470
0005                CALL PLOT(.25,.125,2)                                00001480
0006                CALL PLOT(1.,-.125,2)                                00001490
0007                CALL PLOT(1.,.125,2)                                 00001500
0008                CALL PLOT(.25,-.125,2)                               00001510
0009                CALL PLOT(.25,0.,2)                                  00001520
0010                CALL PLOT(.625,0.,3)                                 00001530
0011                CALL PLOT(.5,.375,2)                                 00001540
0012                CALL PLOT(.75,.375,2)                                00001550
0013                CALL PLOT(.625,0.,2)                                 00001560
0014                CALL PLOT(.625,.375,3)                               00001570
0015                CALL PLOT(.625,.625,2)                               00001580
0016                CALL PLOT(1.,0.,3)                                   00001590
0017                CALL PLOT(1.375,0.,2)                                00001600
0018                CALL PLOT(-XH,-YH,-3)                                00001610
0019                RETURN                                               00001620
0020                END                                                  00001630


FORTRAN IV G1  RELEASE 2.0          ILP            DATE = 80343      14/34/44              PAGE

0001                SUBROUTINE ILP(XIP,YIP,FIP)                          00001640
0002                CALL FACTOR(FIP)                                     00001650
0003                CALL PLOT(XIP,YIP,-3)                                00001660
0004                CALL PLOT(.5,0.,2)                                   00001670
0005                CALL CIRCL(.5,0.,180.,540.,.375,.375,0.)             00001680
0006                CALL PLOT(1.25,0.,3)                                 00001690
0007                CALL PLOT(1.75,0.,2)                                 00001700
0008                CALL PLOT(-XIP,-YIP,-3)                              00001710
0009                RETURN                                               00001720
0010                END                                                  00001730
```

```
FORTRAN IV G1  RELEASE 2.0            STOP          DATE = 80343       14/34/44              PAGE

0001                    SUBROUTINE STOP(XS,YS,FS)                                    00001740
0002                    CALL FACTOR(FS)                                              00001750
0003                    CALL PLOT(XS,YS,-3)                                          00001760
0004                    CALL CIRCL(0.,0.,270.,450.,.25,.25,0.)                       00001770
0005                    CALL PLOT(0.,0.,2)                                           00001780
0006                    CALL PLOT(.25,.25,3)                                         00001790
0007                    CALL CIRCL(.25,.25,180.,540.,.0625,.0625,0.)                 00001800
0008                    CALL PLOT(.375,.25,3)                                        00001810
0009                    CALL PLOT(1.25,.25,2)                                        00001820
0010                    CALL PLOT(-XS,-YS,-3)                                        00001830
0011                    RETURN                                                       00001840
0012                    END                                                          00001850

FORTRAN IV G1  RELEASE 2.0            RTANK         DATE = 80343       14/34/44              PAGE

0001                    SUBROUTINE RTANK(XR,YR,FR)                                   00001860
0002                    CALL FACTOR(FR)                                              00001870
0003                    CALL PLOT(XR,YR,-3)                                          00001880
0004                    CALL PLOT(.375,0.,2)                                         00001890
0005                    CALL CIRCL(.375,0.,180.,540.,.0625,.0625,0.)                 00001900
0006                    CALL PLOT(.5,.3125,3)                                        00001910
0007                    CALL PLOT(.5,-.3125,2)                                       00001920
0008                    CALL PLOT(1.,-.3125,2)                                       00001930
0009                    CALL PLOT(1.,.4375,2)                                        00001940
0010                    CALL FIT(1.,.4375,.75,.375,.5,.3125)                         00001950
0011                    CALL PLOT(-XR,-YR,-3)                                        00001960
0012                    RETURN                                                       00001970
0013                    END                                                          00001980

FORTRAN IV G1  RELEASE 2.0            LTANK         DATE = 80343       14/34/44              PAGE

0001                    SUBROUTINE LTANK(XL,YL,FL)                                   00001990
0002                    CALL FACTOR(FL)                                              00002000
0003                    CALL PLOT(XL,YL,-3)                                          00002010
0004                    CALL PLOT(-.375,0.,2)                                        00002020
0005                    CALL CIRCL(-.375,0.,0.,360.,.0625,.0625,0.)                  00002030
0006                    CALL PLOT(-.5,.3125,3)                                       00002040
0007                    CALL PLOT(-.5,-.3125,2)                                      00002050
0008                    CALL PLOT(-1.,-.3125,2)                                      00002060
0009                    CALL PLOT(-1.,.4375,2)                                       00002070
0010                    CALL FIT(-1.,.4375,-.75,.375,-.5,.3125)                      00002080
0011                    CALL PLOT(-XL,-YL,-3)                                        00002090
0012                    RETURN                                                       00002091
0013                    END                                                          00002092

FORTRAN IV G1  RELEASE 2.0            CVALVE        DATE = 80343       14/34/44              PAGE

0001                    SUBROUTINE CVALVE(XC,YC,FC)                                  00002100
0002                    CALL FACTOR(FC)                                              00002110
0003                    CALL PLOT(XC,YC,-3)                                          00002120
0004                    CALL PLOT(.375,-.125,2)                                      00002130
0005                    CALL PLOT(.375,.125,2)                                       00002140
0006                    CALL PLOT(0.,0.,2)                                           00002150
0007                    CALL PLOT(.375,.0,3)                                         00002160
0008                    CALL PLOT(.875,0.,2)                                         00002170
0009                    CALL PLOT(.875,.125,2)                                       00002180
0010                    CALL PLOT(1.25,0.,2)                                         00002190
0011                    CALL PLOT(.875,-.125,2)                                      00002200
0012                    CALL PLOT(.875,0.,2)                                         00002210
0013                    CALL PLOT(.625,0.,3)                                         00002220
0014                    CALL PLOT(.625,.375,2)                                       00002230
0015                    CALL PLOT(-XC,-YC,-3)                                        00002240
0016                    RETURN                                                       00002250
0017                    END                                                          00002260

FORTRAN IV G1  RELEASE 2.0            VCV           DATE = 80343       14/34/44              PAGE

0001                    SUBROUTINE VCV(XVC,YVC,FVC)                                  00002270
0002                    CALL FACTOR(FVC)                                             00002280
0003                    CALL PLOT(XVC,YVC,-3)                                        00002290
0004                    CALL PLOT(.375,-.125,2)                                      00002300
0005                    CALL PLOT(.375,.125,2)                                       00002310
0006                    CALL PLOT(0.,0.,2)                                           00002320
0007                    CALL PLOT(.375,.0,3)                                         00002330
0008                    CALL PLOT(.875,0.,2)                                         00002340
0009                    CALL PLOT(.875,.125,2)                                       00002350
0010                    CALL PLOT(1.25,0.,2)                                         00002360
0011                    CALL PLOT(.875,-.125,2)                                      00002370
0012                    CALL PLOT(.875,0.,2)                                         00002380
0013                    CALL PLOT(-XVC,-YVC,-3)                                      00002390
0014                    RETURN                                                       00002400
0015                    END                                                          00002410
```

```
FORTRAN IV G1   RELEASE 2.0              SCAP              DATE = 80343        14/34/44                    PAGE

0001                    SUBROUTINE SCAP(XT,YT,FT)                                      00002420
0002                    CALL FACTOR(FT)                                                00002430
0003                    CALL PLOT(XT,YT,-3)                                            00002440
0004                    CALL PLOT(-2.,0.,2)                                            00002450
0005                    CALL PLOT(-1.75,.5,2)                                          00002460
0006                    CALL PLOT(-2.,.5,2)                                            00002470
0007                    CALL PLOT(-2.,-.5,2)                                           00002480
0008                    CALL PLOT(-1.75,-.5,2)                                         00002490
0009                    CALL PLOT(-XT,-YT,-3)                                          00002500
0010                    RETURN                                                         00002510
0011                    END                                                            00002520


FORTRAN IV G1   RELEASE 2.0              HPIPE             DATE = 80343        14/34/44                    PAGE

0001                    SUBROUTINE HPIPE(XHP,YHP,FHP)                                  00002530
0002                    CALL FACTOR(FHP)                                               00002540
0003                    CALL PLOT(XHP,YHP,-3)                                          00002550
0004                    CALL PLOT(1.,0.,2)                                             00002560
0005                    CALL CIRCL(1.,0.,180.,540.,.0625,.0625,0.)                     00002570
0006                    CALL PLOT(-XHP,-YHP,-3)                                        00002580
0007                    RETURN                                                         00002590
0008                    END                                                            00002600


FORTRAN IV G1   RELEASE 2.0              GVALVE            DATE = 80343        14/34/44                    PAGE

0001                    SUBROUTINE GVALVE(XG,YG,FG)                                    00002610
0002                    CALL FACTOR(FG)                                                00002620
0003                    CALL PLOT(XG,YG,-3)                                            00002630
0004                    CALL PLOT(.25,0.,2)                                            00002640
0005                    CALL PLOT(.25,.125,2)                                          00002650
0006                    CALL PLOT(1.,-.125,2)                                          00002660
0007                    CALL PLOT(1.,.125,2)                                           00002670
0008                    CALL PLOT(.25,-.125,2)                                         00002680
0009                    CALL PLOT(.25,0.,2)                                            00002690
0010                    CALL PLOT(-XG,-YG,-3)                                          00002700
0011                    RETURN                                                         00002710
0012                    END                                                            00002720


FORTRAN IV G1   RELEASE 2.0              VGV               DATE = 80343        14/34/44

0001                    SUBROUTINE VGV(XVG,YVG,FVG)                                    00002730
0002                    CALL FACTOR(FVG)                                               00002740
0003                    CALL PLOT(XVG,YVG,-3)                                          00002750
0004                    CALL PLOT(.25,0.,2)                                            00002760
0005                    CALL PLOT(.25,.125,2)                                          00002770
0006                    CALL PLOT(1.,-.125,2)                                          00002780
0007                    CALL PLOT(1.,.125,2)                                           00002790
0008                    CALL PLOT(.25,-.125,2)                                         00002800
0009                    CALL PLOT(.25,0.,2)                                            00002810
0010                    CALL PLOT(.625,0.,3)                                           00002820
0011                    CALL PLOT(.625,.375,2)                                         00002830
0012                    CALL PLOT(-XVG,-YVG,-3)                                        00002840
0013                    RETURN                                                         00002850
0014                    END                                                            00002860


FORTRAN IV G1   RELEASE 2.0              BAFF              DATE = 80343        14/34/44                    PAGE

0001                    SUBROUTINE BAFF(XF,YF,FF)                                      00002870
0002                    CALL FACTOR(FF)                                                00002880
0003                    CALL PLOT(XF,YF,-3)                                            00002890
0004                    CALL PLOT(.25,0.,2)                                            00002900
0005                    CALL PLOT(.625,-.1875,2)                                       00002910
0006                    CALL PLOT(.625,.1875,2)                                        00002920
0007                    CALL PLOT(.25,0.,2)                                            00002930
0008                    CALL PLOT(.75,-.25,3)                                          00002940
0009                    CALL PLOT(.75,.25,2)                                           00002950
0010                    CALL PLOT(1.5,0.,3)                                            00002960
0011                    CALL PLOT(1.25,0.,2)                                           00002970
0012                    CALL PLOT(.875,-.1875,2)                                       00002980
0013                    CALL PLOT(.875,.1875,2)                                        00002990
0014                    CALL PLOT(1.25,0.,2)                                           00003000
0015                    CALL PLOT(-XF,-YF,-3)                                          00003010
0016                    RETURN                                                         00003020
0017                    END                                                            00003030
```

```
FORTRAN IV G1  RELEASE 2.0           HAT           DATE = 80343        14/34/44              PAGE

0001              SUBROUTINE HAT(XHA,YHA,FHA)                                        00003040
0002              CALL FACTOR(FHA)                                                   00003050
0003              CALL PLOT(XHA,YHA,-3)                                              00003060
0004              CALL PLOT(.375,0.,2)                                               00003070
0005              CALL CIRCL(.375,0.,180.,540.,.0625,.0625,0.)                       00003080
0006              CALL PLOT(.5,0.,3)                                                 00003090
0007              CALL PLOT(.875,.25,2)                                              00003100
0008              CALL PLOT(.875,.375,3)                                             00003110
0009              CALL PLOT(.875,-.375,2)                                            00003120
0010              CALL PLOT(.875,-.25,3)                                             00003130
0011              CALL PLOT(.5,0.,2)                                                 00003140
0012              CALL PLOT(-XHA,-YHA,-3)                                            00003150
0013              RETURN                                                             00003160
0014              END                                                               00003170


FORTRAN IV G1  RELEASE 2.0           VAT           DATE = 80343        14/34/44              PAGE

0001              SUBROUTINE VAT(XVA,YVA,FVA)                                        00003180
0002              CALL FACTOR(FVA)                                                   00003190
0003              CALL PLOT(XVA,YVA,-3)                                              00003200
0004              CALL CIRCL(0.,0.,0.,360.,.125,.125,0.)                             00003210
0005              CALL PLOT(.25,.5,3)                                                00003220
0006              CALL PLOT(1.,0.,2)                                                 00003230
0007              CALL PLOT(.25,-.5,2)                                               00003240
0008              CALL PLOT(.25,.5,2)                                                00003250
0009              CALL PLOT(1.,.25,3)                                                00003260
0010              CALL PLOT(1.,-.25,2)                                               00003270
0011              CALL PLOT(1.,0.,3)                                                 00003280
0012              CALL PLOT(2.,0.,2)                                                 00003290
0013              CALL PLOT(-XVA,-YVA,-3)                                            00003300
0014              RETURN                                                             00003310
0015              END                                                               00003320


FORTRAN IV G1  RELEASE 2.0          GLOBE          DATE = 80343        14/34/44              PAGE

0001              SUBROUTINE GLOBE(XGL,YGL,FGL)                                      00003330
0002              CALL FACTOR(FGL)                                                   00003340
0003              CALL PLOT(XGL,YGL,-3)                                              00003350
0004              CALL CIRCL(0.,0.,0.,360.,.0625,.0625,0.)                           00003360
0005              CALL PLOT(.75,0.,2)                                                00003370
0006              CALL CIRCL(.75,0.,180.,540.,.5,.5,0.)                              00003380
0007              CALL PLOT(1.25,-.5,3)                                              00003390
0008              CALL CIRCL(1.25,-.5,270.,450.,.25,.25,0.)                          00003400
0009              CALL CIRCL(1.25,0.,270.,-270.,.25,.25,0.)                          00003410
0010              CALL PLOT(-XGL,-YGL,-3)                                            00003420
0011              RETURN                                                             00003430
0012              END                                                               00003440


FORTRAN IV G1  RELEASE 2.0          RPLUG          DATE = 80343        14/34/44              PAGE

0001              SUBROUTINE RPLUG(XRP,YRP,FRP)                                      00003450
0002              CALL FACTOR(FRP)                                                   00003460
0003              CALL PLOT(XRP,YRP,-3)                                              00003470
0004              CALL PLOT(.875,0.,2)                                               00003480
0005              CALL CIRCL(.875,0.,180.,540.,.0625,.0625,0.)                       00003490
0006              CALL PLOT(1.,.25,3)                                                00003500
0007              CALL PLOT(1.,-.25,2)                                               00003510
0008              CALL PLOT(1.375,-.375,2)                                           00003520
0009              CALL PLOT(1.375,.375,2)                                            00003530
0010              CALL PLOT(1.,.25,2)                                                00003540
0011              CALL PLOT(-XRP,-YRP,-3)                                            00003550
0012              RETURN                                                             00003560
0013              END                                                               00003570


FORTRAN IV G1  RELEASE 2.0          LPLUG          DATE = 80343        14/34/44              PAGE

0001              SUBROUTINE LPLUG(XLP,YLP,FLP)                                      00003580
0002              CALL FACTOR(FLP)                                                   00003590
0003              CALL PLOT(XLP,YLP,-3)                                              00003600
0004              CALL PLOT(-.875,0.,2)                                              00003610
0005              CALL CIRCL(-.875,0.,0.,360.,.0625,.0625,0.)                        00003620
0006              CALL PLOT(-1.,.25,3)                                               00003630
0007              CALL PLOT(-1.,-.25,2)                                              00003640
0008              CALL PLOT(-1.375,-.375,2)                                          00003650
0009              CALL PLOT(-1.375,.375,2)                                           00003660
0010              CALL PLOT(-1.,.25,2)                                               00003670
0011              CALL PLOT(-XLP,-YLP,-3)                                            00003680
0012              RETURN                                                             00003690
0013              END                                                               00003700
```

```
FORTRAN  IV G1   RELEASE 2.0            WCAP            DATE = 80343          14/34/44            PAGE

0001                      SUBROUTINE WCAP(XLG,YLG,FLG)                                  00003710
0002                      CALL FACTOR(FLG)                                              00003720
0003                      CALL PLOT(XLG,YLG,-3)                                         00003730
0004                      CALL PLOT(-1.75,0.,2)                                         00003740
0005                      CALL PLOT(-1.625,.125,3)                                      00003750
0006                      CALL CIRCL(-1.625,.125,45.,315.,.25,.25,0.)                   00003760
0007                      CALL PLOT(-XLG,-YLG,-3)                                       00003770
0008                      RETURN                                                        00003780
0009                      END                                                          00003790
```

```
FORTRAN  IV G1   RELEASE 2.0            WPIPE           DATE = 80343          14/34/44            PAGE

0001                      SUBROUTINE WPIPE(XWP,YWP,FWP)                                 00003800
0002                      CALL FACTOR(FWP)                                              00003810
0003                      CALL PLOT(XWP,YWP,-3)                                         00003820
0004                      CALL CIRCL(0.,0.,0.,360.,.0625,.0625,0.)                      00003830
0005                      CALL PLOT(2.,0.,2)                                            00003840
0006                      CALL CIRCL(2.,0.,180.,540.,.0625,.0625,0.)                    00003850
0007                      CALL PLOT(-XWP,-YWP,-3)                                       00003860
0008                      RETURN                                                        00003870
0009                      END                                                          00003880
```

```
FORTRAN  IV G1   RELEASE 2.0            VPIPE           DATE = 80343          14/34/44            PAGE

0001                      SUBROUTINE VPIPE(XVP,YVP,FVP)                                 00003890
0002                      CALL FACTOR(FVP)                                              00003900
0003                      CALL PLOT(XVP,YVP,-3)                                         00003910
0004                      CALL CIRCL(0.,0.,90.,450.,.0625,.0625,0.)                     00003920
0005                      CALL PLOT(0.,2.,2)                                            00003930
0006                      CALL CIRCL(0.,2.,270.,630.,.0625,.0625,0.)                    00003940
0007                      CALL PLOT(-XVP,-YVP,-3)                                       00003950
0008                      RETURN                                                        00003960
0009                      END                                                          00003970
```

```
FORTRAN  IV G1   RELEASE 2.0            CYLIND          DATE = 80343          14/34/44            PAGE

0001                      SUBROUTINE CYLIND(XCL,YCL,FCL)                                00003980
0002                      CALL FACTOR(FCL)                                             00003990
0003                      CALL PLOT(XCL,YCL,-3)                                        00004000
0004                      CALL CIRCL(0.,0.,0.,360.,.0625,.0625,0.)                     00004010
0005                      CALL CIRCL(0.,0.,180.,-270.,.25,.25,0.)                      00004020
0006                      CALL PLOT(1.5,.25,2)                                         00004030
0007                      CALL CIRCL(1.5,.25,90.,-360.,.25,.25,0.)                     00004040
0008                      CALL CIRCL(1.75,0.,180.,540.,.0625,.0625,0.)                 00004050
0009                      CALL CIRCL(1.75,0.,0.,-90.,.25,.25,0.)                       00004060
0010                      CALL PLOT(.25,-.25,2)                                        00004070
0011                      CALL CIRCL(.25,-.25,270.,-180.,.25,.25,0.)                   00004080
0012                      CALL PLOT(-XCL,-YCL,-3)                                      00004090
0013                      RETURN                                                       00004100
0014                      END                                                         00004110
```

```
FORTRAN  IV G1   RELEASE 2.0            RELBOW          DATE = 80343          14/34/44          PAGE 0001

0001                      SUBROUTINE RELBOW(XRE,YRE,FRE)                               00004120
0002                      CALL FACTOR(FRE)                                            00004130
0003                      CALL PLOT(XRE,YRE,-3)                                       00004140
0004                      CALL CIRCL(0.,0.,270.,630.,.0625,.0625,0.)                  00004150
0005                      CALL CIRCL(0.,0.,180.,270.,.5,.5,0.)                        00004160
0006                      CALL CIRCL(.5,-.5,180.,540.,.0625,.0625,0.)                 00004170
0007                      CALL PLOT(-XRE,-YRE,-3)                                     00004180
0008                      RETURN                                                      00004190
0009                      END                                                        00004200
```

```
FORTRAN  IV G1   RELEASE 2.0            LELBOW          DATE = 80343          14/34/44          PAGE 0001

0001                      SUBROUTINE LELBOW(XLE,YLE,FLE)                               00004210
0002                      CALL FACTOR(FLE)                                            00004220
0003                      CALL PLOT(XLE,YLE,-3)                                       00004230
0004                      CALL CIRCL(0.,0.,0.,360.,.0625,.0625,0.)                    00004240
0005                      CALL CIRCL(0.,0.,270.,360.,.5,.5,0.)                        00004250
0006                      CALL CIRCL(.5,.5,270.,630.,.0625,.0625,0.)                  00004260
0007                      CALL PLOT(-XLE,-YLE,-3)                                     00004270
0008                      RETURN                                                      00004280
0009                      END                                                        00004290
```

12. Use the software listings shown in Exercise 9 to display threads and fasteners of your own design.

13. Use the software listings shown in Exercise 11 to display a process piping diagram like those shown in Figure 4.24 and 4.25.

14. Enter the following short program to display a detail drawing.

```
0001                    CALL PLOTS                                    00000040
0002                    CALL FACTOR(1.66)                             00000041
0003                    CALL TITLE                                    00000050
0004                    CALL DRAW2D                                   00000060
0005          C         CALL SECFRA                                   00000070
0006                    CALL PLOT(18.0,12.0,999)                      00000090
0007                    STOP                                          00000100
0008                    END                                           00000110
```

15. Attach the first subroutine.

```
0001                    SUBROUTINE TITLE                                      00000120
0002                    CALL NEWPEN(5)                                        00000130
0003                    CALL RECT(.5,.5,11.,17.,0.,3)                          00000150
0004                    CALL RECT(.5,.5,.75,1.875,0.,3)                        00000160
0005                    CALL RECT(2.375,.5,.75,3.,0.,3)                        00000170
0006                    CALL RECT(5.375,.5,.75,2.25,0.,3)                      00000180
0007                    CALL RECT(7.625,.5,.75,3.375,0.,3)                     00000190
0008                    CALL PLOT(5.375,.875,3)                                00000200
0009                    CALL PLOT(11.,.875,3)                                  00000210
0010                    CALL PLOT(11.,1.25,3)                                  00000220
0011                    CALL PLOT(17.5,1.25,3)                                 00000230
0012                    CALL PLOT(16.375,.5,3)                                 00000240
0013                    CALL PLOT(16.375,1.25,2)                               00000250
0014                    CALL PLOT(7.625,.5,3)                                  00000260
0015                    CALL PLOT(7.625,1.25,2)                                00000270
0016                    CALL NEWPEN(3)                                         00000280
0017                    CALL SYMBOL(1.375,.875,.125,'7',0.,1)                  00000290
0018                    CALL SYMBOL(.75,.625,.125,'DRAWING NO.',0.,11)         00000300
0019                    CALL SYMBOL(2.625,1.,.125,'ENGINEERING GRAPHICS',0.,20) 00000310
0020                    CALL SYMBOL(2.75,.75,.125,'CLEMSON UNIVERSITY',0.,18)  00000320
0021                    CALL SYMBOL(5.625,1.,.125,'DATE: 11/9/82',0.,13)       00000330
0022                    CALL SYMBOL(5.625,.625,.125,'SCALE: NONE',0.,11)       00000340
0023                    CALL SYMBOL(7.875,1.,.125,'DR. BY: R. PALMER',0.,17)   00000350
0024                    CALL SYMBOL(7.875,.625,.125,'COURSE: EG 411 SEC. 1',0.,21) 00000360
0025                    CALL SYMBOL(12.625,.875,.125,'SECOND FLOOR PLAN',0.,22) 00000370
0026                    CALL SYMBOL(13.375,.625,.125,'TITLE',0.,5)            00000380
0027                    CALL SYMBOL(16.625,.625,.125,'GRADE',0.,5)            00000390
0028                    CALL NEWPEN(1)                                         00000410
0029                    RETURN                                                00000420
0030                    END                                                   00000430
```

16. Attach the second subroutine.

```
0001                    SUBROUTINE DRAW2D                                              00000440
0002                    READ(1,10)NPTS                                                 00000450
0003          10        FORMAT(I4)                                                     00000460
0004                    WRITE(3,20)NPTS                                                00000470
0005          20        FORMAT(//,10X,'THE NUMBER OF POINTS TO BE PLOTTED = ',I4)      00000480
0006                    WRITE(3,30)                                                    00000490
0007          30        FORMAT(//,10X,'THE FOLLOWING DATA POINTS HAVE BEEN READ AND PLOTTE00000500
                        CD:',//13X,'X',14X,'Y',12X'IPEN')                               00000510
0008                    DO60 I=1,NPTS                                                  00000520
0009                    READ(1,40)X,Y,IPEN                                             00000530
0010          40        FORMAT(2(F6.3),I2)                                             00000540
0011                    WRITE(3,50)X,Y,IPEN                                            00000550
0012          50        FORMAT(//,2(10X,F6.3),10X,I2)                                  00000560
0013          60        CALL PLOT(X,Y,IPEN)                                            00000570
0014                    RETURN                                                         00000580
0015                    END                                                            00000590
```

17.   Prepare input data as shown below for Exercises 18, 19, and 20.

THE NUMBER OF POINTS TO BE PLOTTED =   48

THE FOLLOWING DATA POINTS HAVE BEEN READ AND PLOTTED:

X	Y	IPEN
1.500	2.250	-3
15.000	0.0	2
15.000	2.000	2
14.875	2.000	2
14.875	0.125	2
3.125	0.125	2
3.125	1.750	2
3.625	1.750	2
3.625	1.875	2
3.125	1.875	2
3.125	2.250	2
2.750	2.250	2
2.750	2.125	2
3.000	2.125	2
3.000	0.125	2
0.125	0.125	2
0.125	2.125	2
1.750	2.125	2
1.750	2.250	2

0.125	2.250	2
0.125	2.375	2
0.0	2.375	2
0.0	0.0	2
0.0	3.625	3
0.125	3.625	2
0.125	3.750	2
2.500	3.750	2
2.500	3.875	2
0.125	3.875	2
0.125	7.625	2
5.125	7.625	2
5.125	3.875	2
3.625	3.875	2
3.625	3.750	2
5.250	3.750	2
5.250	7.625	2
14.875	7.625	2
14.875	4.500	2
15.000	4.500	2
15.000	7.750	2
0.0	7.750	2
0.0	3.625	2
4.625	1.750	3
13.500	1.750	2
13.500	1.875	2
4.625	1.875	2
4.625	1.750	2
-1.500	-2.250	-3

18.

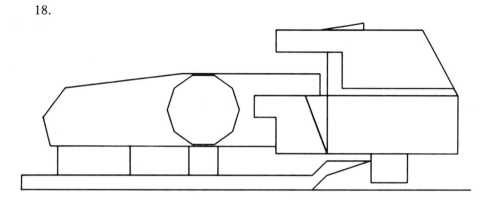

19.

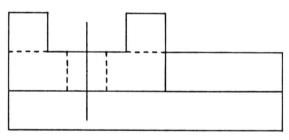

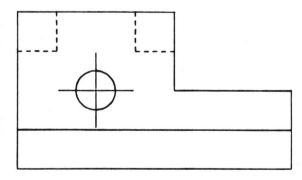
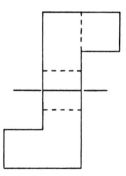

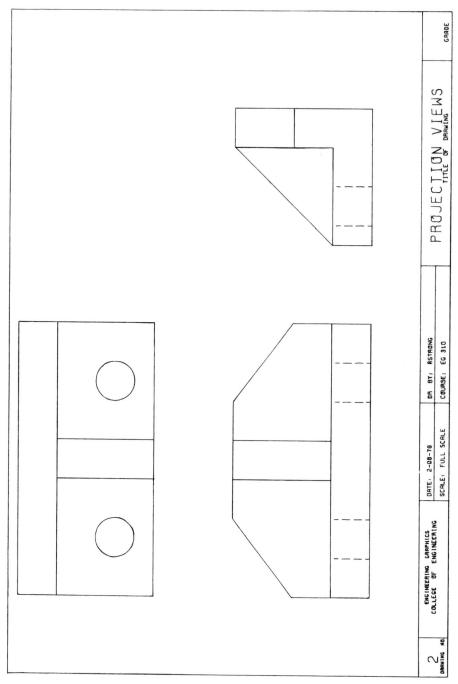

5

Pictorial Representation

In the previous four chapters the importance of plane surfaces in computer graphics was discussed. This 2-dimensional database was used to present everything from working views to planes used as cutting devices. As explained in Chapter 4, a plane can be used to cut through any 3-dimensional space problem and expose the interior detail for dimensioning. The creation of the 3-dimensional solid was not presented.

In Chapter 3, 3-dimensional concepts of DATAPT (Figure 3.15), lines (Figure 3.19), planes (Figure 3.21), and datum (Figure 3.25) were presented. Refer back to them again for further study; they are the foundation concepts for pictorial representation of solid objects.

In this chapter we shall present the use of plane surfaces as boundaries of solids. When a surface forms a boundary completely enclosing a portion of space in three dimensions it becomes a solid. The term "solid" is used in its mathematical sense. A "mathematic solid" is considered to be hollow. It is a wireform container for the object described.

It is constructed of plane surfaces defined by edges. These edges are lines defined by DATAPTS as described in Chapter 3. The first step in solid construction is the information contained in the database. It is in the form of an engineering model, detail drafting model, or some other form. In Figure 5.1 the common types of mathematical solids are shown. Notice that engineering models contain a large number of lines, and that drafting models tend to be much simpler in their database construction. Common wireforms that are of interest to designers and engineers are listed in Table 5.1 and illustrated in Figure 5.1.

Table 5.1 Common Types of Wireform Pictorials

Classification	Number of surfaces
Sphere	1
Cone	2
Cylinder	3
Tetrahedron	4
Prism	5
Hexahedron	6

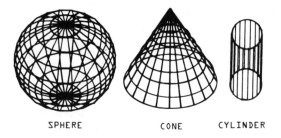

SPHERE   CONE   CYLINDER

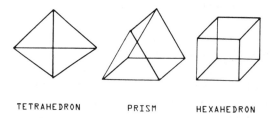

TETRAHEDRON   PRISM   HEXAHEDRON

Figure 5.1 Common types of mathematical solids: sphere, cone, cylinder, tetrahedron, prism, and hexahedron.

PICTORIAL DATABASE

Pictorial drawings/displays are prepared for both the engineering and the drafting functions shown in Chapter 3. The engineering pictorials are mainly geometric models for finite element experimentation, and the drafting pictorials fall into three main groups: axonometric, oblique, and perspective. Common display techniques exist for all three of these types, and before studying each one separately, we will cover these common techniques:

1. Data point specification
2. Line specification
3. Arc specification
4. Object orientation
5. Data collection

Referring again to Chapter 3, we note that a plane surface was defined as at least three points connected in space. The addition of a fourth point not inside the plane creates three additional plane surfaces of a polyhedron. A polyhedron is a composite of points, lines, and planes containing point specifications.

DATA POINT SPECIFICATION

Point specification is important because the display movement must be taken into consideration. For example, suppose the five points shown in Figure 5.2 were:

DATAPT	X	Y	Z	IPEN
1	0.0	0.0	0.0	2
2	2.1	0.0	0.0	2
3	2.1	0.0	1.5	2
4	0.0	0.0	1.5	2
5	0.0	1.5	0.5	2

If we entered these points as shown to a pictorial subroutine Figure 5.3 would result. We would be less than satisfied if we compared that kind of output to the data point specification in Figure 5.2. What went wrong?

First, the data specification is for the points only; it does not specify the location of lines and planes. So what caused the line from the corner of the display screen to the first point? The answer is the IPEN data for DATAPT 1. It is a 2, which means beam is on or line is shown. If we change the first data point specification to:

1   0.0   0.0   0.0   3

and display again with display axis we get an output as shown in Figure 5.4.

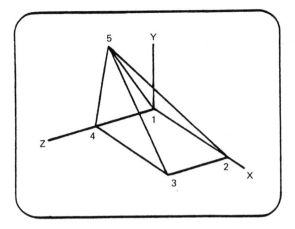

Figure 5.2 Data point specification.

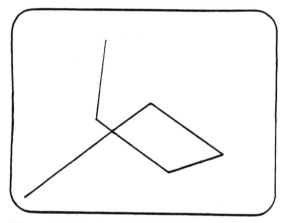

Figure 5.3 Display of data point specifications.

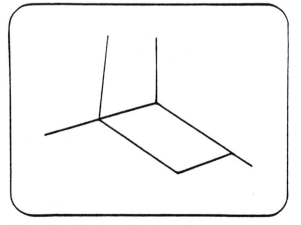

Figure 5.4 Display with axis option on.

Now suppose we add those missing lines to the database as an ICON (point connection list) that would appear as:

ICON = -1,2,3,4,1,5,4,-5,3,-5,2

This is exactly what we need to display Figure 5.5. What did the ICON list do?

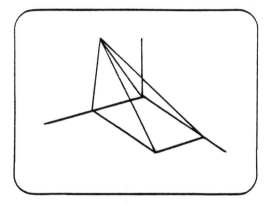

DISPLAY AXIS ON

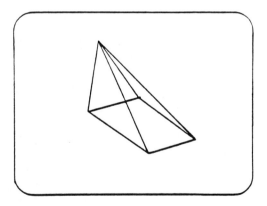

DISPLAY AXIS OFF

Figure 5.5   Pictorial output with ICON data list.

The ICON data says:

```
GOTO 1 WITH PEN UP........-1
GOTO 2 WITH PEN DOWN..... 2
GOTO 3 WITH PEN DOWN..... 3
GOTO 4 WITH PEN DOWN..... 4
GOTO 1 WITH PEN DOWN..... 1
GOTO 5 WITH PEN DOWN..... 5
GOTO 4 WITH PEN DOWN..... 4
GOTO 5 WITH PEN UP........-5
GOTO 3 WITH PEN DOWN..... 3
GOTO 5 WITH PEN UP........-5
GOTO 2 WITH PEN DOWN..... 2
```

LINE SPECIFICATION

You will recall from Chapter 4 that a line generator is used to produce a number of different lines: solid, dashed, broken, center, hidden, missing. A missing line is used to make a wireform appear solid as shown in Figure 5.6. The minus sign in the ICON data list creates a missing line.

The addition of a sixth point in Figure 5.1 creates a six-sided polyhedron called a hexagon. Hexagons are used in combinations to create other pictorial objects. Figure 5.7 represents the use of four hexagons in a single pictorial. They are butted together to form the shape shown. The program used to display Fig-

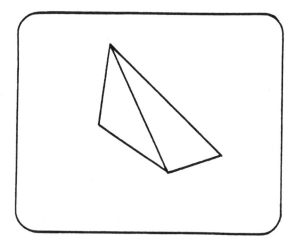

Figure 5.6 Missing line used to create a solid.

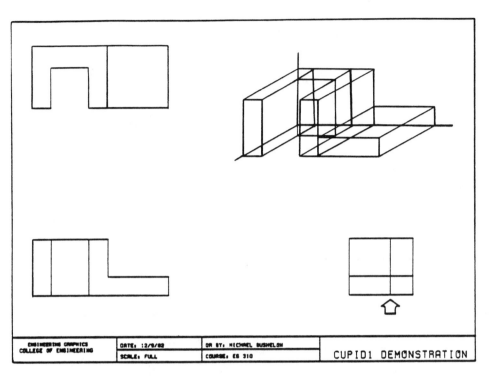

Figure 5.7 Display of hexagons.

ure 5.7 is called CUPID1 and contains a line specification pointer. CUPID1 was also used in Chapter 4 so will not be repeated here, but it is important to note that multiview programs can be used with pictorial displays in a useful manner. The arrow shown in Figure 5.7 locates a case where a hidden line is required in the orthographic representation of the object.

ARC SPECIFICATION

The use of line specification becomes a necessary modification tool when wireforms are combined (as shown in Figure 5.7) and when part features such as fillets and rounds are added (as shown in Figure 5.8). An arc generator for 3-D must be provided for this purpose. Introduced in Chapter 3, it is shown listed in FORTRAN in Figure 5.9. Arcs are usually provided for each of the multiview positions of XARC (front views), YARC (profiles), and ZARC (top views). Each is demonstrated in Figure 5.8.

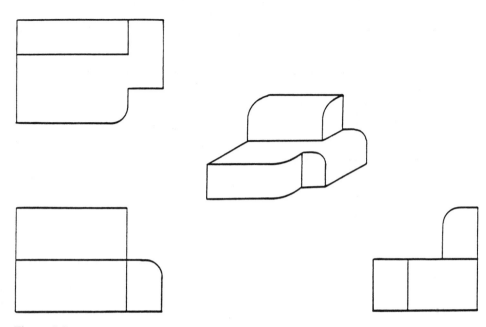

Figure 5.8 Arc specifications.

```
C  *******************************************************************
C  *                                                                 *
C  *   THIS ROUTINE DISPLAYS CIRCULAR ARCS IN THE XPLANE FROM A 3    *
C  *   DIMENSIONAL DATA BASE, WHERE:                                 *
C  *      XP = THE CENTER LOCATION OF THE ARC IN X DIRECTION         *
C  *      YP = THE CENTER LOCATION OF THE ARC IN Y DIRECTION         *
C  *      ZP = THE CENTER LOCATION OF THE ARC IN Z DIRECTION         *
C  *       R = RADIUS OF THE ARC                                     *
C  *      SA = STARTING ANGLE FOR THE ARC                            *
C  *      EA = ENDING ANGLE OF THE ARC IN THETA DEGREES             *
C  *******************************************************************
         SUBROUTINE XARC(XP,YP,ZP,SA,EA,THETA)
         DIMENSION P(400,3)
         PI=3.14159265
         N=EA-SA
         THETA=THETA*PI/180.
         SA=SA*PI/180.
         DO 100 I=1,N
         DZ=R*COS(SA)
         DY=R*SIN(SA)
         P(I,1)=XP
         P(I,2)=YP+DY
         P(I,3)=-ZP+DZ)
  100    SA=SA+THETA
         CALL VANTAC(P,1.,N)
         RETURN
         END
```

Figure 5.9 FORTRAN listing of an arc generator.

214

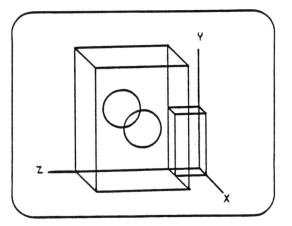

Figure 5.10 Pictorial object ready for orientation.

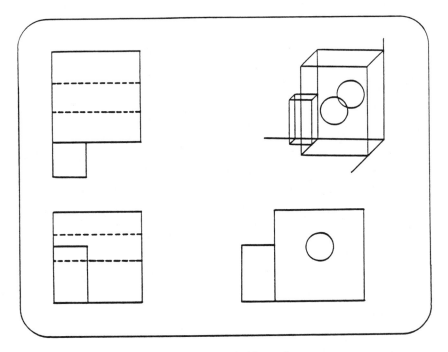

Figure 5.11 CUPID1 display of pictorial orientation.

OBJECT ORIENTATION

In order to visualize how the position of the pictorial is affected by a point, line, and arc specification, assume that the object shown in Figure 5.10 is to be displayed from the worksheet arrangement shown in Chapter 3. For the purpose of orientation, study the display shown in Figure 5.11; this was from the CUPID1 program again.

In Figure 5.11 we see one possible choice of pictorial orientation for display. In Figure 5.12 we see four other possible selections for display. The correct choice is to show those hidden features as visible edges if possible. As long as the pictorial to be defined is placed within the third angle-projection position, namely a positive X, Y, and Z data-gathering system, any change of orientation is acceptable.

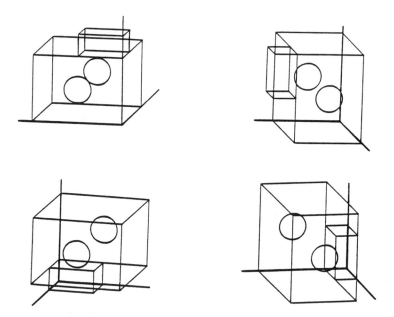

Figure 5.12 Other choices for pictorial orientation.

DATA COLLECTION

The user of a CUPID program is responsible for describing the object to be placed in the 3-D image processor. Figure 5.13 demonstrates this process.

1. Select orientation of the object
2. Digitize the point data (point specification)
3. Add part features (line or arc specification)
4. Determine the order of point connection (ICON)
5. Submit the data to the 3-D image processor

Here we wish only to emphasize the fact that any pictorial representation of a wireform is merely an array of points. To display pictorial objects requires an extension of the 2-D orthographics developed for Chapters 1 through 4.

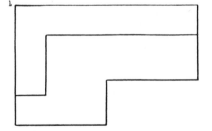

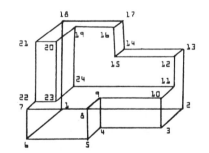

NDATA=2.4

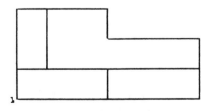

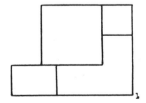

Figure 5.13 Demonstration of data gathering.

THEORY OF PICTORIAL CONSTRUCTION

A 3-dimensional software package, in the FORTRAN language, expands a plotting system's capability to provide more meaningful information in the field of engineering graphics and industrial applications for design. This type of software package is a fully developed system of programs, and it requires only a basic knowledge of programming to operate it.

A stylized system which provides 3-dimensional plots of any data which can be expressed as a function of two variables or in X, Y, and Z coordinates will be developed in this chapter. Using this system, a designer or engineer can quickly take 2-dimensional drawings and provide pictorial drawings of a part from many angles. This series of drawings can then be photographed five frames per pictorial on standard 16-millimeter movie film. By viewing the film the designer can study the part as it turns in space. This technique, called animation, requires hundreds and sometimes thousands of closely related pictorials to be drawn by the computer.

As another application, a user wanting to streamline the production of pictorial images of reasonably simple, "unsculptured" parts and assemblies will find that the program can be used merely as a powerful drafting system. Another application can be the creation of complex pictorials so that a tool designer can verify that the part machined will have the proper dimensions and shape. This program can also be used to 3-dimensionally illustrate a geometric formula, to plot distribution of heat and/or pressure over a surface, or to plot geometrically complete mathematical models of machine parts.

At the present time, it is used on an IBM 370 and on-line CalComp plotter. Users may preview their plots on a 4027 Tektronix CRT before plotting occurs. It was developed upon the existing CalComp software not only as a drafting tool but as a basically new medium for defining 3-dimensional objects.

A 3-dimensional subprogram like CUPID1 expands a plotting system's capability to provide more meaningful information in the drafting function. These types (CUPID1, CUPID2, and CUPID3) of subprograms are not fully developed for pictorial image processing (PIP). But they are an excellent base from which a few programming instructions can be added to produce the type of pictorial desired.

Oblique

This is the simplest of the PIP routines and is shown in Figure 5.14. It should be added to the CUPID1 routines used in Chapter 4 before it is placed in a drafting software package to be used by all drafting personnel.

The PIP routines can be compared directly to the CUPID routines FVIEW, HVIEW, and PVIEW. For example, suppose that a drafter needed just two views

```
C         SUBROUTINE FOR DISPLAYING OBLIQUE
C         PROJECTIONS INSIDE CUPID SOFTWARE
C
          SUBROUTINE PIP1(NDATA,X,Y,A,IPEN,ANG)
          DIMENSION X(100),Y(100),Z(100),IPEN
         +(100), XPLOT(100), YPLOT(100)
          DO 100 I=1,NDATA
          XPLOT(I)= X(I)+Z(I)*COS(ANG/57.3)
          YPLOT(I)= Y(I)+Z(I)*SIN(ANG/57.3)
     100  CALL PLOT XPLOT(I),YPLOT(I),IPEN(I)
          RETURN
          END
```

Figure 5.14 PIP routine for oblique pictorials.

instead of the normal three or six orthographic views? Then the program statements:

CALL FVIEW(NDATA,X,Y,Z,IPEN)

or

CALL HVIEW(NDATA,X,Y,Z,IPEN)

could be used to position a single view, say the top or front in an automated drawing display (see Figures 5.15 and 5.16). The view is positioned by:

CALL PLOT(XTRANS,YTRANS,-3)

where XTRANS is the X location on the display surface and YTRANS is the Y location. Figure 5.16 is the routine for FVIEW, Figure 5.17 is the routine for HVIEW, and 5.18 is the routine for PVIEW.

Axonometric

This is the next PIP routine shown in Figure 5.18. It is very similar to PIP1 which is the logic for the oblique projection. You will notice that there is only one angle of projection used for oblique as shown in Figure 5.14 whereas two angles of projection are used in all axonometric projection.

An axonometric pictorial, also shown in Figure 5.19, is produced when both the horizontal angle (ANG1) and profile angle (ANG2) are greater than zero. If ANG1=0 and ANG2 is greater than zero, an oblique projection results. An axonometric always contains two angles of axis rotation. This produces lines of sight which are perpendicular to the plane of projection, but with the principal faces

```
C        SUBROUTINE FOR DISPLAYING THE TOP
C        ORTHOGRAPHIC VIEW INSIDE CUPID SOFT-
C        WARE SUBPROGRAM KNOWN AS CUPID1
C
         SUBROUTINE HVIEW(NDATA,X,Y,Z,IPEN)
         DIMENSION X(1000),Y(1000),Z(1000),
        +IPEN(1000)
         DO 95 L=1,NDATA
      95 CALL PLOT(X(L),Z(L),IPEN(L))
         RETURN
         END
```

Figure 5.15 FVIEW routine for multiviews.

```
C        SUBROUTINE FOR DISPLAYING AXONOMETRIC
C        PROJECTIONS INSIDE CUPID SOFTWARE
C
         SUBROUTINE PIP2(NDATA,X,Y,Z,IPEN,
        +ANG1,ANG2)
         DIMENSION X(100),Y(100),Z(100),IPEN
        +(100),XPLOT(100),YPLOT(100), PIP(100)
         DO 101 J=1,NDATA
         XPLOT(J)= X(J)*COS(ANG1/57.3)+Z(J)*
        +SIN(ANG1/57.3)
         PIP(J)= X(J)*SIN(ANG1/57.3)*SIN(ANG2
        +/57.3)+Y(J)*COS(ANG2/57.3)
         YPLOT(J)= PIP(J)-Z(J)*COS(ANG1/57.3)
        +*SIN(ANG2/57.3)
     101 CALL PLOT(XPLOT(J),YPLOT(J),IPEN(J))
         RETURN
         END
```

Figure 5.16 HVIEW routine for multiviews.

```
C       SUBROUTINE FOR DISPLAYING THE PROFILE
C       ORTHOGRAPHIC VIEW INSIDE CUPID SOFT-
C       WARE SUBPROGRAM KNOWN AS CUPID1
C
        SUBROUTINE PVIEW NDATA,X,Y,Z,IPEN
        DIMENSION X 1000 ,Y 1000 ,Z 1000 ,
       +IPEN 1000
        DO 90 M=1,NDATA
     90 CALL PLOT Z M ,Y M ,IPEN M
        RETURN
        END
```

Figure 5.17 PVIEW routine for multiviews.

of the object inclined to the plane of projection. The principal faces or axes may be displayed at any angle other than 0 or 90 degrees, since these angles represent orthographic projections. Because these principal surfaces and edges of an axonometric pictorial object are inclined to the plane of projection, the general proportion of the object will vary, depending upon the placement of the object.

Correction in proportion is done before the final display of the pictorial by foreshortening the lines that are inclined to the plane of projection. Therefore, the larger ANG1 and ANG2, the greater the degree of foreshortening.

Foreshortening is handled by adding an additional variable in the subroutine PIP1 or PIP2. It is called SF in PIP1 and reduces the Z data list so that different types of oblique projections can be made, such as cabinet or cavalier projection. In PIP2, SF is used to present isometric, dimetric, and trimetric projections.

```
C       SUBROUTINE FOR DISPLAYING THE FRONT
C       ORTHOGRAPHIC VIEW INSIDE CUPID SOFT-
C       WARE SUBPROGRAM KNOWN AS CUPID1
C
        SUBROUTINE FVIEW(NDATA,X,Y,Z,IPEN)
        DIMENSION X(1000),Y(1000), Z(1000),
       +IPEN(1000)
        DO 90 K=1,NDATA
     90 CALL PLOT(X(K),Y(K),IPEN(K))
        RETURN
        END
```

Figure 5.18 PIP routine for axonometric pictorials.

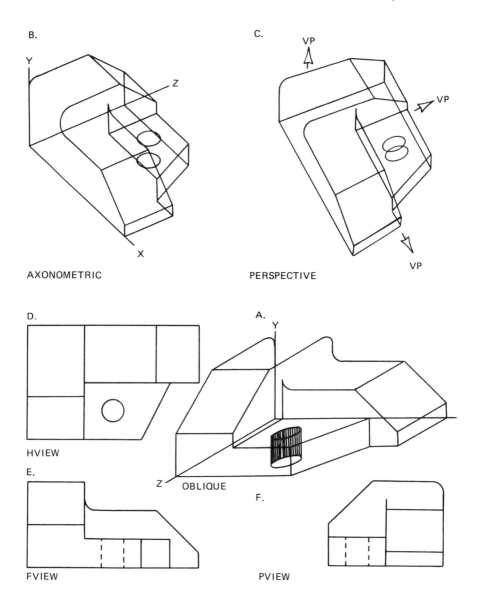

Figure 5.19 Display of A, PIP1; B, PIP2; C, PIP3; D, HVIEW; E, FVIEW; and F, PVIEW.

Figure 5.20 Multiple wireform projection from common database.

Perspective

A perspective drawing is one which more nearly presents an object as it appears to the eye. A third angle (ANG3) is required to be read into a display routine (PIP3). By this time you have guessed that PIP stands for pictorial image processor and 1 = ANG1, 2 = ANG2, and 3 = ANG3. In addition to ANG3, perspective pictorials are based on the fact that all lines (edges) which extend from the observer appear to converge or come together at some distance point.

A stylized pictorial system as defined by the last six subprograms

PIP1, 2 and 3
CUPID1, 2 and 3

provides 3-dimensional plots of any data which can be expressed as:

1. PIP = X,Y,Z,IPEN
2. CUPID = X,Y,Z,ICON
3. Function of two variables to produce a third.

Using this system, a designer or drafter can quickly take database from Chapter 3 and produce pictorial drawings of almost any part. Because the database is stylized, many pictorials can be created from many different angles in a shorter time than would be required to manually prepare one. Consider Figure 5.20: it was produced and output to an electrostatic plotter in six seconds.

METHODS OF PICTORIAL DISPLAY

The pictorials shown in Figures 5.1, 5.7, 5.10, 5.11, and 5.13 are known as a wireforms because they are separate wires representing connections in the database. There are other methods used to present pictorials and these are more common in drafting applications.

This improvement of visualization can instantly provide insights and correlations which might require long scrutiny during the manufacturing process planning, assembly planning, and functional design. A user's imagination can generate an almost unlimited number of applications for pictorials. Pictorials can be an outstanding educational or presentation tool because:

1. They can automatically exclude lines (wires), at user option, so that a reference axis may be used to show orientation. Horizontal, frontal, and profile plane view projections can be created without grid lines for realistic surface definition (see Figure 5.19).

2. Pictorials can be overlapped to show any irregularly spaced DATAPTs and to test the line elimination technique (see Figure 5.21).

3. Pictorial image generators can produce several thousand separate pictorial drawings of a 3-dimensional object, each with a separate viewing angle and viewing distance, including line elimination. This makes possible the creation of inexpensive animated scripts for product simulation or design modification (see Figure 5.22).

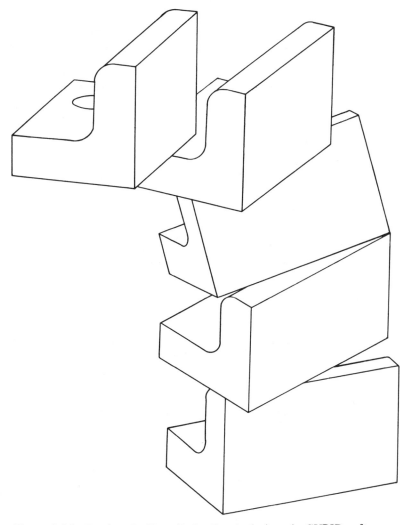

Figure 5.21   Testing the line elimination technique in CUPID software.

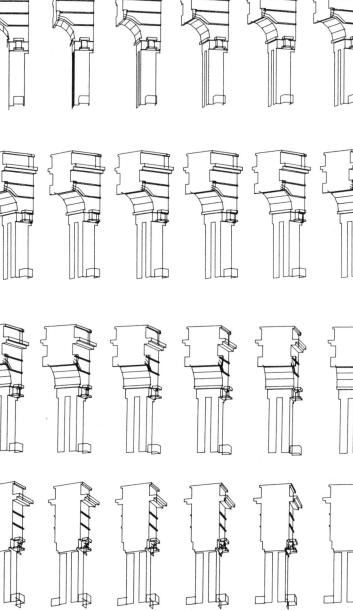

Figure 5.22 3-D objects for animation.

4. Additionally, a database can be plotted from a completely flexible choice of angle to show orthographic and pictorials side-by-side (see Figure 5.19).

5. Pictorial routines are written in simple coding statements as shown in Figure 5.14 and 5.15, so they will operate on the vast majority of computers.

DISPLAY SPECIFICATIONS

To advance beyond the simple point plotting of wireform models, the user replaces the usual CALL PLOTS or CALL INITT with CALL CUPID (see Figure 5.23). All subroutines used in CUPID are designed for X, Y, and Z data input. The program symbology outlined in Chapter 3 is used throughout the logic of CUPID software routines. There are two basic definitional concepts embodied

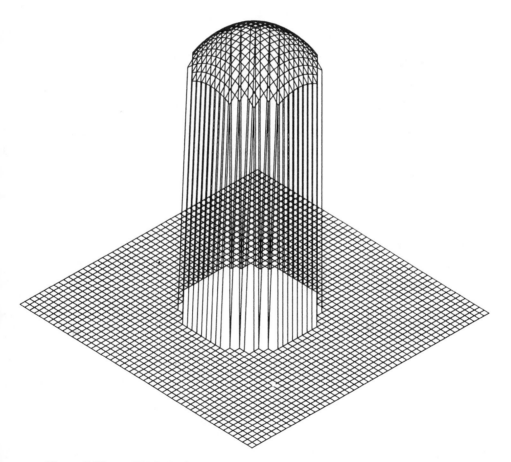

Figure 5.23 CUPID3 display.

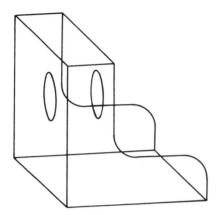

Figure 5.24 Wireform from XPLOT, YPLOT, DATA.

into three layers or versions of CUPID. The first concept is that of a wireform already discussed as an 'ideal' part — a hypothetical solid having perfect form and shape. Nominal part models are also possible (wireforms with lines removed) and are defined via projective geometry. That is, each intersection of a wire is defined in units of X, Y, and Z.

The second basic concept is that the order of and method of point connection is left entirely up to the user. As the part model is placed on the worksheet shown in Chapter 3, each point location is given a number and recorded as a database. This flexibility produces several attributes, as shown on page 230.

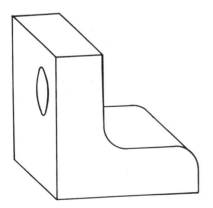

Figure 5.25 Solid form from ELINAT.

```
      SUBROUTINE ELINAT(XPLOT,YPLOT,IPEN,MODE)
C.........................................
C  ON INITAL CALL SET MODE = 1  ..........
C  IPEN = DEVIATION ACCEPTED FROM DATABASE
C  XPLOT = PLOTTER COORDINATE FROM X,Y,Z
C  YPLOT = PLOTTER COORDINATE FROM X,Y,Z
C.........................................
      GOTO(1,2,3)MODE
    1 MODE=1
      X1=XPLOT
      Y1=YPLOT
      PERCEN=FLOAT(IPEN)*.01
      CALL TPLOT(XPLOT,YPLOT,0,0)
      RETURN
    2 GOTO(4,5)MODE1
    4 MODE1=2
    7 X2=XPLOT
      Y2=YPLOT
      IPEN2=IPEN
      S2=(Y2-Y1)/(X2-X1)
      PS2=S2*PERCEN
      SU=S2+PS2
      SL=S2-PS2
      ISS2=(X2-X1)/ABS(X2-X1)
      RETURN
    5 IF(IPEN.EQ.IPEN2)GOTO 6
C.....PEN MODE IS DIFFERENT FROM PREVIOUS.
      CALL TPLOT(X2,Y2,IPEN,0)
      X1=X2
      Y1=Y2
      GOTO 7
C.....PEN MODE IS SAME AS LAST CALL ......
    6 S=(Y-Y1)/(X-X1)
      ISS=(X-X1)/ABS(X-X1)
      IF(S.GT.OR.S.LT.SL.OR.ISS.NE.ISS2)GO
     +TO 8
      X2=X
      Y2=Y
      RETURN
C.....MODE CHANGE, PLOT OLD VECTOR LOCATION
    8 CALL TPLOT(X2,Y2,IPEN2,0)
      X1=X2
      Y1=Y2
      GOTO 7
C.....LAST CALL ..........................
    3 CALL TPLOT(X2,Y2,IPEN,0)
      CALL TPLOT(XPLOT,YPLOT,IPEN,0)
      RETURN
      END
C
C.....CONTROL RETURNED TO CUPID SOFTWARE..
```

1. Models may be shown transparent as in Figure 5.24 or as solid objects as in Figure 5.25.

2. Modifications to part geometry can be made quickly. Notice a line was added in Figure 5.3 to show rounded edge.

3. Line elimination can be completed on a 3-dimensional database that has been transformed into plotter or screen coordinates; XPLOT, YPLOT. This makes line elimination an easier problem and can be done by the subroutine shown on page 229.

Subroutines like ELINATE are necessary if plotters or direct view storage tube displays are used. If CRTs like those shown in Chapter 7 are used, then the use of the subroutine ELINAT is not needed due to the selective erase function. The selective erase function should be used because it is faster for the drafter to point with a light pen then for a subroutine to logically check for visibility in each pictorial in a set of 100 or 1000.

Methods other than subroutine ELINAT and a light pen are also available. One such method is the use of a wireform and surface shading between wires. The drafter may call for shading as many times as necessary to describe the part as a solid. Figure 5.26 demonstrates a wireform model and the same data presented with shading between wires. The surface shading on visible sides covers the wires that appear in the rear of the pictorial. The drafter 'builds up' the desired solid part by joining as many shaded surfaces as necessary. Because this approach produces geometrically complete models, the shading subroutines can can generate any graphic representation of a part that can be defined in a mathematical database. This database is a mapping from 3- to 2-dimensional Euclidean space. The pictorials produced in this manner are still hollow, and if rotated from their base, a designer can go inside the pictorial and look out. Depending upon what the pictorial represents, this can be an advantage.

DATA GATHERING TECHNIQUES

Several methods of obtaining 3-dimensional data points for pictorial display are used. A worksheet method is comparable to the manual X, Y, and Z points obtained in Chapter 4. This is a tedious job at best but is used when other methods are not available. A comparison of 2-dimensional and 3-dimensional data gathering techniques is shown in Table 5.2.

Any of the methods described in Table 5.2 can be used to generate pictorial data. A combination of methods is oftentimes used as shown in Figure 5.27. In Figure 5.27 the drafter is using a digitizer which will record the pictorial data from a movie film. Any combination of methods similar to that in Figure 5.27 is a mechanical technique for recording data from an existing source; a drawing, model, machine part, movie or animation sequence, or the like. The most desired

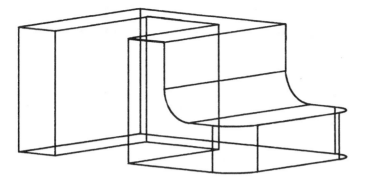

WIREFORM DATA

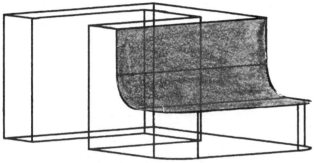

WIREFORM DATA WITH SHADED SURFACE

Figure 5.26 Solids by surface shading.

Figure 5.27 Tektronix researcher digitizes an object projected on a screen. (Copyright 1985 Tektronix, Inc., used with permission.)

Table 5.2 Data Gathering Techniques Used in Plots

Two-dimensional methods	Three-dimensional types
Two-dimensional work sheet	Three-dimensional work sheet
Coordinatograph	Cordax machine
Graphics tablet	Three-dimensional sonic digitizer
On-the-fly digitizer	Laser digitizer
Raster scanner	Wireform model measurer

techniques of multiview projection were explained in Chapter 4. Here the data is gathered in three basic steps. First, the shape of the object is described in straight line segments, usually three or four lines will form a flat surface. This flat surface is then coded for the amount of shade required. Shades of gray can be produced as shown in Figure 5.28 and 5.26. These shading codes can be assigned in any order desired to each surface of a pictorial as illustrated in Figure 5.29.

Second, the coded areas are checked for a logic pattern. Often, shades of gray are used to show light (sun angles) and dark areas of an object as shown in Figure 5.30. In this example, the object is a simple cylinder, but the shade appears as represented in Figure 5.28.

Third, the shaded area is presented as a pictorial object. If the object needs to be refined (i.e., the object looks like Figure 5.29), the number of flat surfaces can be increased to improve the surface shape of the object as shown in Figure 5.31.

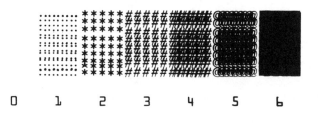

Figure 5.28 Shading code compared to NEWPEN values.

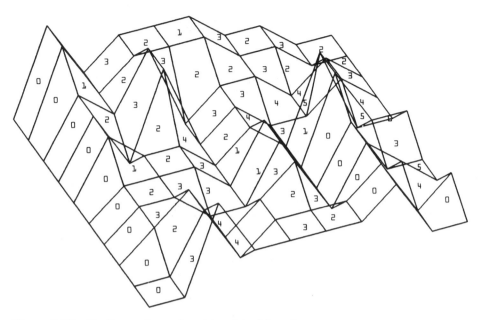

Figure 5.29 Shading codes assigned to pictorial surfaces.

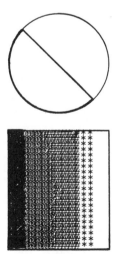

Figure 5.30 Shades of gray to indicate light and dark areas for visualization of a pictorial.

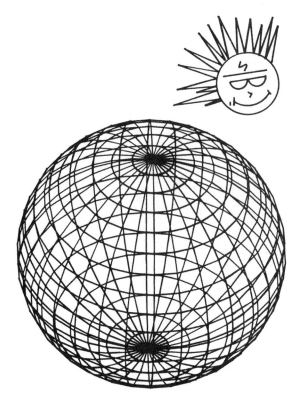

ADDED SURFACES IN TRANSPARENT WIREFORM.

SELECTIVE ERASE FOR SOLID MODEL SHADING.

Figure 5.31 Examples of added surfaces.

DISPLAY OF PICTORIAL DATABASES

The database which describes the pictorial object now contains shading data. A database can include several thousand separate number groups at this point. Always display the smallest size database that will communicate the correct amount of pictorial information to the reader or viewer. A series of examples will illustrate this point for you. In Figure 5.31, we see that as the number of surfaces increase, so do the data elements required to define them. A shaded area requires an additional amount of data to be processed, therefore, the shade produced along the bottom of the pictorial sphere in Figure 5.31 adds to the total database for the pictorial sphere. One way to reduce the amount of data required to display a shaded pictorial is to reduce the number of surface planes. Notice that in Figure 5.32, the number of surface planes has been reduced to a minimum by increasing the length along the Y axis of the object. This produces the shaded pictorial shown in Figure 5.33. The size of the database is now smaller than Figure 5.32 before shading. However, a part of the pictorial still needs additional surface definition, namely where the sizes of the cylinders change diameter and where the smaller cylinder joins the base. The drafter adds the surface planes required and the object is displayed in Figure 5.34.

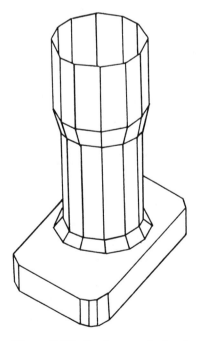

Figure 5.32 Surface ready for shading.

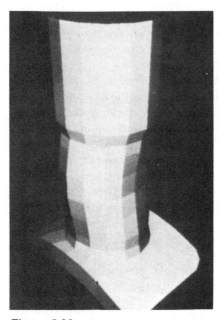

Figure 5.33   Surface displayed on CRT, no line elimination used. (Courtesy Evans and Sutherland Computer.)

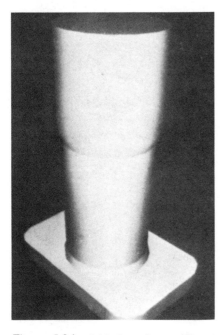

Figure 5.34   Added surfaces. (Courtesy Evans and Sutherland Computer.)

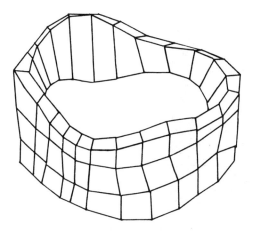

Figure 5.35   Figure before reduction and shading (see Figure 5.36).

Other examples appear in Figures 5.35 and 5.36, where a pictorial database is reduced and then shaded before display. Depending upon the pictorial, this can be an excellent approach. In Figure 5.37, the pictorial is very complex and a reduction of the surfaces to be displayed is not as effective, as shown in Figure 5.38. Often the change of surfaces to be shaded and the SF in one axis will produce dramatic effects as shown in Figure 5.39. Here the same X and Y database was used and Z was scaled before plotting.

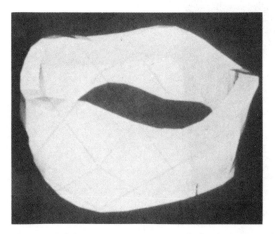

Figure 5.36   Final reduced and shaded pictorial. (Courtesy Evans and Sutherland Computer.)

Figure 5.37 Complex pictorial. (Courtesy Evans and Sutherland Computer.)

Figure 5.38 Complex pictorial: reduced and shaded. (Courtesy Evans and Sutherland Computer.)

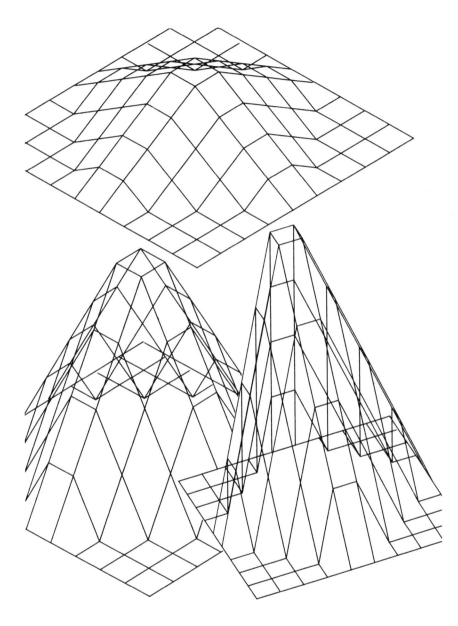

Figure 5.39 Pictorial with same X and Y data, and scaled Z data.

EXERCISES

1. Input the following example program for producing pictorial views.

```
CALL PLOTS
CALL PLOT(0.,3.,-3)
CALL NEWPEN(4)
DIMENSION X(24),Y(24),Z(24),IPEN(24)
DIMENSION PNTS(100,3),ICON(100),VPNT(100,3),VP(3)
DATA X/0.,2.,2.,3*0.,1.,1.,4*0.,4*1.,1.2,1.8,1.2,1.8,4*2./
DATA Y/3*0.,0.,0.,6*2.,0.,2.,1.2,2.,1.2,4*1.,.8,0.,.8,0./
DATA Z/0.,0.,1.,1.,3*0.,1.,1.,0.,1.,1.,0.,0.,4*1.,4*0.,1.,1./
DATA IPEN/3,9*2,3,2,3,2,3,2,3,2,3,2,3,2,3,2/
ANG = 30.
NV=4
DO 1 I=1,NV
1     READ(1,*)VPNT(I,1),VPNT(I,2),VPNT(I,3)
CALL SYMBOL(0.,5.,.2,'DRAWING USING CUPID1',0.0,20)
CALL CUPID1(24,X,Y,Z,IPEN,ANG)
NDATA=24
CALL PLOT(4.,0.,-3)
CALL SYMBOL(4.,5.,.2,'ANIMATION USING CUPID2',0.0,22)
CALL CONVER(X,Y,Z,IPEN,NDATA,PNTS,ICON,NDATA2)
DO 25 I=1,NV
DO 3 J=1,3
3     VP(J)=VPNT(I,J)
CALL PLOT(3.,0.,-3)
CALL ZARC(X(23)-0.2,Y(23),-Z(23),.2,0.,90.,VP)
CALL ZARC(X(21)-0.2,Y(21),-Z(21),.2,0.,90.,VP)
CALL ZARC(X(19),Y(19)+0.2,-Z(19),.2,180.,270.,VP)
CALL ZARC(X(17),Y(17)+0.2,-Z(17),.2,180.,270.,VP)
CALL CUPID2(NDATA2,NDATA,PNTS,VP,ICON)
25    CONTINUE
CALL SYMBOL(5.,5.7,.2,'ANIMATION USING CUPID3',0.0,22)
CALL FACTOR(.75)
CALL PLOT(4.,2.,-3)
CALL CUPID3
CALL PLOT(0.,0.,999)
STOP
END
```

2. Store the following subprogram.

```
SUBROUTINE CUPID1(NDATA,X,Y,Z,IPEN,ANG)
DIMENSION X(100),Y(100),Z(100),IPEN(100),XPLOT(100),YPLOT(100)
COSA = COS(ANG/57.3)
SINA = SIN(ANG/57.3)
DO 10 I=1,NDATA
XPLOT(I) = X(I)+Z(I)*COSA
YPLOT(I) = Y(I)+Z(I)*SINA
10    CALL PLOT(XPLOT(I),YPLOT(I),IPEN(I))
CALL CIRCL(XPLOT(21),YPLOT(21),0.,90.,.2,.2,0.0)
CALL CIRCL(XPLOT(23),YPLOT(23),0.,90.,.2,.2,0.0)
CALL CIRCL(XPLOT(14),YPLOT(14),180.,270.,.2,.2,0.0)
CALL CIRCL(XPLOT(16),YPLOT(16),180.,270.,.2,.2,0.0)
RETURN
END
```

3. Store the following subprogram.

```
SUBROUTINE CONVER(X,Y,Z,IPEN,NDATA,PNTS,ICON,NDATA2)
DIMENSION ICON(100),X(100),Y(100),Z(100),IPEN(100),PNTS(100,3)
DO 7 I=1,NDATA
  PNTS(I,1)=X(I)
  PNTS(I,2)=Y(I)
  PNTS(I,3)=Z(I)
  IF(IPEN(I).EQ.2) ICON(I)=I
7 IF(IPEN(I).EQ.3) ICON(I)=-I
  NDATA2=NDATA
RETURN
END
```

4. Store the following subprogram.

```
SUBROUTINE CUPID2(NP,NC,P,VP,IC)
DIMENSION P(100,3),IC(100),VP(3),PP(100,3)
  A=ARTAN(VP(1),VP(3))
  SA=SIN(A)
  CA=COS(A)
  DO 6 J=1,NP
    PP(J,3)=P(J,3)*CA+P(J,1)*SA
    PP(J,1)=P(J,1)*CA-P(J,3)*SA
6   CONTINUE
  VPP=VP(3)*CA+VP(1)*SA
  A=ARTAN(VP(2),VPP)
  SA=SIN(A)
  CA=COS(A)
  CALL NEWPEN(4)
  DO 7 J=1,NP
    PP(J,2)=P(J,2)*CA-PP(J,3)*SA
7   CONTINUE
  DO 8 J=1,NC
    IF(IC(J).LT.0) GO TO 9
    CALL PLOT(PP(IC(J),1),PP(IC(J),2),2)
    GO TO 8
9     K=-IC(J)
      CALL PLOT(PP(K,1),PP(K,2),3)
8   CONTINUE
RETURN
END

FUNCTION ARTAN(Y,X)
  DATA EPS/0.001/
  AX=ABS(X)
  AY=ABS(Y)
  IF(AX.GT.EPS.AND.AY.GT.EPS) GO TO 1
  IF(AX.LT.EPS.AND.AY.LT.EPS) GO TO 3
  IF(AX.LT.EPS) GO TO 2
3 ARTAN=0.0
  RETURN
2 ARTAN=(3.14159*AY)/(Y*2.0)
  RETURN
1 ARTAN=ATAN2(Y,X)
  RETURN
END
```

5. Store the following subprogram.

```
SUBROUTINE ZARC(XP,YP,ZP,R,SANG,EANG,VP)
DIMENSION P(100,3),IC(100),VP(3)
PI=3.14159265
N=IFIX(EANG-SANG)
THETA=(EANG-SANG)/N
THETAR=THETA*PI/180.
SRANG=SANG*PI/180.
DO 1 I=1,N
DX=R*COS(SRANG)
DY=R*SIN(SRANG)
P(I,1)=XP+DX
P(I,2)=YP+DY
P(I,3)=-ZP
SRANG=SRANG+THETAR
1   CONTINUE
NP=N
NC=N
IC(1)=-1
DO 999 I=2,NP
999 IC(I)=I
CALL CUPID2(NP,NC,P,VP,IC)
RETURN
END
```

6. Stop at this point and test part of the program shown in problem 1. Output only the portion that calls CUPID1 as shown below.

DRAWING USING CUPID1

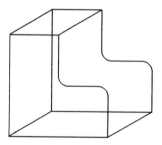

7. Input the additional subprogram.

```
SUBROUTINE CUPID3
DIMENSION X(300),Y(300),Z(300)
ICNT=0
DO 200 J=1,10
DO 300 K=1,10
ICNT=ICNT+1
X(ICNT)=J
Y(ICNT)=K
READ(1,*)Z(ICNT)
300 CONTINUE
200 CONTINUE
S1=.707
C1=.707
DO 1 I=1,4
CALL SURF(X,Y,Z,ICNT,S1,C1)
CALL PLOT(13.,0.,-3)
1   S1=S1+.5
RETURN
END
```

8. Output the second part of the program.

ANIMATION USING CUPID2

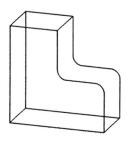
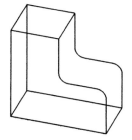

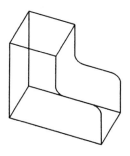
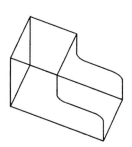

9. Input the last subroutine.

```
SUBROUTINE SURF(A,B,C,N,S1,C1)
DIMENSION A(300),B(300),C(300),BUFR(300),P(20,20)
DATA AXLN/3.0/
AXLN=5.
AXLN1=AXLN+0.001
XH=0.0
YH=0.0
ZH=0.0
XL=100.
YL=100.
ZL=100.
NN=10
DO 1 I=1,N
IF(XH.LE.A(I))XH=A(I)
IF(YH.LE.B(I))YH=B(I)
IF(ZH.LE.C(I))ZH=C(I)
IF(XL.GE.A(I))XL=A(I)
IF(YL.GE.B(I))YL=B(I)
IF(ZL.GE.C(I))ZL=C(I)
1 CONTINUE
DO 2 I=1,N
A(I)=(A(I)-XL)/(XH-XL)*AXLN
B(I)=(B(I)-YL)/(YH-YL)*AXLN
C(I)=(C(I)-ZL)/(ZH-ZL)*AXLN
2 CONTINUE
DO 3 I=1,NN
DO 4 J=1,NN
P(I,J)=0.
4 CONTINUE
3 CONTINUE
DO 5 I=1,N
IX=A(I)/AXLN1*NN+1.
IY=B(I)/AXLN1*NN+1.
IF(C(I).GT.P(IX,IY))P(IX,IY)=C(I)
5 CONTINUE
DO 6 I=1,NN
X=I*AXLN/NN
SX=X
IP=3
DO 7 J=1,NN
X=SX
Y=J*AXLN/NN
Z=P(I,J)
CALL ROTATE(X,Y,Z,S1,C1)
CALL PLOT(X,Y,IP)
IP=2
7 CONTINUE
6 CONTINUE
DO 8 I=1,NN
Y=I*AXLN/NN
SY=Y
IP=3
DO 9 J=1,NN
Y=SY
X=J*AXLN/NN
Z=P(J,I)
CALL ROTATE(X,Y,Z,S1,C1)
CALL PLOT(X,Y,IP)
IP=2
9 CONTINUE
8 CONTINUE
RETURN
END
SUBROUTINE ROTATE(X,Y,Z,S1,C1)
DATA  C2/.404/,S2/-.587/
SY=Y
Y=Z*C2+X*C1*S2 +Y*S1*S2+5.
X=SY*C1-X*S1+10.
RETURN
END
```

10. Test the last part of the program.

ANIMATIØN USING CUPID3

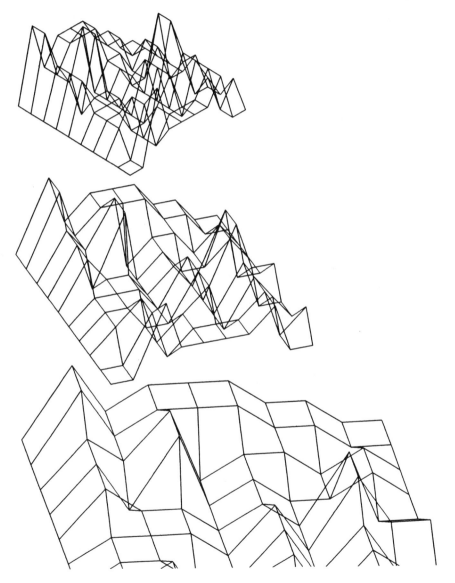

11. Database problem

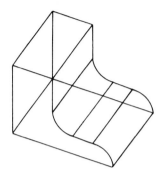

12. ICON problem

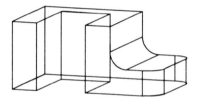

13. Digitizing problem

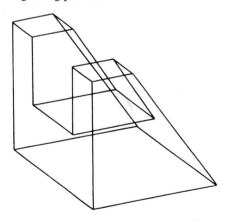

14. Database problem

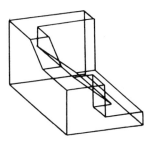

15. ICON problem

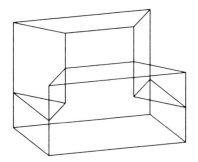

16. Digitizing problem

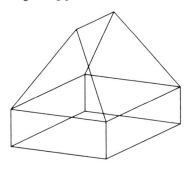

6

Computerized Descriptive Geometry

Computerized descriptive geometry (CDG) is a computer/automated system
which manipulates 3-dimensional databases. CDG has provided the designer
with an effective tool for satisfying the graphical as well as the quantitative de-
mands that occur in the design process. The advantages of using a CDG system
to fully use the information that is available during the early stages of the design process are explored in this chapter. Also discussed are the more obvious
features of a CDG system for constructing, modifying, viewing, and analyzing
spatial relationships.

The introduction of a CDG system which can meet the requirements for the
design, documentation, analysis, and fabrication of a product is the main thrust
of this chapter. The rapid rate of CDG system usage for these tasks in many manufacturing industries closely parallels similar developments in the more conventional interactive graphics systems (IGSs) described in Chapter 1. A further parallel has been the discovery that the most effective way to use the capabilities of
CDG was to institute database management devices at the early stages of the design process. Just as was the experience with IGSs, meeting this objective reduces the amount of effort required to bring a project from conception to
fruition.

Only recently have computer graphics been utilized to any significant degree
in a production mode to create drawings for industries. Most of the initial work
occurred at a few universities and at several large automotive and aircraft manufacturers.

STORAGE OF POINTS, LINES, PLANES, AND SOLIDS

The bulk of the work done on a CDG system involves the storage of 3-dimensional points. These points are then used to define straight lines, planes, and solids. Figure 6.1 illustrates a CDG coordinate plotting system for points, lines, and planes. This system consists of a right-handed Cartesian coordinate location for each of the 3-dimensional points used. Points are located by specifying the location from the origin in Figure 6.1. A point located (0,0,0) is the origin of the system. A point located (5,0,0) can be found 5 units to the right of the origin, (0,5,0) would specify a point 5 units above the origin, and (0,0,5) would specify a point 5 units in front of the origin. In this fashion any point may be located as shown in Figure 6.2.

A CDG system displays the entire cartesian coordinate system as shown in Figure 6.1 or just the points as shown in Figure 6.2. Sometimes a combination of the two displays is useful when checking point locations. The coordinate display system can also be positioned for viewing as a pictorial or as a flat orthographic view (top, front, side). Figure 6.3 represents an orthographic display of the cartesian coordinate planes viewed from the top and front.

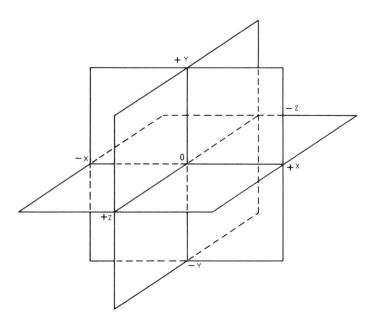

Figure 6.1 CDG coordinate system.

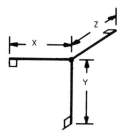

Figure 6.2 Point location measured from origin in X, Y, and Z directions.

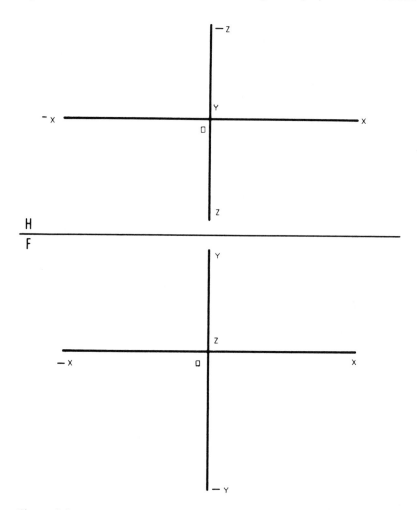

Figure 6.3 Orthographic display of cartesian coordinate planes.

Simple objects may now be displayed either as a pictorial as shown in Figure 6.4 or as orthographic views shown in Figure 6.5. This is possible because of the CDG workstation which allows an operator to choose proper display techniques.

A typical work station is shown in Figure 6.6. In this illustration, the operator is using a light pen in her right hand to select menu items, such as move, turn, and reset, from the bottom of the CRT. The left hand is free to use a function box which contains thirty-two lighted pushbuttons. A typical work procedure is to select image functions with the left hand (a depressed button activates firmware) and position them with the right hand. This method of using a CDG consists of hardware, firmware, and software that set the basic graphics-handling potential of the system. The manner in which a user will approach a descriptive geometry problem will be determined by the hardware/ software that is backing up each of the push buttons.

It really is not important in this section of the text whether hardware or software is more important, as both are featured by different CDG system manufacturers. Both the software (light-pen-controlled) and hardware (push-button-controlled) are needed to provide a complete system. With the advent of programmable microprocessors and the introduction of *firmware,* the gray area at the interface between software and hardware has narrowed.

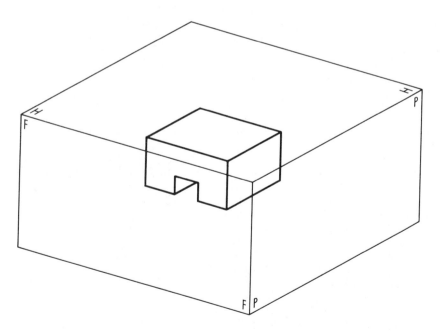

Figure 6.4 Display points used to describe a simple pictorial.

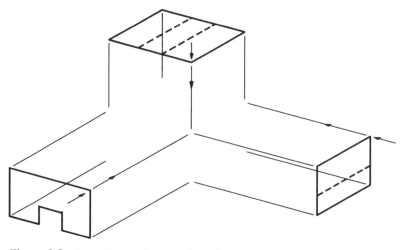

Figure 6.5 Same data points used to describe orthographic views.

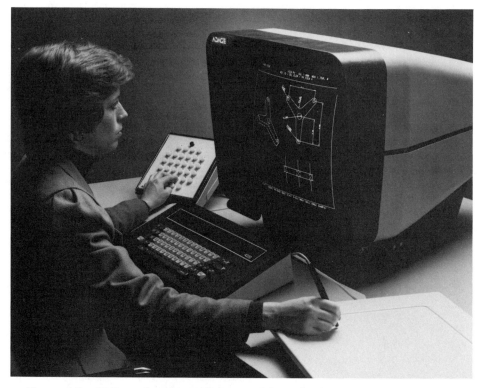

Figure 6.6 CDG workstation. (Courtesy Adage, Inc.)

To input or store points, lines, or planes in a CDG system, any one of three types of commands may be employed. The first type, composed of *system commands,* is the set of instructions that are standard to any computer-graphics operating system and were explained in detail in Chapters 1 through 5 of this text. These instructions usually consist of all the basic graphics-handling operations common to all applications. Instructions to move, copy, rotate, dimension lines, store, and plot are all part of the system command repertoire. These commands are preprogrammed by the vendor of the CDG.

The second type, *user commands,* is commonly thought of as programs that are written by a user to enhance the basic capabilities of the CDG for unique needs. Every company has its own unique and special needs. For example, Figure 6.7 is a typical process control application in which such variables as temperature, pressure, and radiation levels are continuously monitored and updated within a power plant. The information is displayed in a descriptive manner rather than as a table of values. A more common application of descriptive geometry might be a company that makes a line of custom gears programming a special routine to automatically generate a gear tooth involute. The mathematics for this calculation may be proprietary, and therefore the user may wish to create this program in-house. By writing a user command (usually in a common programming language such as FORTRAN), the CDG customer has complete control of its use. In addition, he has added a powerful tool to the CDG that greatly increases its productivity.

To ensure the integrity of the CDG operating system (system commands), it is important to keep the user command software separated from the general operating system. This is done by providing "handles" in the operating system to allow user commands to access and modify the drawing database but not modify the operating system software.

The third method is known as *macros.* They are system and user commands combined to form more powerful commands. In addition, a macro may involve the use of graphics language to increase its capability. The main difference between a macro and a user command is the ease of implementation. Drafters and designers, as well as programmers, write macros. Macros are often written and implemented within 5 minutes of conceptualization. They provide the user with a flexible tool that permits quick creation of a command language sometimes referred to as a geometric calculator.

DIGITIZING OF SPATIAL GEOMETRY

A system for digitizing spatial geometry is simply an organizational scheme that allows a drawing to be represented in a numerical form. In Chapters 1 through 4 databases were restricted to 2-dimensional straight-line drawings. The X, Y coordinates of each line were stored in a table. In Chapter 5 we became more so-

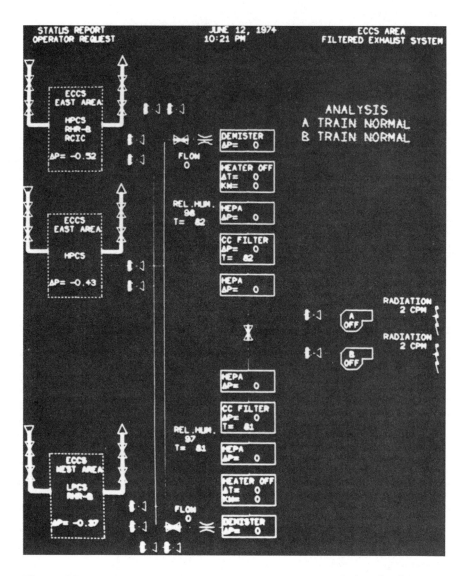

Figure 6.7   CDG process control application. (Courtesy Imlac, Inc.)

phisticated; the databases evolved to handle more complex geometries more efficiently. Three-dimensional arcs, curves, surfaces, and parts were just a few of the component types that 3-D-type programs could handle.

Digitizing an existing drawing may be compared to making a tracing. The drawing is taped onto a graphics tablet. The user than indicates with an electronic pencil the beginnings, corners, and ends of lines. Predefined template parts may be used to add subassemblies to memory. See Figure 6.8.

A relatively fast method of getting a drawing into a computer database, digitizing is very successful in CDG applications. Whenever the design data lies on a grid, it is a very popular method of inputting data. If grids are not used and the drawing is digitized at full scale, the actual hardware accuracy of a graphics tablet is about 0.025 millimeter. However, the ability of a good draftsperson to consistently position a pen on a drawing in a typical production environment is about 0.50 millimeter. Drawings for mechanical design do not lie on grid; therefore if accurate database and 3-dimensional models are desired, this method of digitizing is not acceptable. Some design firms have experimented with digitizing a nongrid drawing onto a grid overlay and then increasing the accuracy via geometric construction routines.

Digitizing in the third dimension, given orthogonal views, may be achieved with the tablet and pen by interactively declaring the third dimension for digitized geometry. Three-dimensional models constructed in this manner will contain sufficient accuracy for technical illustrations. A 3-dimensional database is used to represent a 3-dimensional object in a numerical form. To accomplish this in an efficient manner, a "wireform model" representation of the object is often used. The wireform consists of lines in space that are used to represent the edges of an object. A cube therefore can be represented by twelve straight lines (the twelve edges). This method of digitizing a solid is acceptable for polyhedral surface objects but can be awkward to use when representing complex shapes such as might be found in a casting or in digitizing a bottle. For these types of objects, more sophisticated sysetms for digitizing have now been developed. A 3-dimensional surface digitized by laser techniques has been used to describe flat, revolved, or completely irregular, sculptured surfaces.

A limited set of 3-dimensional surface digitizers has been developed, but their use among CDG users has been negligible. The current state of the art finds 3-dimensional digitizing done as wireforms. The wireform is the most popular method of digitizing 3-dimensional objects, with surface digitizers showing great promise but limited use. The wireform model is relatively easy to digitize on a CDG and is stored in a straightforward manner in the database. These models have been used to represent a variety of both simple and complex shapes. A digitized wireform may be recalled and displayed in much the same way that a drawing is created. Instead of calling plots, the CDG user adds "wires" in space. Much spatial information and manipulation can be derived by

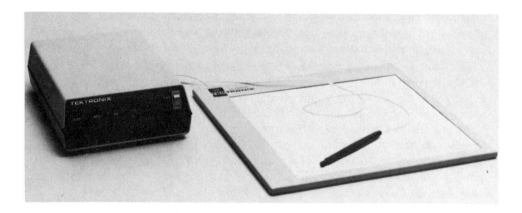

Figure 6.8 Graphics tablet. (Copyright 1985 Tektronix, Inc., used with permission.)

the engineer from these pictorial computer models, as their behavior is consistent with the actual physical object being modeled.

The main advantage of wireforms must be weighed against the disadvantage: The edges and not the surfaces themselves are represented in the database, and many operations that require surface information are difficult to implement. For example, the intersection of a plane and a wireform gives us a series of points (end views of edges), not visible edges. The user must interact with the CDG system to connect the end views to create a section. Compared to the methods used in Chapter 4, this is a time-consuming task because the order of point connection is not always clear. The "true-section" cut, explained in Chapter 4, could be created automatically.

PROJECTION OF POINTS, LINES, PLANES, AND SOLIDS

Before a 3-dimensional database can be utilized with a CDG to project an image, it must be placed in system memory. The method of digitizing just explained is only one method of obtaining a database. Another method is known as *interactive construction.* This method of constructing a database is the most natural to a user familiar with descriptive geometry skills. True, it is done at the CDG work station and not at the drawing board; but the similarities are remarkable. By using the electronic pen, tablet, alphanumeric keyboard and function box, the designer constructs a descriptive geometry solution in much the same way that is used at a conventional drawing board.

First, the user "turns the key" that activates his work station. This is usually a set of procedures and alpha codes that allows the operator to use the CDG station. Doing the "housekeeping" jobs is also referred to as a manner of turning on or starting up the system. Next the user enters a single string command such as

CALL BEGIN

or depresses a single function button. This "sets the page" on the CRT. One of the common pages used on CDG systems is the familiar HF reference plane with working space above and below:

H
_____
F

In this mode the CDG will accept X and Y data below the reference plane and place X and Z data above the plane. Perhaps the most primitive method of interactive construction is to input the X, Y, and Z coordinates of the beginning and end of every line from the keyboard. A more natural method is to use the light pen to indicate the ends of the lines or freehand-sketch the desired lines of the problem as shown in Figure 6.9. CDG features, including grids and locks, can be used to straighten lines and provide a method of accurately sketching a problem to specified sizes. The use of a design grid is like using graph paper in H and F views. Freehand light pen lines may be placed to the nearest grid intersection, ensuring a length that is a multiple of the grid spacing. A line entered via a keyboard will be positioned exactly where specified.

In most descriptive and vector geometry problems only one line in a view is absolutely positioned, the first one. This is usually entered from the keyboard, because of its accuracy. All other lines are positioned relative to the first line. With this in mind, a user may minimize the amount of information that must be typed from the keyboard. If a line needs to be added between the ends of two already-existing lines, it should only be required that the ends be touched by the light pen and that the proper function button be pushed to display the line between the indicated points. It should never be necessary to have the user type all the X, Y, Z coordinates for the entire drawing.

Once enough information is displayed above and below the HF plane, the user may select a single working view space to add more detailed bits of graphics. This single view space will be framed with a rectangular box to indicate the viewing plane. A menu bar is placed below a viewing surface for easy touch of the light pen. See Figure 6.10 (single window).

/ MOVE / TURN / SIZE / RESET / SET / GRID / OVERLAY / 1 2 3

This philosophy carried through the design and use of a CDG will greatly increase the productivity of the system. If the user wishes to "go back" to a two-view relationship, the added lines from the single view are now located in the opposite view as shown in Figure 6.11.

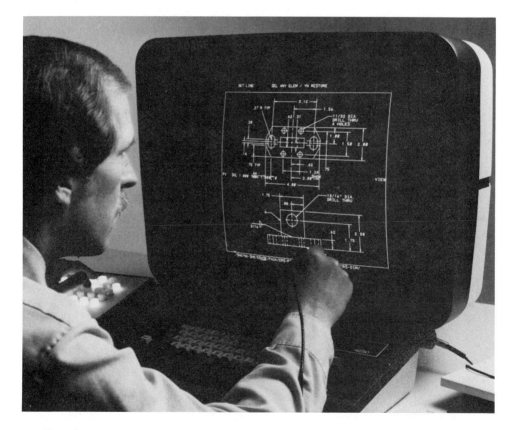

Figure 6.9   User in two-view mode of CDG. (Courtesy Adage, Inc.)

A CDG should also have a comprehensive set of geometric routines to allow the user to build onto the drawing by geometric relationships. A 3-dimensional set of geometric routines similar to those described for 2-dimensional illustration in Chapter 2 is available. Other examples of geometric routines are included in the following sections.

Figure 6.10   User in single-view mode of CDG. (Courtesy Adage, Inc.)

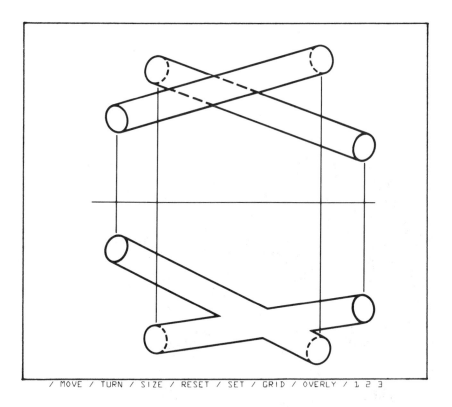

/ MOVE / TURN / SIZE / RESET / SET / GRID / OVERLY / 1 2 3

Figure 6.11   CDG operator places added lines in multiviews.

TRUE LENGTH OF LINE SEGMENTS

One of the problem-solving tools that is common to almost every other engineering graphic technique is that of determining the true length of a line segment. A line segment is displayed on the CRT by directing a stream of electrons to hit the phosphor coating of the screen. When this happens light is emitted. Due to the nature of the electron beam and the screen, there are five ways to produce a line segment.

1. *Beam deflection.* The electron beam is deflected by both magnetic and electrostatic fields. An advantage of the CRT is that the beam has little inertia and can be moved at very high speeds compared to a plotting pen.

2. *Beam modulation.* By modulating either the cathode or the control grid of the CRT, the beam can be turned off while it is being moved to location and then turned on at the proper spot.

3. *Beam cross section.* The beam is focused with an electrical lens system. Several cross-sectional shapes of the beam pattern may be displayed on the screen. The movement of these cross-sectional shapes can generate a line segment.

4. *Image persistence.* The type of phosphor used inside the CRT can determine the type of line segment presented to the viewer. Phosphors are classified in the time to decay from view. Short-term phosphors may cause flicker on the screen.

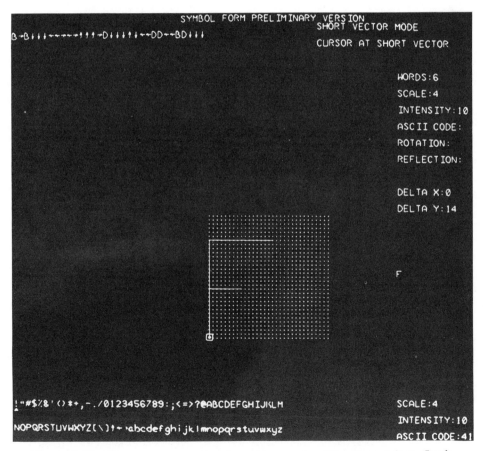

Figure 6.12 Character generation by vector mode. (Courtesy Adage, Inc.)

5. *Color.* There is a broad spectrum of colors available to the viewer. Phosphors are available which will emit white, green, blue, yellow, red, or orange light.

Every line segment displayed on a CRT, either oblique or true length, must employ one or more of the above techniques. The speed at which lines are displayed is so fast that most users do not stop to consider the techniques involved. In Chapter 6 we learned that the following line segments could be displayed at the press of a button:

H
───
F

Both of the characters H and F are composed of three short line segments. The reference plane edge dividing the two views is made up of one long line segment. In Figure 7.2, an enlargement of the character F, the control grid is clearly shown. The normal size of the character is shown directly to the right of the enlargement. All of the line segments in Figure 6.12 appear in true length because of the 2-dimensional nature of the presentation.

When 3-dimensional notation for line segments is used the displayed line segments may be true length or oblique. A graphics user may display the two-view mode function and enter the line coordinates from the keyboard:

                                                    . (40,5)B

                       . (13,1)A
    H
    ───
    F
                       . (13,3)A

                                                    . (40,4)B

Point A has coordinates of $X = 13$, $Y = 3$, and $Z = 1$; while point B has coordinates of $X = 40$, $Y = 4$, and $Z = 5$. The points are displayed in both views according to their locations. A dark line segment appears between the two points, as the beam was turned off during the move. A bright line segment could have been displayed as easily.

An experienced graphics observer can tell the line segment is oblique and must be manipulated in order to find its true length. Many techniques exist for this: auxiliary projection shown in Figure 6.13, rotation shown in Figure 6.14, and mathematical calculation. The first two methods are more time-consuming than the third. The following software listing can provide the true length in a fraction of a second.

```
C   *****************************************************************
C   *                                                               *
C   *   THIS PROGRAM COMPUTES THE TRUE LENGTH OF A LINE SEGMENT     *
C   *   THAT IS DESCRIBED AS STARTING POINT A AND ENDING POINT B.   *
C   *                                                               *
C   *****************************************************************
C         READ ABSOLUTE COORDINATE LOCATIONS FOR A AND B
          READ(1,*) AX,AY,AZ,BX,BY,BZ
          X=AX-BX
          Y=AY-BY
          Z=AZ-BZ
          TL=(X**2+Y**2+Y**2)**.5
          WRITE(3,*) TL
          STOP
          END
```

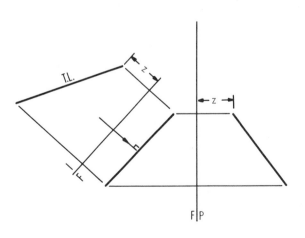

Figure 6.13 True length by auxiliary projection.

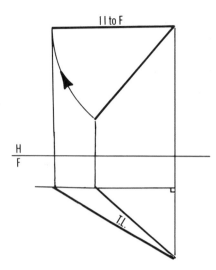

Figure 6.14   True length by rotation.

TRUE SIZE OR SHAPE DESCRIPTIONS

The next most often used geometric solution is that of finding the true size or area of a plane surface. A minimum of three line segments is required to close the plane surface and could be displayed in two-view mode as

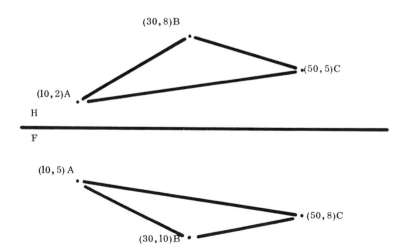

Here the line segments are displayed in bright vectors for ease of visualization. The graphics user may position the cross hairs of the joy stick over each of the points to be input. After each point is located by the joy stick, the space bar is depressed. This send the X, Y, and Z coordinates of the point into a software routine that accepts them and solves for the true length of each of the sides of the plane surface. The true lengths are then used to compute the true area of the plane surface. This information is printed on the CRT screen at a convenient location, usually above the menu display area of the screen. The following program listing will calculate and display the true area of the plane surface being studied:

```
C  ****************************************************************
C  *                                                              *
C  *   THIS PROGRAM COMPUTES THE AREA OF A PLANE SURFACE A,B,C    *
C  *                                                              *
C  ****************************************************************
C          READ THE ABSOULTE COORDINATE LOCATIONS FOR THE PLANE
           READ(1,*) AX,AY,AZ,BX,BY,BZ,CX,CY,CZ
           XA=AX-BX
           XB=BX-CX
           XC=CX-AX
           YA=AY-BY
           YB=BY-CY
           YC=CY-AY
           ZA=AZ-BZ
           ZB=BZ-CZ
           ZC=CZ-AZ
           TLA=(XA**2+YA**2+ZA**2)**.5
           TLB=(XB**2+YB**2+ZB**2)**.5
           TLC=(XC**2+YC**2+ZC**2)**.5
           IF(TLA.LT.TLB.OR.TLC) GOTO 10
           IF(TLB.LT.TLA.OR.TLC) GOTO 11
           IF(TLC.LT.TLA.OR.TLB) GOTO 12
        10 IF(TLB.LT.TLC) GOTO 50
           GOTO 40
        11 IF(TLA.LT.TLC) GOTO 50
           GOTO 40
        12 IF(TLA.LT.TLB) GOTO 60
        40 AREA=TLB*TLC/2.
           WRITE(3,*) AREA
           STOP
        50 AREA=TLA*TLB/2.
           WRITE(3,*) AREA
           STOP
        60 AREA=TLC*TLA/2.
           WRITE(3,*) AREA
           STOP
           END
```

If all the lines of a surface appear in true length in a single view, that view displays the true size and shape of the plane surface. Two methods are commonly used to display true shape on the CRT: developmental and projective. The developmental method is similar to a sheet-metal layout in that the correct contour of a surface can be obtained by set procedure. It is the method by which a sufficient number of lines which lie in the plane are shown in true length in the opposite view. From these lines a folded template can be transferred to a flat surface. If the template is cut out of the flat surface and folded together, the true size and shape of the 3-dimensional object can be constructed.

The procedure for displaying the true size of a plane surface by projection requires only one true length line segment. It may be the edge of the plane described by the data points, or it may be a construction line within the plane surface. The automatic methods for either are available for display on the graphics CRT. After the true length has been established an end view of the true length is necessary. The software program necessary to display this end view must use the Y datapoint information if the end view is to appear in the horizontal plane of projection:

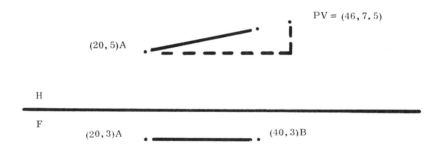

The Y datapoint information is the same for both points A and B because the true length appears in the horizontal plane of projection. The Y information is placed along the same line of sight as the true length line segment. The FORTRAN program computes the point view (PV) location in three statements:

PV=TL+BY
$XPV=(Y**2-PV**2)**.5$
$ZPV=(Z**2-PV**2)**.5$

The CRT screen can be lighted by a single command:

SET(XPV,ZPV)

where the point view is displayed at the end of the true length line in the horizontal (H) view. Of course point views can be programmed to appear in the frontal (F) or profile (P) view by using X,Z information for frontal and Z,Y information for the profile.

Once the true length of a line segment is found as a point view, the entire plane surface can be located as an edge view:

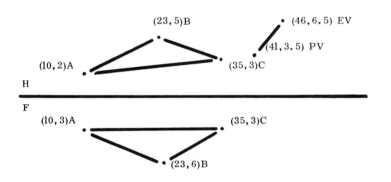

This is done by the construction of point EV and then calling for a bright line segment between PV and EV. Most applications for CRT graphic terminals used in the construction of descriptive-type problems start with the representation of a single point in adjacent views. By adding an additional point, a line segment can be formed. Three or more points may form a plane surface, while a number of planes may be used to represent an object. Software programs have been written to display most of the geometric relationships in problem solving; see Table 6.1.

Table 6.1 Software Available for Descriptive Geometry

Display routine	Code	Figure demonstration
True length	TL	6.13-6.14
Slope of TL line	M	6.15
Bearing	BRG	6.16
Intersecting lines	IL	6.17
Parallel lines	PL	6.18
Point views	PV	6.19
Line in a plane	LP	6.20
Edge views	EV	6.21
True shape	TS	6.22
Piercing point	PP	6.23
Intersection of planes	IP	6.24
Angle between planes	DA	6.25

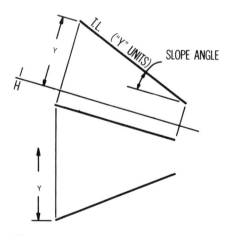

Figure 6.15 Slope of a line.

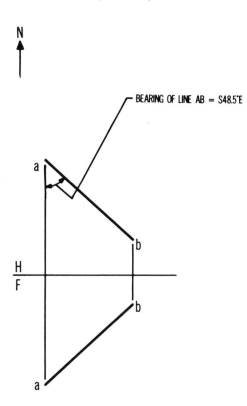

Figure 6.16 Bearing of a line.

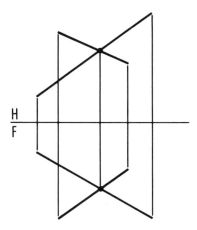

Figure 6.17 Intersecting lines.

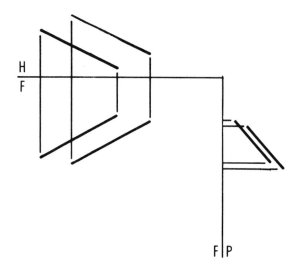

Figure 6.18 Parallel lines.

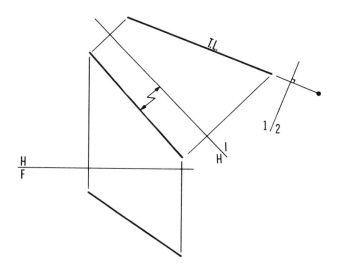

Figure 6.19 Point view of a line.

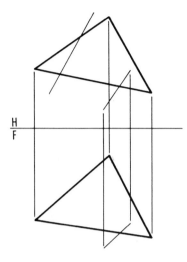

Figure 6.20   Line in a plane.

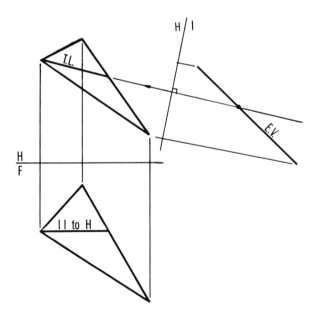

Figure 6.21   Edge view of a plane.

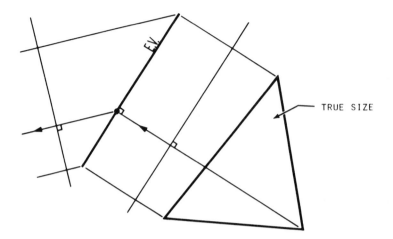

Figure 6.22 True size of a plane.

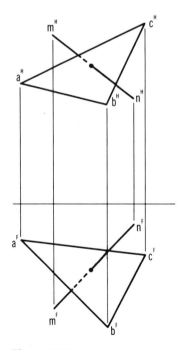

Figure 6.23 Piercing point of line and a plane.

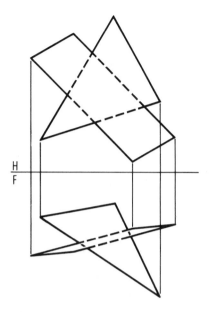

Figure 6.24 Intersection of planes.

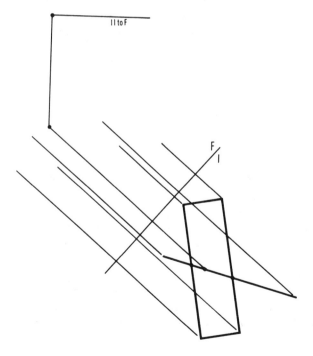

Figure 6.25 Angle between plane surfaces.

CDG IN THE DESIGN PROCESS

The design process consists of several stages that mark the development of an idea into a product. A modified version of the design process seen in most modern descriptive geometry textbooks is shown in Figure 6.26. It has been modified to better illustrate the areas where CDG graphics play an important role in communicating information. Each stage will be examined to determine the correct use of a CDG interactive graphics system in the design process.

Conceptualization

At this stage of the design process, the engineer begins to collect first impressions of the solution to a design problem. Most often this solution is based on past experiences of the engineer in working with similar problems. Therefore the solution can be documented by modification of past solutions stored in computer memory. This situation of creating a "new" design by modifying an already-existing design is a good candidate for a CDG system. The old solutions are retrieved on the CDG screen, and the new features are added by "editing" a copy of the existing design. A layout can be constructed from the trial solution in computer memory. This is the most desirable stage of the design process at which to use a CDG. It will allow all the successive design stages to build onto the database that is formed at this point. The work-hours required to create a layout using a CDG is not much different from those for manual methods. The advantages of the CDG consist of greater accuracy, ease of manipulation, and assembly of different parts. If the layout requires many standard components or redundant geometries such as mirrored outlines or repeated patterns, the total design documentation can be greatly reduced by the techniques learned in Chapters 1 through 5.

Engineering Analysis

After the creation of the layout drawings, the designer will experiment with the design to determine its validity. One of these analyses is the geometric verification of how the design will fit together. This involves the determination of allowance and interference; on a CDG system this can be greatly improved through the use of visual inspection templates. The inspection of the design parameters can be accomplished interactively with the user, indicating what dimensions or distances she wishes to use for the template. This new concept is similar to the old manual go/no-go gages used in the machine shop, but here the computer creates the gages as 3-dimensional templates to visually check the 3-dimensional wireform design. Since auxiliary views are quickly generated from the 3-dimensional wireform, visual checks for spatial relationships can be rapidly determined.

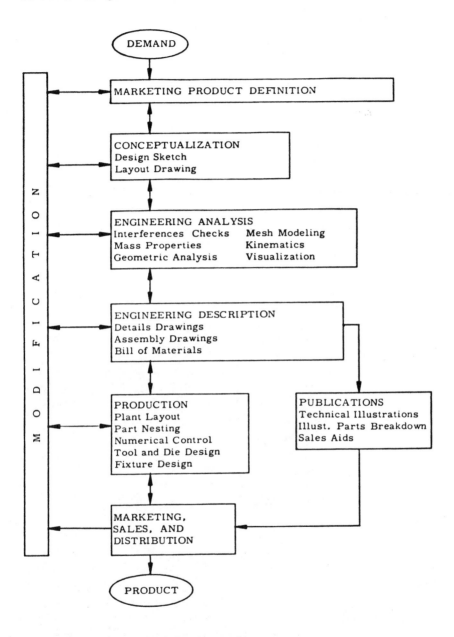

Figure 6.26   CDG in the design process.

The ability to create axonometric, perspective, or stereo views with pictorial programming greatly enhances the designer's ability to visualize the object before it is actually produced. In addition to direct interference analysis, the designer can quickly overlay and build multiple part assemblies and visually or arithmetically check clearances. Figure 6.27 shows an engineer as he touches the menu item

/   /   /   /   /   /   / OVRLY /

with the light pen. The item checked for interference in this case is a fuel tank design for an airplane wing section. A variety of properties that can be difficult if not impossible to calculate at the drawing board can be automatically deter-

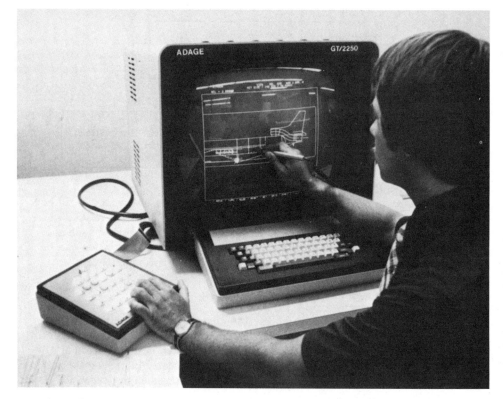

Figure 6.27   Designer touches OVRLY to fit fuel tanks in wing section.

mined with the CDG system. A good example of this is the volume calculation of the fuel tanks for the entire wing.

If a stress analysis program such as FLING* is to be used to evaluate the design, the CDG can be used to interactively create the nodes and elements needed to describe the shape of the part. A program such as FLING allows the designer to use the captured geometry to efficiently create boundary conditions and interior nodes. Since this finite element mesh model is graphically constructed by the engineer, the visual feedback provides a good, effective method of reducing errors in the node list and element connectivity data. (It should be noted that FLING cannot be done on the minicomputer of the CDG and must be fed via a communications link to the host mainframe where the actual analysis is performed. The results are fed back to the CDG for display, evaluation, and further interconnection.)

Engineering Description

The engineering description stage of the design process is devoted to the creation of working drawings for manufacture. This work is done by a draftsperson since the design information is communicated to manufacturing through the use of technical drawings. The design and drafting functions are not necessarily done in separate departments because drafting describes the layout drawing so that the individual detail drawings may be displayed and plotted. The layout already exists in the CDG system; it is not necessary for the draftsperson to redraw the basic parts. The concern is modifying the layouts to conform to the company drafting standards and providing the fabrication notes.

The 3-dimensional wireform model is the reference for the construction of the detailed drawings. The modification of the model to yield a detailed drawing can be done by the use of menu items. The draftsperson may want to relocate a section of layout; the following item is touched with the light pen:

/ MOVE /   /   /   /   /   /   /

Then the portion of graphics to be moved is touched by the pen. The draftsperson is now free to position the graphics at will. Remember, the wireform initially defines lines (edges) and bounded surfaces in space. To use menu items and construct a variety of views (front, right, top, etc.) information and draftsperson's direction must now be given with the model that defines how a line should appear when viewed at a particular angle. Additional engineering drawing re-

---

*Finite element program developed at Lockheed, Georgia plant.

quirements such as cross-hatching, notes, and dashed lines may also have to be added to the drawing. The answer is to allow the draftsperson to use the CDG to its fullest capacity by interaction with the database to produce correct views.

Hidden Line Uses and Applications

The hidden line removal problem is a special case of this general freedom of interaction with the CDG. Simply, it is the desire to make those lines of a 3-dimensional wireform that are not visible from a vantage point appear as dashed lines. Both interactive and mathematical techniques have been used to remove hidden lines or make them dashed. The selection of vantage points was described in Chapter 5, and they are part of the pictorial program. These mathematical routines will work with severely restricted wireforms and will usually require large amounts of computer time. The interactive methods used with a CDG where the user indicates which lines or parts of lines should be hidden or dashed will work on all 3-dimensional wireforms and will sometimes be faster than the mathematical ones.

   Since the CDG is a CRT screen, groups of lines can be moved by the menu item MOVE. With the use of the menu items,

---

/   /   /   / RESET / SET /   /   /

---

lines may be "turned off," making them invisible yet still present. This technique is extremely useful during the detailing stage of the working drawing development.

Techniques for Technical Illustration

An additional use of the SET/RESET level of visibility is in illustration of parts for publication. Individual parts, (for example, a gear shaft housing and idler gear) may be placed on different levels. If only the housing is to be emphasized, the levels containing the shaft and gears may be RESET. Another spin-off from the CDG wireform model is the creation of illustrations for service manuals and sales aids. The creation of an exploded assembly view showing the order of assembly of a complex part is greatly simplified through the use of a CDG system. The basic part geometry need not be recreated, as it exists in memory. The technical illustrator positions the component parts according to his judgment and then makes the artistic touch-up to create the illustration. The procedure is very similar to the "paste-up" methods now in use.

Production

This stage of the design process is concerned with the actual fabrication of the design. The best known manufacturing uses of interactive CDG systems is the creation of numerical control (N/C) tapes. Since the design is represented in a 3-dimensional database, it makes sense to use this information to determine the tool motion needed to machine the part. A parts programmer uses the CDG to direct the N/C sequences and techniques used to machine the part. The N/C programmer is relieved by the CDG system of the tedious, error-prone calculations needed to specify the tool paths. The CDG may give either an APT file or other standard N/C machine language output or perform the postprocessing through CADAM via the IBM 370.

In addition to N/C, fixture design for conventional machine tooling can be done on a CDG. In the design of a fixture, the piece part may be redrawn more than a dozen times. If the part involves complex geometry, the number of auxiliary views may be great. The CDG will produce as many views as needed at high speeds from the designer's data base in memory. The CDG not only provides quick copies at the desired scale and orientation but also provides a tool to determine fixture clearances, angles, surface normals, and section cuts. Interactive nesting techniques developed for CDG systems allow manufacturers to lay out irregular-shaped patterns on stock size sheets to minimize waste. After the parts are laid out on plates, N/C cutting routines can be used to assess and visualize the cutter path.

EXERCISES

1. Select a CDG work station and sign on the system (the instructions for this will be located in the notebook you prepared for the exercises in Chapter 1. CDG systems are called refresh graphic systems and as such have light pens and function boxes. Oftentimes a large computer center does not provide this "stand-alone" operational mode. Check to make sure that a set of software exists for the selection buttons of the CDG work station.

2. Begin working with the refresh system by building single points in space. Two points in the horizontal plane of projection (above the HF display) and two related points in the frontal plane of projection are stored as one line segment having X, Y, and Z coordinate locations. Practice connecting the points with dark and light vectors. Connect lines to form planes and planes to form solids as shown below.

3. Display point C as shown above. Consider this point as part of a pictorial object.

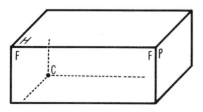

4.   Display point C from above as part of an orthographic projection.

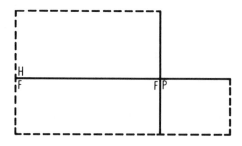

5.   Add a second point to form a line.

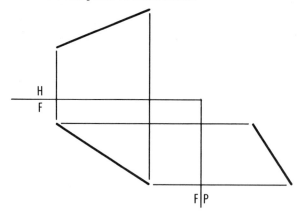

6.   Add a third point to form a plane.

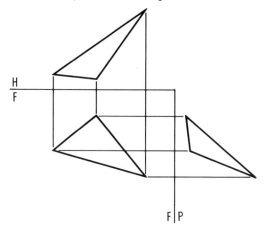

7. Add additional points to the display to form a solid.

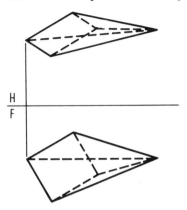

8. Continue the solid building process with auxiliary views.

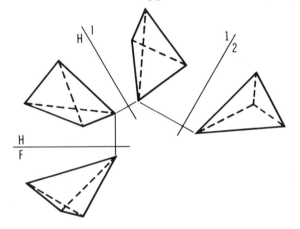

9. Find the true length (TL).

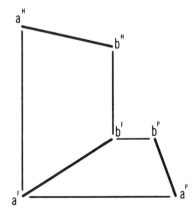

10.   Find the slope of the line.

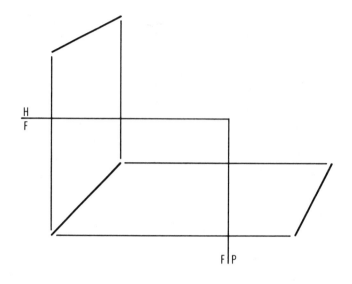

11.   Find the bearing of the line.

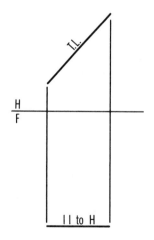

12. Find the intersection of the lines.

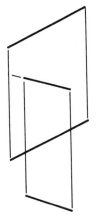

13. Find the parallel lines in a profile view.

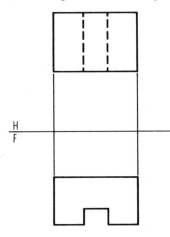

14. Find the point view of the line.

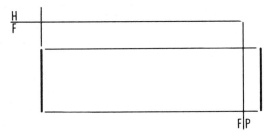

15.   Find the location of the line in the various planes.

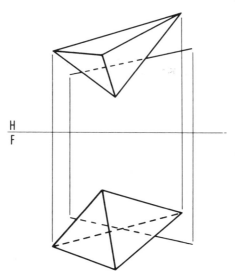

16.   Find the edge view of the plane.

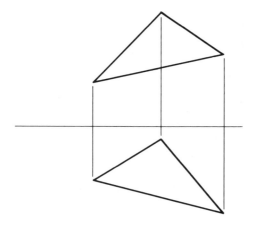

17.   Find the true size of the plane.

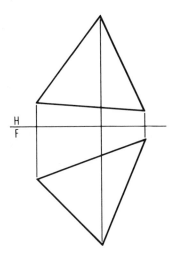

18.   Find the piercing point of the line and plane.

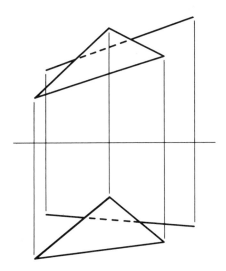

19.   Find the intersection of the planes.

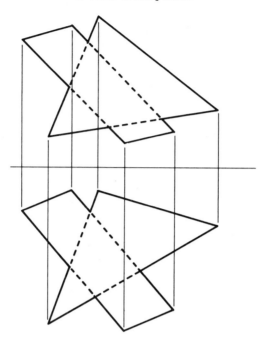

20.   Find the angle between the planes.

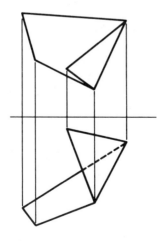

7

DVST Graphics Terminals

The DVST graphics terminal, as an interactive input/output device, represents the single most powerful extension to modern-day computer graphics and design. It enables the designer to communicate with a computer in his own medium and most natural form. It also allows the computer to answer in a form that is compact, descriptive, and most appropriate for a design situation. It provides a means for a common language between human and machine.

The DVST computer display terminals are capable of displaying both alphanumeric characters and graphic data. Once written, the display remains visible until it is erased, and it is not necessary to continually refresh the information put up on the screen. The DVST is an upper and lower case ASCII terminal.

Some DVST terminals offer, in addition, a write-through capability, in which both stored and refreshed information may be displayed. These terminals have a display area of 14.5 inches by 10.9 inches, and the user has the option of four character sizes.

TERMINAL CONTROL SYSTEM

The terminal control system for DVST makes the terminal as easy to use as a pencil and a piece of paper. The detailed programming and general I/O handling are contained with the system; as a result the basic terminal capabilities are made available to the user in a natural and practical manner.

The terminal control system subroutines communicate with each other primarily through the terminal status area. The package gives many graphing conveniences to the user. Bright and dark vectors (line segments) as well as points may be displayed on the terminal screen. A bright vector, which can be seen on the screen, is caused by one of the "draw" routines. A "move" routine will cause a dark vector, the invisible equivalent of a bright vector; a "point" routine causes the display of a bright spot or point. The following section deals with some of the subroutines which output bright and dark vectors and points using terminal screen coordinates. The values of these coordinates should be from $\emptyset$ to 1023 for X directions. The Y-axis coordinates should not exceed 780 to remain visible on the screen.

TERMINAL CONTROL SUBROUTINES

By allowing the terminal control system to monitor alphanumeric (A/N) output rather than using FORTRAN READ and WRITE statements, it is possible to maintain terminal status, especially the tracking of the beam position. This tracking is required for tab and margin control as well as for facilitating the mixture of A/N and graphic output. As with graphic output, alphanumeric output is buffered, or stored, until a routine is called to dump the buffer, or until the buffer is full.

ANMODE

At times the user may wish to output A/N data other than through the terminal control system. In such cases it is the user's responsibility to insure that the terminal is in A/N mode. This can be done by using ANMODE. It is not necessary to call ANMODE when using the terminal control system routines as they will automatically call it whenever necessary. ANMODE can be used to dump the output buffer.

CALLING SEQUENCE:

CALL ANMODE

BELL

An audible tone may be output at any time to call the user's attention to a particular event. Often a sustained audible output, which may be generated by a series of calls to the bell routine is used for an alarm. The "bell" may be sounded while in any mode except GIN (Graphic Input) mode and has no affect on terminal status.

CALLING SEQUENCE:

CALL BELL

CSIZE

Provides the current character height and width in raster units. The characters are measured in screen coordinates. This subroutine is useful for imposing alphanumeric characters on graphic displays, primarily in the case of labeling. It allows the user to see where his label ought to be placed to coincide with grid lines and tic marks. When dealing with the multiple character sizes available on the DVST terminal, this routine is especially helpful.

CALLING SEQUENCE:

CALL CSIZE (IHROZ, IVERT)

Parameters Returned:

IHORZ   the horizontal character dimension, including inter-character space; the horizontal distance between two periods.

IVERT   the vertical distance, as above, including interline spacing.

Figure 7.1 demonstrates a use of CSIZE.

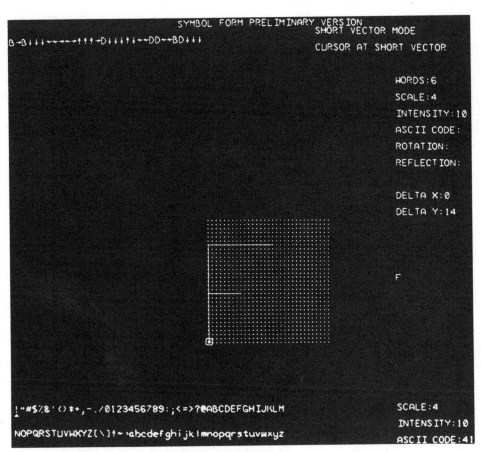

Figure 7.1 Character generation by vector mode.

Dash

Dashed lines of nearly infinite variety may be drawn through the use of the terminal control system in both virtual and screen space. The four basic dashed line subroutines are DSHABS, DSHREL, DASHA, and DASHR. These routines are analogous to DRWABS, DRWREL, DRAWA, and DRAWR; each dashed line subroutine, however, has a third, integer-format argument. This third argument controls the type of dashed line displayed, and it can take any integer value from –1 to the largest integer the computer can accept.

CALLING SEQUENCES:

>   CALL DSHABS (IX, IY, L)
>   CALL DSHREL (IX, IY, L)
>   CALL DASHA (X, Y, L)
>   CALL DASHR (X, Y, L)

IX, IY (integer) and X, Y (real) are the coordinates the dashed line is drawn to and L is the dash type specification.

Software dashed lines may be specified on any graphics display terminal with a concatenation of the following code numbers:

>   1 - 5 raster units, visible
>   2 - 5 raster units, invisible
>   3 - 10 raster units, visible
>   4 - 10 raster units, invisible
>   5 - 25 raster units, visible
>   6 - 25 raster units, invisible
>   7 - 50 raster units, visible
>   8 - 50 raster units, invisible

Example:

>   CALL DSHABS (2ØØ, 7ØØ, 3454)

The software also uses single digits to specify (L):

>   –1 causes a move
>
>   0 causes a draw
>
>   9 alternate visible and invisible segments between data points.

Example:

CALL DSHABS ($2\emptyset\emptyset$, $7\emptyset\emptyset$, -1)

Draw

The three functions which do line drawing by referring to screen coordinate locations are MOVABS, DRWABS, and PNTABS. "ABS" stands for absolute; the drawing is called absolute because it is measured from a fixed point, the origin ($\emptyset$, $\emptyset$). The arguments of these routines are always in integer format.

MOVABS. The argument of MOVABS is the pair of coordinates of the point to which a move is desired. Output starts at the stored current beam position. This position is updated after every line draw or other output command.

CALLING SEQUENCE:

CALL MOVABS (IX, IY)

Example:

CALL MOVABS ($1\emptyset\emptyset$, $15\emptyset$)

This call generates a move to ($1\emptyset\emptyset$, $15\emptyset$) so that drawing can proceed from there.

DRWABS. This generates a bright vector from the current beam position to the coordinates given and updates the appropriate variables in the Terminal Status Area.

CALLING SEQUENCE:

CALL DRWABS (IX, IY)

Example:

CALL MOVABS ($1\emptyset\emptyset$, $5\emptyset$)
CALL DRWABS ($3\emptyset\emptyset$, $5\emptyset$)

These calls cause a move to ($1\emptyset\emptyset$, $5\emptyset$) and a subsequent line to be drawn from ($1\emptyset\emptyset$, $5\emptyset$) to ($3\emptyset\emptyset$, $5\emptyset$).

PNTABS. Similarly, PNTABS moves to the coordinates given as arguments and displays a point there. See Figure 7.2.

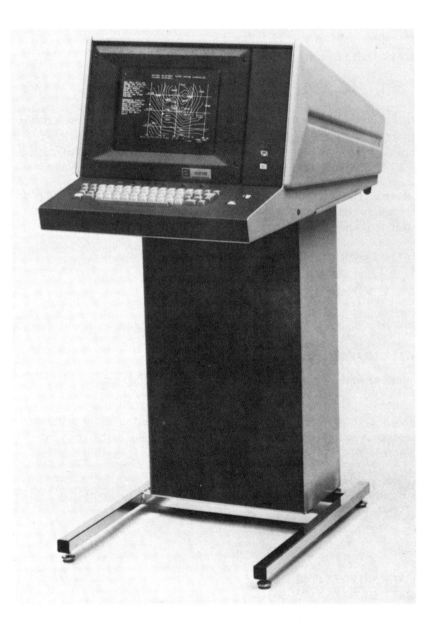

Figure 7.2 Model 4012 CRT graphics terminal. (Copyright 1985, Tektronix, Inc., used with permission.)

CALLING SEQUENCE:

CALL PNTABS (IX, IY)

Example:

```
CALL INITT (3Ø)
CALL MOVABS (3ØØ, 2ØØ)
CALL DRWABS (5ØØ, 2ØØ)
CALL DRWABS (5ØØ, 4ØØ)
CALL DRWABS (3ØØ, 4ØØ)
CALL DRWABS (3ØØ, 2ØØ)
CALL PNTABS (4ØØ, 3ØØ)
CALL FINITT (Ø,767)
```

It is often easier to draw lines by indicating how many horizontal and vertical screen units to move *relative* to the last beam position. Negative relative movement is to the right or up. DRWREL, MOVREL, and PNTREL perform relative drawing in screen units. They have the same syntax as DRWABS, MOVABS, and PNTABS.

Example:

Draw the same box as in Figure 7.4 with relative vectors.

```
CALL INITT (3Ø)
CALL MOVABS (3ØØ, 2ØØ)
CALL DRWREL (2ØØ, Ø)
CALL DRWREL (Ø, 2ØØ)
CALL DRWREL (-2ØØ, Ø)
CALL DRWREL (Ø, -2ØØ)
CALL PNTREL (1ØØ, 1ØØ)
CALL FINITT (Ø, 767)
```

ERASE

The terminal screen may be erased without changing the mode or beam position. The terminal control system will prevent generation of additional output until the erase is completed.

CALLING SEQUENCE:

CALL ERASE

FINITT

When terminating a program which uses the terminal control system, it may be desirable to return the terminal to alphanumeric mode and move the cursor to a point that will not interfere with any previous output. All output to the terminal is buffered, or stored, until the user calls a routine that dumps the buffer, or until the buffer is full.

FINITT automatically performs these functions. It terminates the program and outputs the contents of the buffer. Its arguments designate the position of the alphanumeric cursor upon program termination. FINITT should be used, depending on the computer system, either in conjunction with or in place of a FORTRAN STOP statement.

CALLING SEQUENCE:

CALL FINITT (IX, IY)

Parameters Entered:

IX - the screen x-coordinate of the position to which the beam is moved before program termination.

IY - the screen y-coordinate of the beam termination position.

HDCOPY

The user who is equipped with the DVST hardcopy unit may have the computer generate a hardcopy of the screen contents at any time. This may be accomplished while in any mode and does not affect the terminal control system status. The system will prevent generation of additional output until the hardcopy is completed. See Figure 7.3.

CALLING SEQUENCE:

CALL HDCOPY

Figure 7.3 Hard copy unit for 4012 unit. (Copyright 1985, Tektronix, Inc. used with permission.)

HOME

This terminal control subroutine moves the alphanumeric cursor to the upper left corner of the DVST screen.

    CALLING SEQUENCE:

    CALL HOME

INITT

The first subroutine called in a DVST display program. INITT requires the rate of character transmission from the computer to the terminal as an input parameter in order that appropriate delays may be produced during screen erasure and hardcopy generation. This will prevent loss of data on remotely connected terminals while they are not ready.

CALLING SEQUENCE:

CALL INITT (IBAUD)

Parameter Entered:

IBAUD - the transmission (baud) rate in characters per second.

KCM

The function routine KCM transforms centimeters to screen units. It provides the number of raster units in (RC) centimeters.

CALLING SEQUENCE:

Variable = KCM (RC)

Parameter Ended:

RC - the number of centimeters.

Parameter Returned:

KCM - the number of raster units in (RC) centimeters.

Example:

KCM is a means of determining a screen position when the user wishes to work with virtual units.

IX = KCM (3.5)

CALL DRWREL (IX, 0)

KIN

The function routine KIN transforms inches to screen units. It provides the number of raster units in (RI) inches.

CALLING SEQUENCE:

Variable = KIN (RI)

Parameter Entered:

RI - the number of inches.

Parameter Returned:

KIN - the number of raster units in (RI) inches.

Example:

KIN is a means of determining a screen position when the user wishes to work with virtual units.

IX = KIN (1.4)

CALL DRWREL (IX, 0)

Line

Line control for the DVST may be called from NEWLIN, LINEF, CARTN, HOME, BAKSP, or NEWPAG.

CALLING SEQUENCES:

Generates a line feed and carriage return.

CALL NEWLIN

Generates a line feed.

CALL LINEF

Generates a carriage return.

CALL CARTN

Moves the alphanumeric cursor to the upper left corner of the screen.

CALL HOME

Generates a backspace.

CALL BAKSP

Erases the terminal screen and returns the alphanumeric cursor to the HOME position.

CALL NEWPAG

MOVE

MOVEA, DRAWA, and POINTA are analogous to MOVABS, DRWABS, and PNTABS, but they allow points outside the virtual window to be referenced. Only those points or portions of bright vectors (line segments) which fall within the window boundaries, however, will be displayed; this is known as "clipping".

CALLING SEQUENCE:

CALL MOVEA (X, Y)
CALL DRAWS (X, Y)
CALL POINTA (X, Y)

Parameters Entered:

X - the horizontal virtual (real) coordinate to which a bright or dark vector is drawn or at which a point is displayed.

Y - the vertical virtual (real) coordinate to which a bright or dark vector is drawn or at which a point is displayed.

Point

MOVER, DRAWR, and POINTR draw straight lines, move, and display points, respectively, relative to the current beam position. They are analogous to MOVREL, DRWREL, and PNTREL, except that they deal with user rather than screen units and clipping, as described above, may occur.

RECOVR

RECOVR updates the terminal to match the terminal status area variables. It is useful following output to the terminal which is outside the terminal control system (e.g., a FORTRAN WRITE).

CALLING SEQUENCE:

CALL RECOVR

RESET

This routine accomplishes the same function as INITT but it does not call for a new page.

CALLING SEQUENCE:

CALL RESET

RESTAT

The DVST may be restored to any previously saved state at any time by providing the status restoring routine with the 60-word real array in which the previous terminal status area was stored.

CALLING SEQUENCE:

CALL RESTAT (RARRAY)

Parameter Entered:

RARRAY - the 60-word array containing previously stored terminal state.

RROTAT

A graphic figure drawn with relative coordinates may be rotated at any angle relative to its original display position.

CALLING SEQUENCE:

CALL RROTAT (DEG)

Parameter Entered:

DEG - the angle of rotation relative to the position of the original display.

RSCALE

A graphic figure drawn with relative coordinates may be rescaled by any factor which is compatible with the virtual window definition; that is, a figure will be clipped if its dimensions exceed the limits of the virtual window.

CALLING SEQUENCE:

CALL RSCALE (FACTOR)

Parameter Entered:

FACTOR - the rescaling factor relative to the original size of the display.

SCURSR

The graphic cursor may be used to specify screen coordinates directly. Calling
SCURSR will activate the graphic cursor, allowing the user to position it. The
cursor position is transmitted to the computer when a keyboard character is
struck. This character along with the input position is returned as arguments by
SCURSR. The terminal control system compensates for effects on the beam
position caused by the graphic cursor.

CALLING SEQUENCE:

CALL SCURSR (ICHAR, IX, IY)

Parameters Returned:

ICHAR - a keyboard character, 7-bit ASCII right-adjusted.

IX   - the screen x-coordinate of the graphic cursor.

IY   - the screen y-coordinate of the graphic cursor.

Figure 7.4 demonstrates a use of the screen cursor.

SEELOC

SEELOC allows the user to locate on the screen the last position of the graphic
beam if he has generated output outside the terminal control system (e.g., a
FORTRAN READ or WRITE). Thus, the beam may be updated.

CALLING SEQUENCE:

CALL SEELOC (IX, IY)

Parameters Returned:

IX - the screen X-coordinate of the beam.

IY - the screen Y-coordinate of the beam.

SEEMOD

SEEMOD returns the value of common variables indicating the status of the
hardware dashed line type, Z-axis mode, and DVST mode.

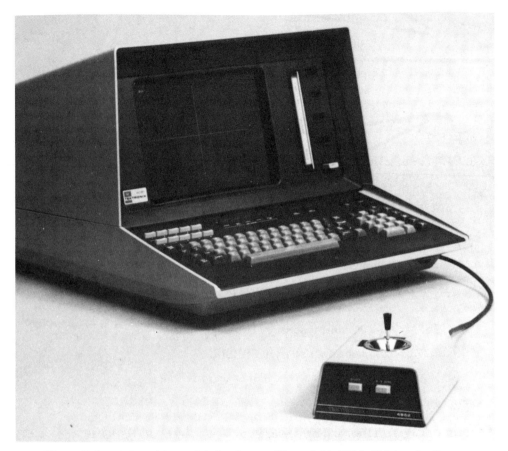

Figure 7.4 CRT and joy stick hardware. (Copyright 1985, Tektronix, Inc. used with permission.)

CALLING SEQUENCE:

CALL SEEMOD (LINE, IZAXIS, MODE)

Parameters Returned:

LINE   - the hardware line type in effect

IZAXIS - the hardware Z-axis mode

MODE - the software mode:

$\emptyset$ = alphanumeric
1 = vector
2 = point plot
3 = incremental plot
4 = dash

SEETRM

SEETRM returns the common variables which identify DVST speed, type, character size, and the maximum range of addressable points (4096 or 1024).

CALLING SEQUENCE:

CALL SEETRM (ISPEED, ITERM, ISIZE, MAXSR)

Parameters Returned:

ISPEED - the baud rate in characters per second which has been set in INITT

ITERM - the terminal type set in TERM

ICSIZE - the character size set in CHRSIZ

MAXSR - the maximum screen address set in TERM.

SETMRG

This routine sets the left and right margins to be used by CARTN, HOME, and NEWPAG.

CALLING SEQUENCE:

CALL SETMRG (MLEFT, MRIGHT)

Parameters Entered:

MLEFT - the screen coordinate at which a line of alphanumeric output starts. Its value should always be greater than $\emptyset$ and less than the maximum screen coordinate (1023 or 4095) or the right margin value.

MRIGHT - the screen coordinate at which a line of A/N output ends. Its value should always be greater than MLEFT and less than the maximum screen coordinate (1023 or 4095).

SETTAB

The routine SETTAB takes a given tab setting in screen coordinates and inserts it into the given tab table. If the tab is full, the maximum setting will be lost in order that a lessor tab setting may be inserted. Although duplicate tab settings are not inserted, SETTAB does not generally check the tab setting for validity nor does it know whether the given tab table is horizontal or vertical.

CALLING SEQUENCE:

CALL SETTAB (ITAB, ITBTBL)

Parameters Entered:

ITAB   -   tab setting in either X or Y coordinates.

ITBTBL -   the horizontal or vertical tab table (Array Name).

To remove a tab selectively, its position in screen coordinates (ITAB) must be entered along with the proper tab table. Non-zero values which do not correspond to a current tab setting are ignored. If the value of the tab position is $\emptyset$, the entire tab table will be removed.

CALLING SEQUENCE:

CALL RSTTAB (ITAB, ITBTBL)

Parameters Entered:

ITAB   -   the X or Y screen coordinate of the tab to be removed. If the number is $\emptyset$, all tabs in the tab table designated will be removed.

ITBTBL -   the horizontal or vertical tab table (Array Name).

TCSLEV

This routine returns the last date of modification for the terminal control system as well as the level number.

CALLING SEQUENCE:

CALL TCSLEV (LEVEL)

Parameter Returned:

LEVEL - a three element integer array where:

> Level 1 = the year of modification.
> Level 2 = the julian day.
> Level 3 = the level number.

VCURSR

It is often useful to be able to retrieve virtual rather than screen coordinates with the graphic cursor. The routine VCURSR allows you to use the graphic cursor. After the cursor has been positioned, its screen coordinates may be transmitted to the computer by striking a keyboard character. VCURSR transforms the input data into virtual coordinates according to the current window definition. The virtual cursor does not affect the beam position.

The transformation which VCURSR effects assumes that all of the screen is a continuation of virtual space with the scale implied by the current window.

CALLING SEQUENCE:

CALL VCURSR (ICHAR, X, Y)

Parameters Returned:

ICHAR - a keyboard character, 7-bit ASCII, right-adjusted.

X - the virtual x-coordinate of the graphic cursor.

Y - the virtual y-coordinate of the graphic cursor.

Window

So far, to display a drawing in virtual space the entire screen has been used. But any rectangular portion of the screen can be used as a display area. This display area is called the screen window, and it is defined by the subroutines SWINDO and TWINDO. The two subroutines stand in the same relation to each other as do VWINDO and DWINDO (see Sections 3.3 and 3.4); like all arguments in screen terms, the arguments of SWINDO and TWINDO are in integer format.

CALLING SEQUENCE:

CALL SWINDO (MINX, LENX, MINY, LENY)

Parameters Entered:

MINX - the minimum horizontal screen coordinate.

LENX - the horizontal extent of the rectangle.

MINY - the minimum vertical screen coordinate.

LENY - the vertical extent of the rectangle.

CALLING SEQUENCE:

CALL TWINDO (MINX, MAXX, MINY, MAXY)

Parameters Entered:

MINX - the minimum horizontal screen coordinate.

MAXX - the maximum horizontal screen coordinate.

MINY - the maximum vertical screen coordinate.

MAXY - the maximum vertical screen coordinate.

A second method of defining a virtual window may be employed by using the subroutine DWINDO. DWINDO uses a calling sequence similar to that of VWINDO.

CALLING SEQUENCE:

CALL DWINDO (XMIN, XMAX, YMIN, YMAX)

Parameters Entered:

XMIN - the minimum horizontal user coordinate.

XMAX - the maximum horizontal user coordinate.

YMIN - the minimum vertical user coordinate.

YMAX - the maximum vertical user coordinate.

EXERCISE

1. If a CDG work station is not available, the exercises from Chapter 6 may be worked on a DVST graphic terminal that has a storage tube with write-through capability. Constant motion cannot be displayed on the hardware, but the calculations and simulation by software can be done. Check the JCL information in your notebook and work the set of exercises on either type of equipment.

8

Automated Vector Analysis

Automated vector analysis is the study of graphic statics with computer assistance. The application of graphic statics to the solution of structural problems has been in wide use by engineers and architects for many years. The addition of computer graphics to this method is fairly new and is called computerized vector geometry (CVG). Like computerized descriptive geometry (CDG), it contains powerful tools for problem solution. CVG representation of the forces which act in various members of a structural framework possesses many advantages over manual solution; the key advantage, beyond presenting a graphical picture of the stresses, are that most problems can be solved with the speed and accuracy of the computer.

With the CDG skills outlined in Chapter 6, stresses may be obtained much more accurately than the various members can be sized, since in sizing we must select, from a handbook, members capable of withstanding loads equal to or greater than the design load. Using CVG, the designer computes a size and then applies a factor of safety* when designing any and all structures.

Problems in statics are customarily solved by either graphical or algebraic methods. In this chapter the author has assumed that the reader is familiar with one or the other. With no previous background in statics, the reader will gain little from the study of how to automate it. Before proceeding further, review the following common terms of graphic statics shown in Table 8.1.

---

*The factor of safety allows for unforeseeable hazards and labor defects or structural weaknesses. It is defined as ultimate strength divided by allowable unit stress.

Table 8.1 Common Terms of Graphic Statics

Statics	Force	Elements of force
Vector	Tension	Compression
Shear	Equilibrium	Equilibrant
Magnitude scale	Structural scale	Coplanar
Noncoplanar	Concurrant	Noncurrant
Resultant of a force	Moment of a force	Couples
Funicular polygon	Space diagram	Stress diagram
Load line	Reactions	Free-body diagram

Many excellent references for studying the terminology listed exist. The reader should consult a reference source if any of the terms listed are unclear. We shall begin the study of automated vector analysis by building directly upon the skills learned in Chapter 6.

Line segments were labeled starting point and ending point in Chapter 6 because they were not vectors. They were known as scalar values. In Chapter 8 we shall deal with line segments known as vectors. This is the name applied to a line of scaled length which represents the magnitude and direction of a force. An arrowhead placed on the line, usually at the end, shows the "sense" (which way the force acts). The next noticeable difference is that vectors use Bow's notation for labeling. For example, CDG notation looks as follows for a line segment:

A
$_{(X, Y)}$ ——————————————— B $_{(X, Y)}$

while CVG notation using Bow's notation looks like

You will note the space around the vector has been labeled. Both are referenced AB, the first representing a frontal projection of a line segment. The use of the scalar notation

$A_{(X,Y)}$ and $B_{(X,Y)}$

indicated that locations X and Y were used to define the location. A complete description must include another orthogonal view, i.e.,

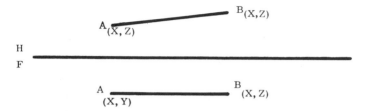

The horizontal view contains the true length of the scalar AB. In the case of a vector it, too, will appear orthographically as a directed line segment which may or may not be in true length in any of the principal views:

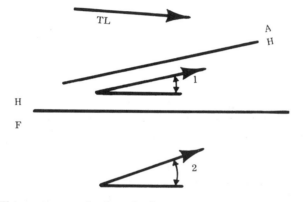

This vector may be described as

$$AB = TL \underline{|}^\odot 1, {}^\odot 2$$

Here vector notation is used to say the following: A vector AB is TL vector units long (magnitude) and the angles from the polar references are 1 and 2.

Vector notation should not be confused with Bow's notation. Bow's notation is the labeling of a diagram to read around two or more vectors called "joints." The reading is made in a clockwise direction for convenience.

RESULTANTS

If a group of vectors describing a system are in equilibrium, the system is said to be balanced. The resultant of this system is always zero. Systems are either balanced or unbalanced. Vectors represent abstract quantities of the physical system. Two or more vectors acting together are required to describe a system. To solve a problem in which vectors are used, a resultant is often found. It is found by the use of two diagrams. One is called the space diagram; it shows the relationship in the physical system and indicates how the vectors are applied. The second is called the stress diagram and is built from the space diagram to determine characteristics of the system, i.e., balanced or unbalanced.

Suppose we look at a simple two-vector diagram:

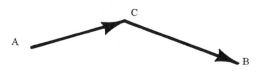

If the two vectors act simultaneously at point A, the result will be a path shown as dashed from A to B:

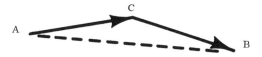

The resultant then is the result of two or more vectors acting at the same time upon a system. If the vectors act independently, the path taken will be A to C to B or along the vector lines. When only two vectors are contained in the system, a principle of the parallelogram of forces is employed in finding the resultant of two vectors acting on a body. By using the same example the body would be moved directly along the diagonal connection of the parallelogram (R):

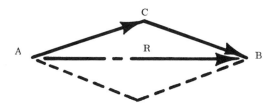

A computer graphics program can now be written to handle all two-vector diagrams of a coplanar nature (see Figure 8.1).

```
C     ***************************************************************
C     *                                                             *
C     *    THIS IS AN AUTOMATED VECTOR ANALYSIS PROGRAM FOR THE     *
C     *    SOLUTION OF PARALLELOGRAM OF FORCES OR THE ADDITION OF   *
C     *    VECTORS CONTAINED IN A COPLANAR SYSTEM.  THE PROGRAM     *
C     *    DISPLAYS THE VECTORS AS SOLID LINES AND THE RESULTANTS   *
C     *    AS DASHED LINE SEGEMENTS.  CONSTRUCTION SCALE = 1 GDU    *
C     *    TO INPUT THE FOLLOWING INFORMATION                       *
C     *         X & Y LOCATION OF A,B,C WHERE:                      *
C     *              A= POINT OF APPLICATION                        *
C     *              B= END POINT OF SYSTEM                         *
C     *              C= MIDPOINT OF SYSTEM                          *
C     ***************************************************************
      CALL PLOTS
      DIMENSION X(3),Y(3)
      READ(3,*) X(1),Y(1),X(2),Y(2),X(3),Y(3)
C     DISPLAY THE SYSTEM OF VECTORS
      CALL AROHD(X(1),Y(1),X(3),Y(3),.125,0.,16)
      CALL AROHD(X(3),Y(3),X(2),Y(2),.125,0.,16)
      CALL DASHP(X(1),Y(1),.1)
C     COMPUTE VECTOR LENGTHS
      X1=X(3)-X(1)
      X2=X(2)-X(3)
      X3=X(2)-X(1)
      Y1=Y(3)-Y(1)
      Y2=Y(2)-Y(3)
      Y3=Y(2)-Y(1)
      TL=(X1**2+Y1**2)**.5
      TLA=(X2**2+Y2**2)**.5
      TLB=(X3**2+Y3**2)**.5
C     PRINT VECTOR QUANTITIES
      WRITE(1,*)TL,TLA,TLB
      CALL PLOT(0.,0.,999)
      STOP
      END
```

Figure 8.1 Automated vector analysis program.

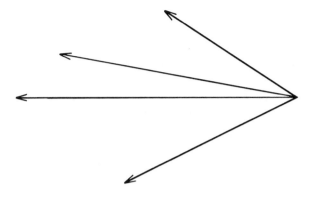

Figure 8.2 Space diagram for concurrent coplanar system of vectors.

RESULTANT OF A SYSTEM OF FORCES

Figure 8.2 illustrates a space diagram for a system of concurrent coplanar forces of given magnitude and directions. This system can be previewed on the DVST by the following program:

```
C   ******************************************************************
C   *                                                                *
C   *   DISPLAY PROGRAM FOR SYSTEM OF CONCURRENT COPLANAR VECTORS.   *
C   *                                                                *
C   ******************************************************************
        CALL PLOTS
        CALL AROHD(5.,6.,4.5,8.,.125,0.,16)
        CALL AROHD(5.,6.,7.,6.,.125,0.,16)
        CALL AROHD(5.,6.2,5.,.125,0.,16)
        CALL AROHD(5.,6.,3.6,.125,0.,16)
        CHARACTER * 3 ICHAR
        DIMENSION X(8),Y(8),HT(8),ICHAR(8),ROT(8),NCHARS(8)
        DATA X/4.,7.1,6.4,3.2,5.,6.,6.,4.2/
        DATA Y/7.4,6.,5.,4.,7.,6.2,5.8,5./
        DATA HT/8*.125/
        DATA ICHAR/'A  ','B  ','C  ','D  ','150','130','100','225'/
        DATA ROT/4*0.,300.,0.,300.,45./
        DATA NCHARS/8*3/
        DO 100 I=1,8
  100   CALL SYMBOL(X(I),Y(I),HT(I),ICHAR(I),ROT(I),NCHARS(I))
        CALL PLOT(12.,0.,999)
        STOP
        END
```

After the system is displayed we may want to find the single force (resultant) which will have the same effect as the four vectors. One method of solution would be to consider the system as two sets of double vectors to be added. The method for this will now be presented. The procedure would be to repeatedly apply the principle of the parallelogram of forces. Doing this, we can determine a single force which will produce the same result as the four vectors. We should input the forces in clockwise order and start with vectors A and B. The coordinate locations of A,B, and the point of concurrency are input to the program with the following result.

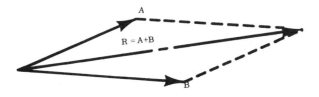

Now R and C are combined without erasing the screen:

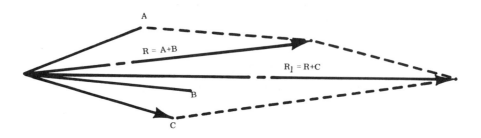

R_1 and D are added together to find the resultant of the total system:

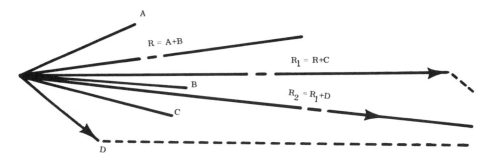

Obviously the system is not in equilibrium because R_2 has direction and magnitude. The use of the parallelogram program for solving complex systems is not recommended. An advanced program has been written for the construction of a stress diagram. A stress diagram uses the coordinate locations of the space diagram and redraws the diagram by combining one vector to another (maintaining true direction and length). This is much quicker than constructing a series of parallelograms.

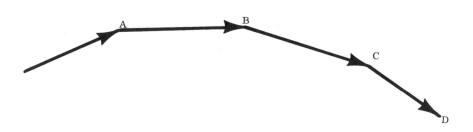

The "tip to tail" technique clearly shows any result or opening. The system is balanced or in equilibrium if the stress diagram closes. If an opening occurs, then a resultant exists or an equilibrant is needed to close and balance the system.

DETERMINING RESULTANT AND POINT OF APPLICATION

The general term for the process of replacing a group of vectors by a single vector is combination or composition. This process is the addition of two or more vectors. The opposite process, that of replacing a single vector by two or more vectors having the same effect, is called resolution. Each vector in the new system is called a component of the given vector. Resolution and composition are useful techniques when studying nonconcurrent systems of vectors.

Nonconcurrent, coplanar forces may be combined to show a point of application. The combination or addition will illustrate a common resultant:

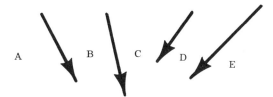

In this system, four vectors are separated by Bow's notation: A, B, C, D, and E. They are not concurrent, and they do not act parallel. By using the DVST and the advanced program for addition of vectors, the tips are connected to each tail:

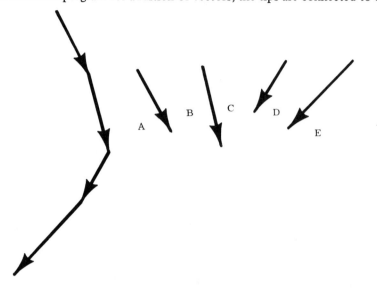

This clearly shows that a resultant is present. The magnitude of the resultant can be computed and displayed, but the point of application has not been located. The graphics input (GIN) mode of the terminal can be used to locate a convenient point beside the plotted information. This point is called a pole point. From the pole point, PLOT's are connected to each tip and tail:

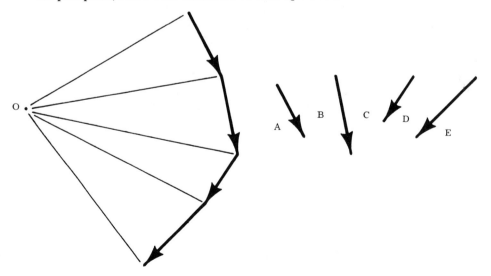

A call to alpha mode can now be used for convenient labeling of points and diagrams used so far in the solution process:

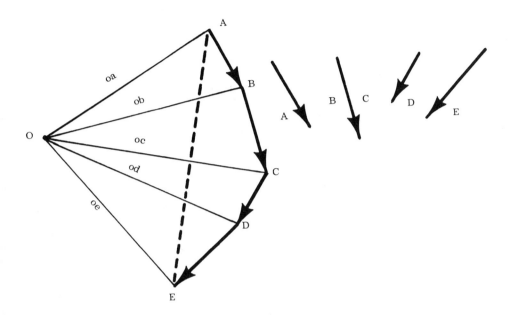

The last steps in the location of the point of application would be the construction of the funicular polygon in the GIN mode:

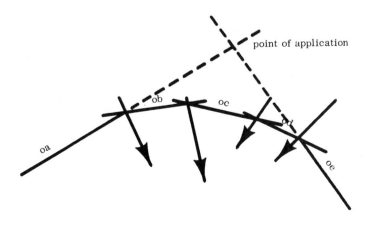

The resultant has already been computed for magnitude and displayed for direction; with the aid of the GIN mode, the point of application was found. With the alpha mode all labeling of the construction steps was completed:

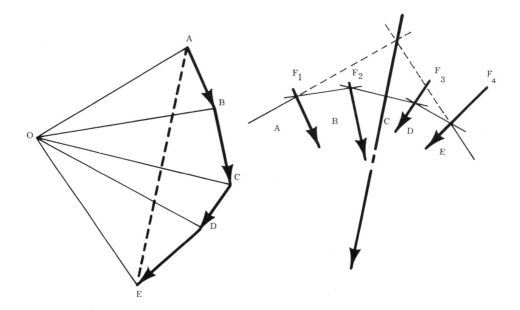

EQUILIBRANTS

If a single vector is added to an unbalanced system to produce equilibrium, that vector is known as an equilibrant. The equilibrium in an unbalanced system will always have the same location and magnitude as the resultant of that system but will have the opposite sense. The subroutine for displaying the equilibrant is as follows:

```
C  ****************************************************************
C  *                                                              *
C  *   SUBROUTINE FOR DISPLAY OF EQUILIBRANT IN A SYSTEM STRESS   *
C  *   DIAGRAM.   XLOC,YLOC= STARTING POINT, XTIP,YTIP= END POINT *
C  *                                                              *
C  ****************************************************************
         SUBROUTINE EQUALB(XLOC,YLOC,XTIP,YTIP)
         CALL AROHD(XLOC,YLOC,XTIP,YTIP,.125,0.,16)
         RETURN
         END
```

Many statics problems can be worked because an equilibrant can be added to a system or the system is already in a state of equilibrium.

Example: Let us assume that the wheel in the space diagram is to be pushed over a block:

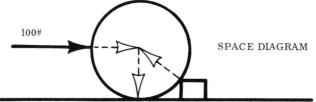

SPACE DIAGRAM

The horizontal force tending to push the wheel is applied level with the centerline of the wheel. A stress diagram of the concurrent system can be displayed on the DVST because we know the system is in equilibrium:

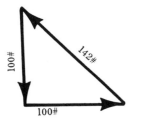

The stress diagram indicates the direction and magnitudes of the forces in the balanced system. As shown in the space diagram, the lines of action of the three forces meet in a common point (concurrency), and the stress diagram closes (equilibrium). A slight increase in horizontal force will produce motion.

The next question that might be asked is whether or not the centerline is the most ideal place to apply a pushing force if labor saving is important. Two other points of application are selected and analyzed:

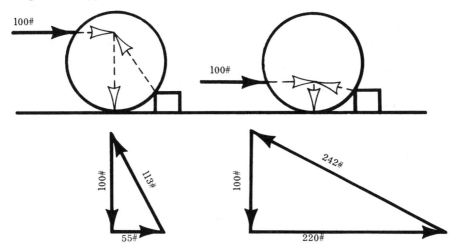

Space diagrams are programmed as subpicture problems, as described in Chapters 1 through 5. The computer program for constructing the wheel space diagram would be as follows:

```
C ***********************************************************************
C *                                                                     *
C *  DISPLAY PROGRAM FOR WHEEL SPACE DIAGRAM USED IN CHAPTER 8.         *
C *                                                                     *
C ***********************************************************************
      CALL PLOTS
      CALL CIRCL(4.5,3.25,0.,360.,1.5,1.5,0.)
      CALL RECT(3.75,2.,.25,.25,3)
      CALL AROHD(.5,3.25,1.5,3.25,.125,0.,16)
      CALL DASHP(3.0,3.25,.1)
      CALL DASHP(3.0,1.75,.1)
      CALL PLOT(3.0,3.25,3)
      CALL DASHP(4.2,2.2,.1)
      CALL AROHD(.5,3.25,3.,3.25,.125,0.,06)
      CALL AROHD(4.2,2.2,3.,3.25,.125,0.,06)
      CALL AROHD(3.0,3.25,1.5,3.25,.125,0.,06)
      CALL PLOT(12.,0.,999)
      STOP
      END
```

The equilibrium diagram, sometimes called a free-body diagram, is drawn from a more general type of program written for coplanar-type problems. It appears below:

```
C ***********************************************************************
C *                                                                     *
C *  PROGRAM FOR CONSTRUCTING FREE-BODY DIAGRAM OF COPLANAR             *
C *  PROBLEM WHERE NV= NUMBER OF VECTORS, PX= POINT OF ORIGIN           *
C *  PY= POINT OF ORIGIN IN Y DIRECTION, AND XARRAY,YARRAY ARE          *
C *  LOCATIONS IN X AND Y FOR DISPLAY VECTOR LOCATIONS.                 *
C *                                                                     *
C ***********************************************************************
      CALL PLOTS
      READ(1,*) NV,PX,PY
      DIMENSION XARRAY(NV),YARRAY(NV)
      DO 10 I=1,NV
   10 READ(1,*) XARRAY(I),YARRAY(I)
      CALL PLOT(PX,PY,3)
      DO 20 J=1,NV
   20 CALL AROHD(XARRAY(J),YARRAY(J),XARRAY(J+1),YARRAY(J+1),.12
     +5,0.,16)
      CALL PLOT(12.,0.,999)
      STOP
      END
```

Before leaving the concept of computer display for balanced systems, it is important to mention that a complete treatment of equilibrium has not been presented here. A few ideas and methods of programming displays have been given as examples of how this may be displayed in the type of terminal explained in Chapter 7. A typical list of examples of equilibrium diagrams might include

1. Forces required to resist wedging actions
2. Stresses in jib cranes
3. Stresses caused by deflected weights
4. Stresses in cable problems
5. Force acting on braces and formwork
6. Solving for reactions
7. Inverse proportion force problems
8. Simple truss stresses
9. Weights on ladders and temporary structures
10. Forces required to move objects

SPACE DIAGRAMS

The use of simple "diagrams in space" has been illustrated in the two previous sections, "Resultants" and "Equilibrants." To explain the two concepts and solve static problems, two separate diagrams were employed. One diagram, called the space diagram, will now be expanded to include nonconcurrent, noncoplanar uses. The other diagram, called a stress or vector diagram, will be covered in detail in the next section.

All computer displays have thus far been 2-dimensional (coplanar), described in X and Y locations. To display noncoplanar space diagrams, X, Y, and Z locations must be known. A subroutine for displaying noncoplanar vectors has been developed:

```
C    ****************************************************************
C    *                                                              *
C    *   SINGLE VECTOR DISPLAYED AS A NONCOPLANAR IMAGE IN FRONT     *
C    *   AND TOP VIEWS.   INPUT LOCATION OF HF LINE (XL,YL) AND 3     *
C    *   DIMENSIONAL LOCATION FOR START AND END OF VECTOR.           *
C    *                                                              *
C    ****************************************************************
      SUBROUTINE VECTOR(XL,YL,XTIP,YTIP,ZTIP,XTAIL,YTAIL,ZTAIL)
C     DISPLAY THE HF REFERENCE LINE
      CALL PLOT(XL,YL,3)
      CALL PLOT(XL+6.,YL,2)
      CALL SYMBOL(XL,YL+.1,.2,'H',0.,1)
      CALL SYMBOL(XL,YL-.3,.2,'F',0.,1)
C     DISPLAY FRONT VIEW OF VECTOR LOCATION
      CALL AROHD(XTAIL,YTAIL,XTIP,YTIP,.125,0.,16)
      ZTAIL=ZTAIL+YL
      ZTIP=ZTIP+YL
C     DISPLAY TOP VIEW OF VECTOR
      CALL ARHOD(XTAIL,ZTAIL,XTIP,ZTIP,.125,0.,16)
      RETURN
      END
```

The bulk of vector geometry problems fall into the noncoplanar category. Therefore computer assistance and graphical displays play an important role in the visualization of a statics problem. Bow's notation also comes in handy in labeling more than one view of a single system of vectors. This is illustrated in the concurrent, noncoplanar system represented here.

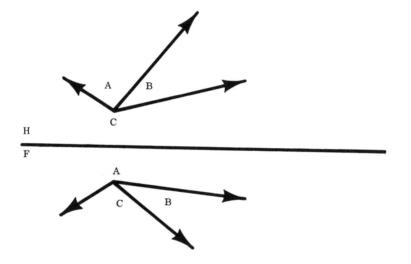

By this method, letters or numbers are placed on both sides of each line of action shown in the space diagram, and each vector is described by the two letters between which it lies.

The space diagram shown can be displayed by the following lines in a program:

```
CALL VECTOR(.5,3.,1.5,2.,1.,2.25,2.5,.5)
CALL VECTOR(.5,3.,3.5,1.5,2.,2.25,2.5,.5)
CALL VECTOR(.5,3.,3.5,4.25,2.25,1.,2.25,2.5,.5)
```

In the case of nonconcurrent vectors a similar use of CALL VECTOR can be used to display the following:

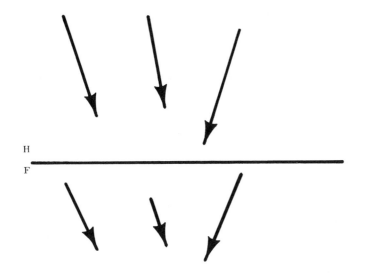

with the FORTRAN lines in a program stated as follows:

```
CALL VECTOR(.5,3.,2.,1.5,1.,1.5,2.5,2.5)
CALL VECTOR(.5,3.,3.,1.5,1.,2.75,2.25,2.5)
CALL VECTOR(.5,3.,3.6,1.,.5,4.1,2.8,2.25)
```

Conventional plotting subroutines can be used in a program to display a space diagram for a system of noncoplanar forces. The use of a space diagram in "setting" a problem is important; a series of coplanar and noncoplanar examples will illustrate this.

Example 1. The first space diagram shows a weight lodged between two inclined surfaces:

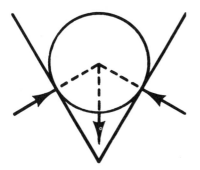

The following program was used to display the space diagram:

```
C  ******************************************************************
C  *                                                                *
C  *   PROGRAM FOR SPACE DIAGRAM OF WEDGING ACTION BETWEEN TWO       *
C  *   INCLINED SURFACES PROGRAMMED FOR CALCOMP PREVIEW ON DVST.     *
C  *                                                                *
C  ******************************************************************
        CALL PLOTS
        CALL AROHD(1.75,2.25,2.3,2.6,.125,0.,16)
        CALL AROHD(3.,2.25,3.,1.75,.125,0.,16)
        CALL AROHD(4.25,2.25,3.6,2.6,.125,0.,16)
        CALL PLOT(4.25,3.75,3)
        CALL PLOT(3.,1.5,2)
        CALL PLOT(1.75,3.75,2)
        CALL CIRCL(3.75,3.,0.,360.,.75,.75,0.)
        CALL PLOT(2.3,2.6,3)
        CALL DASHP(3.,3.,.1)
        CALL DASHP(3.,2.25,.1)
        CALL PLOT(3.,3.,3)
        CALL DASHP(3.6,2.6,.1)
        CALL PLOT(12.,0.,999)
        STOP
        END
```

Example 2. The second space diagram illustrates a jib crane supporting a load.

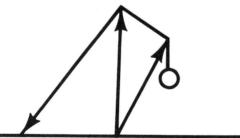

The following program will display the space diagram:

```
C  ******************************************************************
C  *                                                                *
C  *   PROGRAM TO DISPLAY STRESS IN A JIB CRANE __ DVST OUTPUT       *
C  *                                                                *
C  ******************************************************************
        CALL PLOTS
        CALL PLOT(2.75,6.,3)
        CALL PLOT(6.,6.,2)
        CALL PLOT(4.5,8.,3)
        CALL PLOT(5.25,7.5,2)
        CALL AROHD(4.5,8.,3.,6.,.15,0.,16)
        CALL AROHD(5.25,7.5,5.25,7.,.125,0.,16)
        CALL CIRCL(5.3,6.8,0.,360.,.125,.125,0.)
        CALL PLOT(0.,0.,999)
        STOP
        END
```

Example 3. The third space diagram illustrates a type of support frame commonly used in overhanging loads:

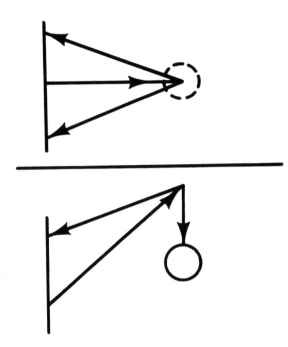

The following program will display example 3:

```
C  *****************************************************************
C  *   EXAMPLE #3, NONCOPLANAR DISPLAY FOR DIRECT DVST OUTPUT     *
C  *****************************************************************
       CALL  INITT(240)
       CALL  DISVEC(1.5,3.,4.,2.75,1.25,2.,2.,1.25)
       CALL  DISVEC(1.5,3.,2.,2.,.5,4.,2.75,1.25)
       CALL  DISVEC(1.5,3.,2.,2.,2.,4.,2.75,1.25)
       CALL  DISVEC(1.5,3.,4.,1.75,1.25,4.,2.75,1.25)
       CALL  CIRCL(4.25,1.5,0.,360.,.25,.25,0.)
       CALL  CIRCL(4.25,4.25,0.,360.,.25,.25,.5)
       CALL  FINITT(0,0)
       STOP
       END
```

For this application VECTOR could not be named the same as a system routine, so an identical subroutine named DISVEC for "display vector" was written.

VECTOR DIAGRAMS

The "vector" or stress diagram is displayed for determining certain characteristics of the system. The stress diagram represents the magnitudes and directions of the forces called for in the space diagram.

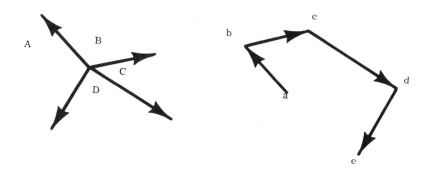

The program presented earlier for displaying systems in equilibrium can be used to present stress diagrams of a tip to tail nature if they are concurrent and coplanar. Nonconcurrent, coplanar systems may use all three:

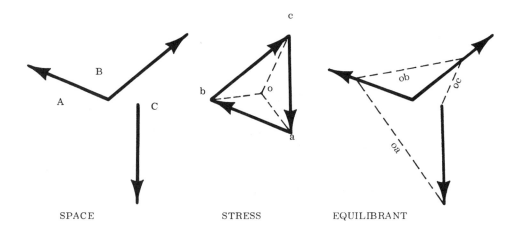

SPACE   STRESS   EQUILIBRANT

The subroutine **VECTOR** is used to display the stress diagram for noncoplanar systems of forces. The solution of a noncoplanar system of vectors to
determine the state of equilibrium is similar to coplanar methods. When concurrent vectors are present, the parallelogram method can be used:

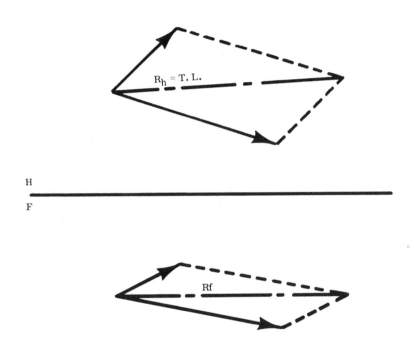

Figure 8.3 was displayed with the call VECTORS. In this example the resultant
was located in both the horizontal and frontal planes of projection. A resultant
was determined from CDG techniques and displayed at R(TL). Figure 8.4 illustrates stresses in a system of concurrent, noncoplanar members.

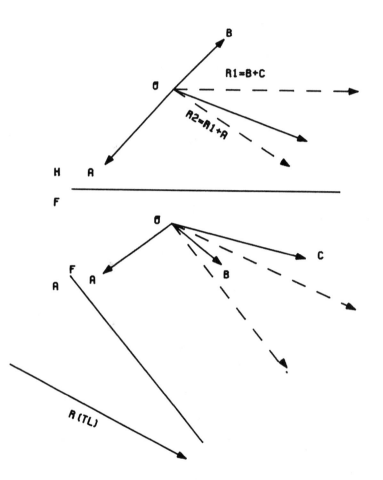

Figure 8.3 Call VECTORS plotted on an HP flat bed plotter.

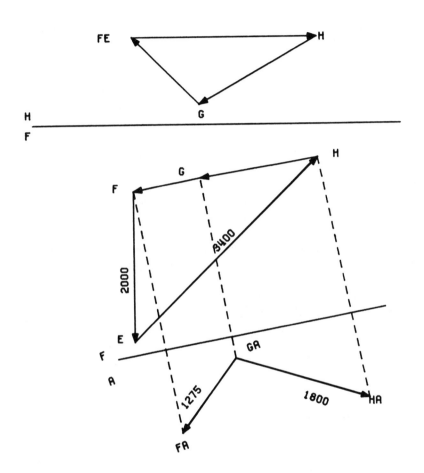

Figure 8.4 Stresses in a system of concurrent, noncoplanar members.

SIMPLE STRUCTURE ANALYSIS

Figure 8.5 illustrates the combination of space and stress diagrams to determine
the stresses in a simple structure. The loads are laid out in a straight line (load
line). This is displayed first, at a scale suitable for the CRT screen, and then the
stress diagram is displayed around it. By providing a calculation section inside
the display program, the forces in the members can be determined and printed.
The tendency for the structure to slide at R1 and R2 is shown by C'X and YC'.
This stress must be balanced by a tie member (equilibrant) across the base.

Figure 8.6 shows a ladder leaning against a wall. This stress diagram shows the
approximate pressure against the wall and the floor. Calculated values will be approximate since coefficients of friction between the different materials will be
left out. The stress has been combined with the space diagram to show the
weight of the ladder by the vector AB and the pressure against the wall by CB.
The vector CB also represents the horizontal thrust at the foot of the ladder.

Figure 8.7 shows a simple form of roof truss with supporting loads. To determine the stresses in the members, it is necessary to designate the loads and members in some convenient method. This should be done with Bow's notation. The
labels for members must be read in a clockwise direction. For example, the left
rafter member at the joint R1 is BE. If read about the joint at the top, this same
member would be EB.

When determining the size of a member required to carry a given load, it is
important to know the kind of stress (tension or compression) of the force and
the length of the required member. Stress diagrams for simple structures contain
both tension and compression vectors. A tension vector tends to cause stretch-
ing, separation, or pulling apart. It is labeled with a minus sign and is read
"pulling away" from a joint or point of application:

A compression vector causes shortening, the state of being compressed. It is
labeled with a plus sign and is read "pushing in" on a joint or point of application:

To illustrate simple structure analysis by computer display, refer to example
3. Here the display program for the space diagram was given. To show stresses
and spatial relationships involving noncoplanar members in this framework, two

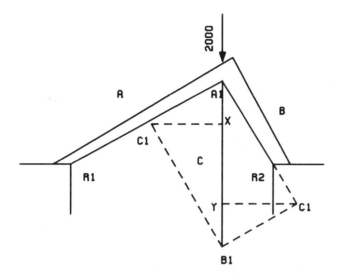

Figure 8.5 Combination of space and stress diagram for simple structure analysis.

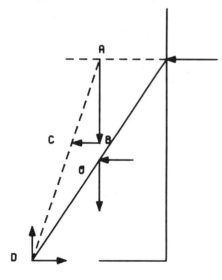

Figure 8.6 Ladder problem.

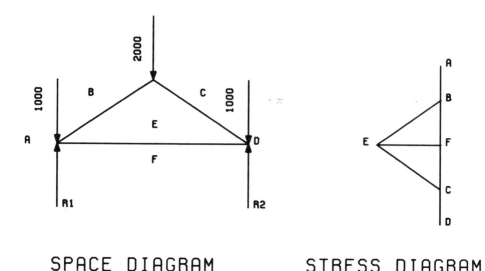

SPACE DIAGRAM   STRESS DIAGRAM

Figure 8.7 Roof truss analysis.

related views must be added. To display the members in true length, auxiliary views of some of the vectors must be displayed also. The free-body diagram, which is a portion of the space diagram from example 3, shows the sense (+ or -) of the forces in the members.

When displaying the problem for solution, start with the known load of 2000 pounds. Some convenient scale to fit the CRT may be selected for laying out the load. The load (FE) is vertical; the vector will display as a point in the top view and true length in the front view. From the top and bottom of the load line (FE) shown in example 3, lines are displayed which are, respectively, parallel to members CD, AD, and BD in the front view of the space diagram. These lines intersect at point H.

Vectors CD and AD align in the front view of the stress diagram. Their individual lengths will be found after displaying the top view of the stress diagram and displaying the necessary auxiliary views,

1. From the top view of FE (point view), display a line which is parallel to member BD in the space diagram; the length of this vector is determined by projection (CDG) from point H.
2. Line FH is known; lines are displayed from H and F, parallel to corresponding members in the top view of the space diagram.

3. The intersection of the lines displayed in step 2 cross at point G. Point G may now be placed in the front view.
4. The true lengths of the vectors FG and GH have been determined by auxiliary views, displayed on the screen, and values calculated for printout.

TRUSS DESIGN AND ANALYSIS

When computerized vector geometry is used to design a truss, computer displays are used to determine stresses in the various members of the truss. Any structure must be designed to carry its own weight in addition to the specified weights or loads. For convenience in this section, we shall assume that the weight of the truss is included with the given loading. The weights of roofing members can also be determined by the following:

Steel: $W = 1/2al (1 + 1/101)$
Wood: $W = 3/4al (1 + 1/101)$

where l = span in feet
       a = distance in feet between adjacent trusses
       W = weight in pounds of a single truss

Figure 8.8 shows a typical solution when determining stresses in the members of a truss. The truss is anchored at both ends and is subjected to dead loads concentrated at points where the truss members frame (connect) together. When analyzing stresses by CVG, the space diagram is displayed first. Bow's notation is applied, and the stress diagram is written as follows:

1. Start by displaying the load line and dividing it proportionally between the reactions at both fixed ends.
2. The load line is vertical, since the loads acts vertically. The length of the load line represents the sum of the loads when displayed to scale.
3. The loads in this example are symmetrical, the reactions R1 and R2 are equal, or 4000.
4. The first line in the stress diagram should be displayed horizontally through point G and toward the left edge of the screen so it cuts vector BH displayed through B on the load line and is parallel to truss member BH in the space diagram.
5. All vectors in the stress diagram should be labeled by a call Alpha as they are plotted (remember that the CRT is used to preview information sent to the pen plotter). The load line is labeled, load by load, before displaying the vectors representing the truss members.

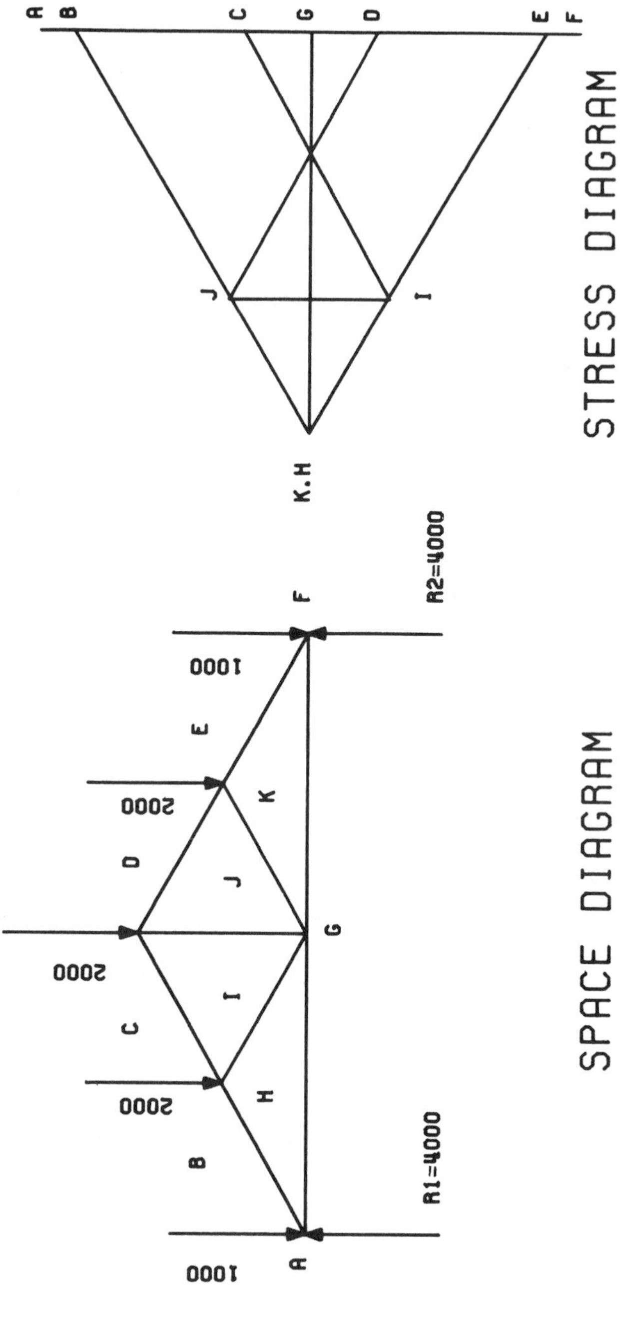

STRESS DIAGRAM

SPACE DIAGRAM

Figure 8.8   Analysis of roof truss with anchored ends and multiple dead loads.

6. Each joint in the space diagram, from left to right, must be matched by a closed polygon in the stress diagram. The completed stress diagram is a series of closed polygons (equilibrium diagrams).
7. Each vector in the stress diagram is parallel to the corresponding member in the space diagram. While each vector in the stress diagram is automatically at the same scale as used to plot the load line, individual member stresses can be calculated and displayed for our use.

EXERCISES

1. Load the CVG software into the refresh or storage tube systems. (Refer to exercise 1 of Chapter 1.) Model generation is definitely the most time-consuming part of the CVG analysis. In each of the cases used for the exercises in this chapter, the model is provided. Recall the program BEAM. You will note that a simple beam is supported at both ends. Three loads are carried by the beam. These loads are shown as "vectors." Combine these vectors tip to tail. Does the diagram close? Is the system in equilibrium?
2. The system displayed in exercise 1 was a coplanar problem. Using this same model, we can solve for the reactions at the right and left ends of the beam. Recall program SWING. Here a child's swing set is displayed with the loads displayed for you. Solve for the reactions right and left.
3. Recall WEIGHT. This program displays a space diagram of a weight wedged between two inclined surfaces. Prepare a vector diagram (in equilibrium) at the construction scale 1 inch = 100 pounds. Solve for the amount of force necessary to release the weight.
4. Recall JIB. This program displays a space diagram of a jib crane supporting a load of 2 kips. Solve for the amount of force in each of the crane members.
5. Recall FRAME. This program illustrates a type of support frame commonly used in overhanging loads. Solve for the amount of force in each member.

9

Computer-Generated Charts and Graphs

The use of the computer to systematically produce charts or graphs during the design process has been well documented by a number of computer graphics hardware companies. The most common form of documentation has been a collection of programed groups together under an operating system (Tektronix Advanced Graphic Package, for example). Either charts or graphs can be produced.

Webster's Dictionary defines a chart as a sheet showing facts graphically or in tabular form or as a graph showing changes in temperature, variation in population, or prices. A graph is defined as a diagram representing the relationship between two or more factors by means of a series of connected points or by bars, curves, or lines.

It is obvious that the editors of the dictionary regard the two terms as synonymous. Most recent engineering graphics texts do not distinguish between the two. The author, however, thinks a distinguishing difference should be made for computer applications and will define the two as follows:

Chart: A more or less pictorial computer graphics presentation of facts. It should be pointed out that facts presented by charts are easy to read and are quite meaningful to the lay person. Therefore, charts are seen in newspapers, magazines, and the like.

Graph: A presentation of data plotted in one of the many formats where each point is connected with the following adjacent point by a line. There may be more than one set of data per sheet. Graphs are used by engineers to illustrate trends, to predict, to develop an equation for a certain behavior, to present results of test data obtained in experiments, and to correlate the observations of natural phenomena.

ANALYSIS OF DESIGN DATA

Before a proposed design is accepted, it must be subjected to a careful analysis. During this process the computer data provided must be evaluated and interpreted by the engineer. Most frequently, data are submitted in numerical form, and interpretation is often a lengthy and difficult procedure. Thus, to ensure that the engineer and each member of the design team understands all aspects of the project, it is convenient to convert numerical computer data to a more customary form which will permit ready understanding.

Before selecting the type of chart or graph to illustrate the design data, consideration must be given to its use. If it is to be used to determine numerical values or reading numbers, it would be a quantitative chart or graph. If it is used to present comparative relationships, it is called qualitative. Since there are many types of programs available to present data, the purpose must be established before the graph or chart is created.

Creating a Basic Graph

To create a graph it is necessary to prepare the data which are to be plotted. Two data lists will be necessary: one for the horizontal (X) values and one for the vertical (Y) values. The lists will include in the first position the number of data values to be plotted. The rest of the positions in the list contain the data values. Each list will be called an array.

```
DIMENSION XDATA(7), YDATA(7)
DATA XDATA/6., 1., 2., 3., 4., 5., 6./
DATA YDATA/6., 211., 114., 306., 453., 291., 325./
```

The first line is a standard FORTRAN dimension statement assigning the names XDATA and YDATA to the two arrays and setting the length of each to 7. The second line contains the number of data points (6) followed by the actual data values for the X axis. The third line sets Y. Once the data are in a usable form, five call statements will produce the graph:

```
CALL INITT(30)
CALL BINITT
CALL CHECK(XDATA, YDATA)
CALL DSPLAY (XDATA, YDATA)
CALL FINITT(0, 700)
```

The call to INITT initializes the Tektronix terminal. The parameter 30 indicates that transmission is at thirty characters per second. BINITT begins the AG-II (Advanced Graphing Package). CHECK has two arguments, the names of the

```
DIMENSION XDATA(7),YDATA(7),YDATA1(7)
DATA XDATA/6.,1.,2.,3.,4.,5.,6./
DATA YDATA/6.,211.,114.,306.,354.,291.,325./
DATA YDATA1/6.,367.,300.,179.,238.,320.,210./
CALL INITT(240)
CALL BINITT
CALL CHECK(XDATA,YDATA)
CALL DSPLAY(XDATA,YDATA)
CALL CPLOT(XDATA,YDATA1)
CALL FINITT(0,700)
STOP
END
```

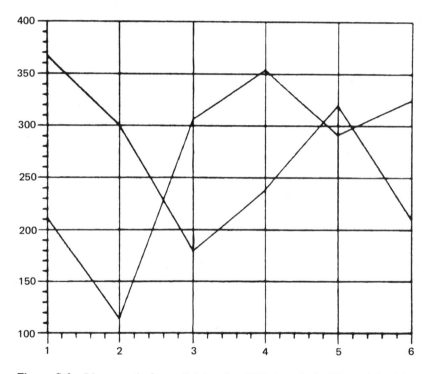

Figure 9.1 Line graph from Tektronix 4010 terminal. (Copyright 1985 Tektronix, Inc., used with permission.)

data arrays to be plotted. DSPLAY plots the graph on the face of the CRT. FINITT terminates use of the AG-II package.

It is often desirable to plot two sets of data on the same plot. With regard to adding a second data curve to the plot we just created, refer to Figure 9.1. Since the second curve will be plotted on the same graph as the first, the widest range of data should be plotted first. The same horizontal values will be used, so only one array for another curve (YDATA 2) has been added to the program. An additional call statement has been added immediately after the call to DSPLAY. It will plot the second curve:

CALL CPLOT(XDATA, YDATA2)

many options are available for reproducing the graph. Figure 9.1 is a call to HCOPY or a "thermo"-type copy of the CRT screen. This type of reproduction is quick, but its appearance is not suitable for a technical report or business report. A call for plotter output will improve the quality of the reproduction. Figure 9.2 is an example of a Tektronix pen plotter graph. In this example the data points have been labeled by

CALL SYMBL(N)

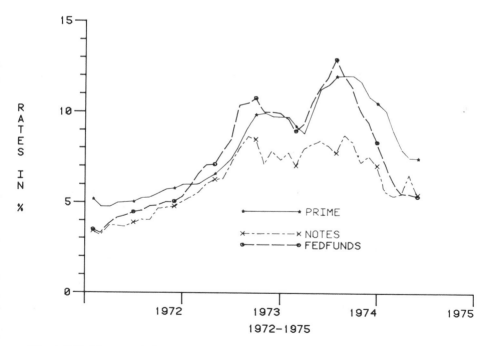

Figure 9.2 Line graph from Tektronix pen plotter. (Copyright 1985 Tektronix, Inc., used with permission.)

where N equals an integer 0 to 11. Figure 9.3 introduces the use of the twelve symbols for labeling data points.

Examples of Design Data Analysis

The eight examples in Figures 9.4 through 9.11 have been selected to illustrate some of the display techniques that can be used for computer-generated charts and graphs.

```
DIMENSION XARRAY(4),YARRAY(7)
DATA XARRAY/-1.,6.,22.,2.4/
DATA YARRAY/6.,211.,114.,306.,354.,291.,325./
CALL INITT(240)
CALL BINITT
CALL SYMBL(6)
CALL CHECK(XARRAY,YARRAY)
CALL DSPLAY(XARRAY,YARRAY)
CALL TINPUT(I)
CALL FINITT(0,700)
STOP
END
```

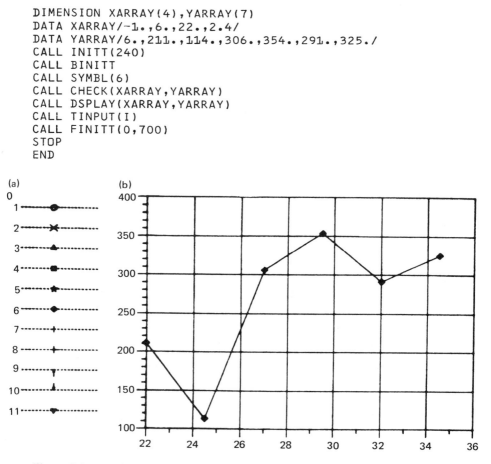

Figure 9.3 (a) Symbols available for point plotting. (b) Line graph using point plotting. (Copyright 1985 Tektronix, Inc., used with permission.)

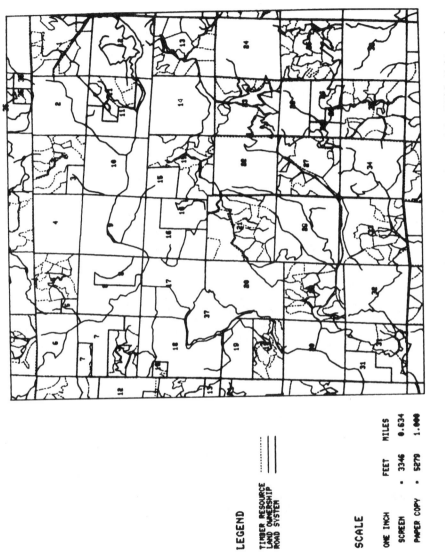

LEGEND

TIMBER RESOURCE ....
LAND OWNERSHIP   =======
ROAD SYSTEM

SCALE

ONE INCH	FEET	MILES
SCREEN	3346	0.634
PAPER COPY	5279	1.000

Figure 9.4 Textronix hard copy of chart displaying timber resources. (Copyright 1985 Tektronix, Inc., used with permission.)

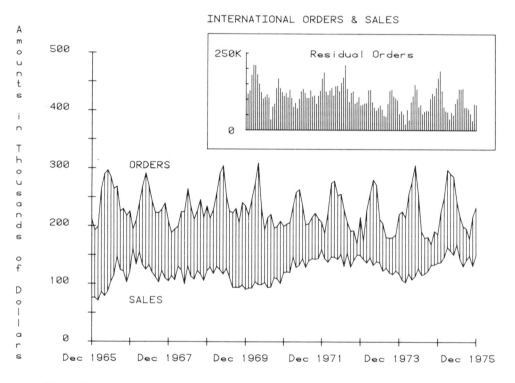

Figure 9.5 Displays of two sets of data using routine for shading. (Copyright 1985 Tektronix, Inc., used with permission.)

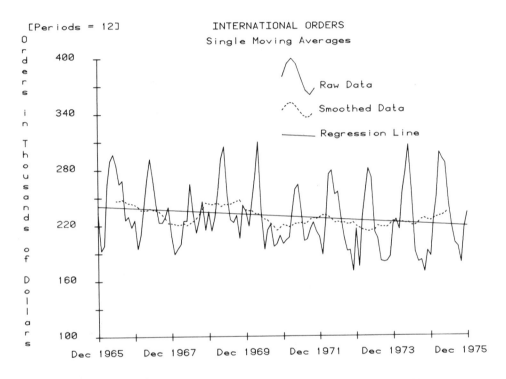

Figure 9.6 Displays of three sets of data using routine to form stepped lines. (Copyright 1985 Tektronix, Inc., used with permission.)

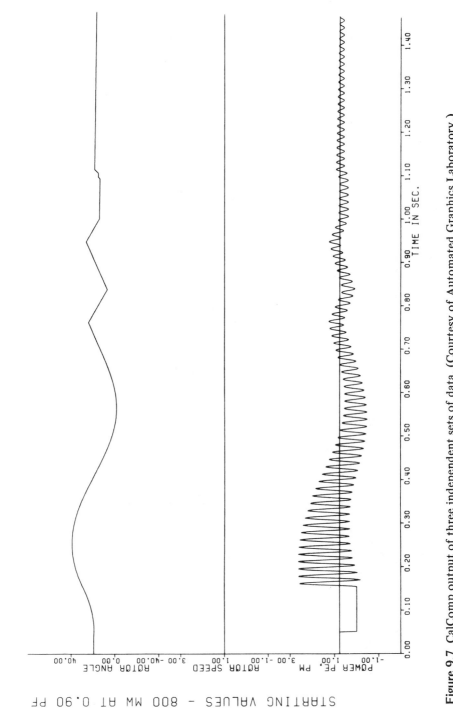

Figure 9.7 CalComp output of three independent sets of data. (Courtesy of Automated Graphics Laboratory.)

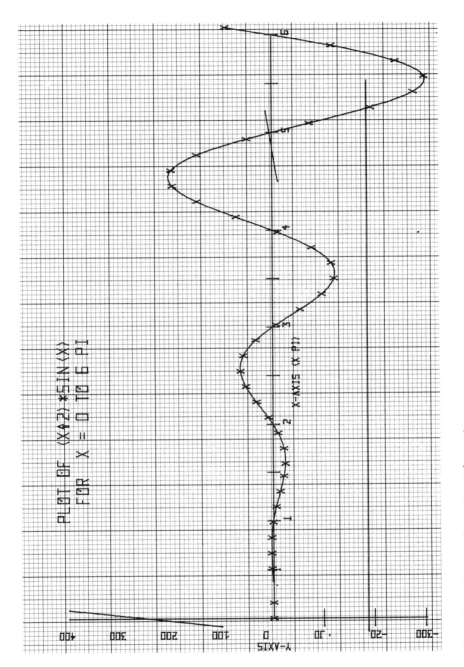

Figure 9.8 Display of equation information.

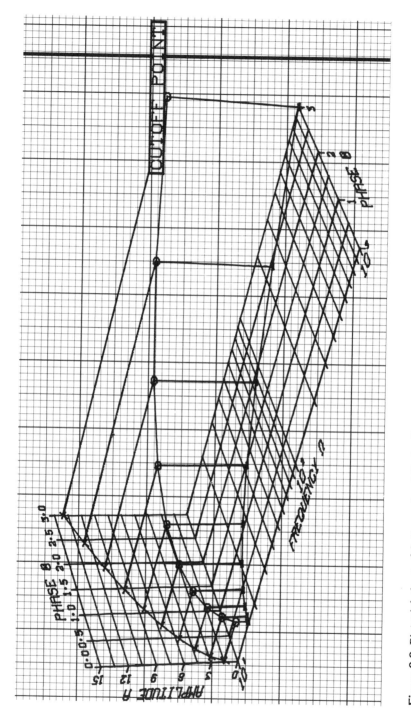

Figure 9.9 Pictorial chart of 3-dimensional Bode diagram.

344

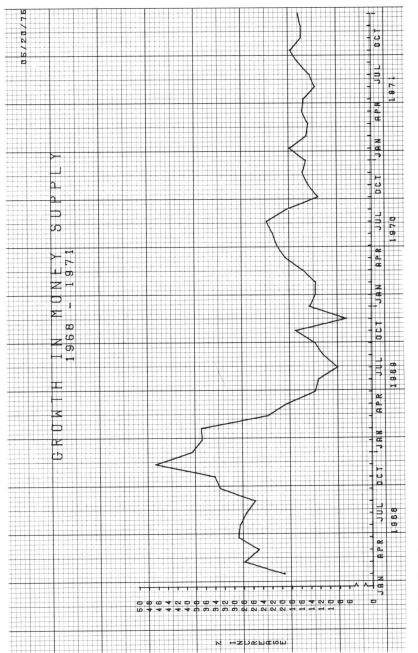

Figure 9.10 Use of multiline in a graph.

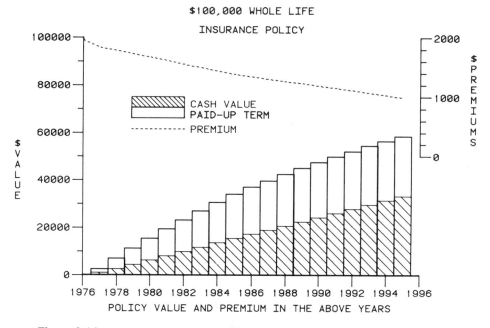

Figure 9.11 Bar chart and use of shading. (Copyright 1985 Tektronix, Inc., used with permission.)

LINEAR GRAPHS

The majority of engineering graphs are plotted in rectangular coordinate format. This format is generally grided to form 1/20-inch squares (Figures 9.8 and 9.10). Others are plotted in centimeters or in 1/10-, 1/8-, or 1/4-inch squares. The larger squares make the graph easier to read. Variables selected for the abscissa (X) and ordinate (Y) are chosen showing the independent variables as X and the dependent variables as Y. It is important to choose the correct scaling since this has an effect on the slope of the curve. The slope of the curve provides a visual impression of the degree of change in the dependent variable for a given increment of the independent variable. Always try to create the correct impression when programming graphs for computer output.

The ranges of scales should ensure effective and efficient use of the area available. If a chart is quantitative, the intersection of the axis need not be at the origin (zero) of the coordinates. However, if the chart is qualitative, both the ordinate and the abscissa generally should have the value of zero at the intersection. The arithmetic scale numbers should be 1, 2, 3, . . . ; 2, 4, 6, . . . ; or 5, 10,

15 . . . . Of course these units may be multiples of 0.1, 0.01, and 10, 100, and 1000. The use of too many digits in the scale numbers should be avoided. The scale caption can be designated as "100s," "millions," or "10^5."

The plotted points on the graph should be identified. If more than one curve is plotted on a sheet, then a different SYMBL may be used; refer to Figure 9.3. After all points have been plotted the curve must be displayed by CALL DSPLAY. If the data are continuous, the curve will be smooth, and if discontinuous, each adjacent points should be connected with a straight line. When displaying the curve for continuous data the curve should be an average of the plotted points. This is done by a short linear form:

DATA YARRAY/-1., 6., 1., 2./

The first element is -1, indicating the method of expansion (linear). The second element is the number of data points to be plotted, while the third is the first value to be displayed. The last element is the amount by which the value is to be incremented for each data point. Therefore the DATA STATEMENT would cause the values 1, 3, 5, 7, 9, and 11 to be selected.

After the curve has been determined it should then be displayed according to line type. This may be done by

CALL LINE(IVALUE)

where IVALUE = 0 unless changed by a call to LINE. The following IVALUES may be used:

0	SOLID	———————————————
1	LONG DASH	— — — — — — — — — —
2	SHORT DASH	-------------------
3	DASH DOT	-. -. -. -. -. -. -. -. -.
4	DOT	. . . .
−1	NO LINE	
−2	VERTICAL BAR	
−3	HORIZONTAL BAR	
−4	POINT PLOT	

Multiple curves on a linear graph make excellent use of different line types. A simple method of displaying a second curve was shown in Figure 9.1. Here the second curve fit nicely on the scales selected. However, if the second curve has data values which extend outside the first data limits, the curve will be clipped at the edge of the screen. See Figure 9.12. To prevent this from occurring, the user may make all the calls to display the first curve followed by calls to DINITX or

```
DIMENSION XDATA(4),YDATA(7),YDATA1(7)
DATA XDATA/-1.,6.,1.,1./
DATA YDATA/6.,211.,114.,306.,354.,291.,325./
DATA YDATA1/6.,367.,458.,168.,238.,620.,210./
CALL INITT(240)
CALL BINITT
CALL CHECK(XDATA,YDATA)
CALL DSPLAY(XDATA,YDATA)
CALL LINE (34)
CALL CPLOT(XDATA,YDATA1)
CALL TINPUT(K)
CALL FINITT(0,700)
STOP
END
```

NOTE: The call to TINPUT is used as a pause throughout this
       so the user can study the graph or make a hard copy.

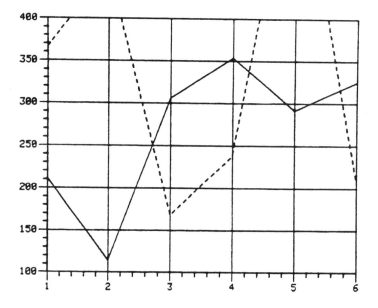

Figure 9.12 Example of clipping. (Copyright 1985 Tektronix, Inc., used with permission.)

```
DIMENSION XARRAY(7),YARRAY(7),ZARRAY(7)
DATA XARRAY/6.,22.,24.5,27.,29.5,32.,34.5/
DATA YARRAY/6.,211.,114.,396.,354.291.,325./
DATA ZARRAY/6.,366.,458.,198.,235.,620.,478./
CALL INITT(240)
CALL BINITT
CALL SLIMX(200,800)
CALL CHECK(XARRAY,YARRAY)
CALL DSPLAY(XARRAY,YARRAY)
CALL DINITY
CALL YLOC(-100)
CALL LINE(34)
CALL YFRM(4)
CALL XLAB(0)
CALL XFRM(0)
CALL CHECK(XARRAY,ZARRAY)
CALL DSPLAY(XARRAY,ZARRAY)
CALL TINPUT(IVY)
CALL FINITT(0,700)
STOP
END
```

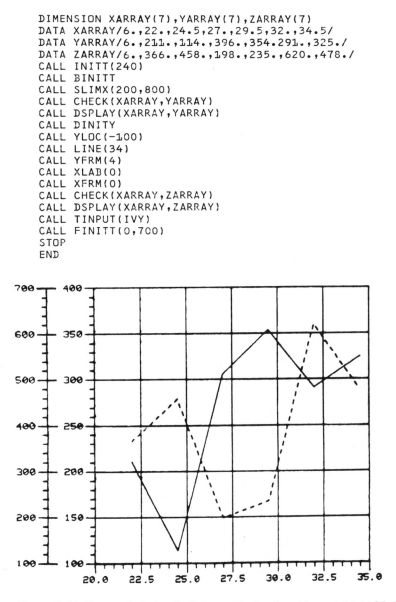

Figure 9.13 Proper "windowing" to avoid clipping. (Copyright 1985 Tektronix, Inc., used with permission.)

DINITY. An axis location change is necessary to prevent the new label values from being printed over the old ones; these techniques will be discussed in the remaining sections of this chapter. For now we are concerned with

CALL DINITX
CALL DINITY

These subroutines reinitialize the label values of the X and Y axis, allowing the drawing of an additional curve with new label values. All values related to labeling the axes are set to zero so that new values can be computed for the display of an additional curve. Figure 9.13 shows the same sets of data plotted with a CALL DINITY to avoid the clip at the top of the screen.

By studying Figure 9.13, you will note that CALL SILIMX(200, 800) has been used. This is a screen window location. If no reference is made to window size, then the window is the size of the screen. On a Tektronix terminal there are 1024 visible addressable units along the X axis and 781 on the Y axis with 128

Figure 9.14 Tektronix 4006 terminal with graphic displays. (Copyright 1985 Tektronix, Inc., used with permission.)

units to the inch. These unit designations are used to show screen location. A full screen plotting surface can be described as 0 to 1023 in X and 0 to 780 in Y. The limits of the plotting area may be set directly in screen units by calling either SILIMX or SILIMY in the form

CALL SILIMX(NX, NY)

where NX is the X-axis screen minimum in tek units and NY is the X-axis maximum. This would limit the width of the plotting window. SILIMY would be called to set the height of the plotting window.

In most cases the "window techniques" described above can be useful in the arrangement of linear graphs. In some cases the range of the data is so large that the plotting window becomes extremely small. Figure 9.14 is a photograph of three graphs displayed on a Tektronix screen; here setting and resetting windows has allowed the graphs to be displayed as one. In the case of the lower right-hand bar chart, the information has been compressed into a window size unsuitable for presentation. For proper display the same information is given in Figure 9.11.

To avoid overcrowding a graph, data setting limits may be used:

CALL MNMX(ARRAY, AMIN, AMAX)

Where ARRAY is the data array for which the minimum and maximum are to be found, AMIN is the minimum array value and AMAX is the maximum array value. MNMX is used internally to determine data limits and may be useful to the user in setting the minimum and maximum values for multiple overlapping curves.

LABELING THE AXES

Axes may be labeled by establishing an array of the ASCII equivalents of the characters to be displayed (see Table 9.1). The user then moves to the starting poing and calls either HLABEL (horizontal label routine) or VLABEL to display the axis label. The instruction

CALL HLABEL(5, ISTRIN)

would display the five characters of TITLE contained in the string ISTRIN horizontally. VLABEL is used the same way for 90-degree orientation or vertical

352   Computer-Generated Charts and Graphs

CONTROL				HIGH X & Y GRAPHIC INPUT				LOW X				LOW Y			
NUL	0	DLE	16	SP	32	ø	48	@	64	P	80	`	96	p	112
SOH	1	DC1	17	!	33	1	49	A	65	Q	81	a	97	q	113
STX	2	DC2	18	"	34	2	50	B	66	R	82	b	98	r	114
ETX	3	DC3	19	#	35	3	51	C	67	S	83	c	99	s	115
EOT	4	DC4	20	$	36	4	52	D	68	T	84	d	100	t	116
ENQ	5	NAK	21	%	37	5	53	E	69	U	85	e	101	u	117
ACK	6	SYN	22	&	38	6	54	F	70	V	86	f	102	v	118
BEL (BELL)	7	ETB	23	'	39	7	55	G	71	W	87	g	103	w	119
BS (BACK SPACE)	8	CAN	24	(	40	8	56	H	72	X	88	h	104	x	120
HT	9	EM	25	)	41	9	57	I	73	Y	89	i	105	y	121
LF (LINE FEED)	10	SUB	26	*	42	:	58	J	74	Z	90	j	106	z	122
VT	11	ESC	27	+	43	;	59	K	75	[	91	k	107	{	123
FF	12	FS	28	,	44	<	60	L	76	\	92	l	108	|	124
CR (RETURN)	13	GS	29	-	45	=	61	M	77	]	93	m	109	}	125
SO	14	RS	30	.	46	>	62	N	78	^	94	n	110	~	126
SI	15	US	31	/	47	?	63	O	79	_	95	o	111	RUBOUT (DEL)	127

Table 9.1 ASCII Equivalents

labels. Figure 9.15 is a display of this. A more direct test of the HLABEL routine might be the alphabet displayed.

```
DIMENSION ISTRG(26)
DATA ISTRG/65, 66, 67, 68, 69, 70, 71, 72, 73, 74, 75, 76, 77, 78, 79, 80,
+81, 82, 83, 84, 85, 86, 87, 88, 89, 90/
CALL INITT(30)
CALL BINITT
CALL HLABEL(26, ISTRG)
CALL FINITT(0, 700)
STOP
END
```

A BCDE F GHIJK LMNO PQRS TUVWXY Z

A direct test for the VLABEL routine using digit plotting is as follows:

```
DIMENSION KSTRG(22)
DATA KSTRG/48, 32, 49, 32, 50, 32, 51, 32, 52, 32, 53, 32, 54, 32, 55, 32,
+56, 32, 57, 32, 58, 32/
CALL INITT(30)
CALL BINITT
CALL VLABEL(22, KSTRG)
CALL FINITT(0, 700)
STOP
END
```

```
0
1
2
3
4
5
6
7
8
9
```

Alphanumeric labels can be displayed with calls to HLABEL and VLABEL. For special character generation inside graph labels, CALL NOTATE should be used as

CALL NOTATE(LX, IY, LENCHR, ISTRIN)

```
DIMENSION XDATA(4),YDATA(7), ISTRIN(5)
DATA XDATA/-1.,6.,1.,1./
DATA YDATA/6.,211.,114.,306.,354.,291.,325./
DATA ISTRIN/84,73,84,76,69/
CALL INITT(240)
CALL BINITT
CALL CHECK(XDATA,YDATA)
CALL DSPLAY(XDATA,YDATA)
CALL MOVABS(500,730)
CALL HLABEL(5,ISTRIN)
CALL TINPUT(K)
CALL FINITT(0,700)
STOP
END
```

Figure 9.15 Labels and titles. (Copyright 1985 Tektronix, Inc., used with permission.)

where IX, IY replaces CALL MOVABS. It designates the beginning point of the label in screen coordinates. LENCH is the length of the character string for the given label, while ISTRIN is the string or characters in integers from 0 to 127.

Axis labels may also be justified right, left, or center by the use of

CALL JUSTER(LENGTH, ISTRING, KEY, IFILL)

LENGTH is the total length of the character string, including fill characters (spaces). ISTRING is the array of characters in ASCII equivalents. KEY is an integer that designates if the string is to be right-, left-, or center-justified:

+: right-justified
-: left-justified
0: centered

IFILL is the character in ASCII code used as filler (usually 32). JUSTER provides the information necessary for a call to NOTATE, which displays the label.

PLOTTING THE DATA

To plot the data and complete the graph, the location of the axes must be known. This is done by calling XLOC and YLOC; these subroutines specify the location of the axes with tick marks and labels. The values placed in these subroutines are in tek-point units, with a positive value indicating the distance above the X-axis screen minimum or to the right of the Y-axis screen minimum and a negative value indicating the distance in the opposite direction. The instruction

CALL XLOC(50)

will change the location of the X axis by fifty tek-point units to the right of its present location.

Subroutines to establish the original location of the axes in relation to the right and upper edges of the screen window are

CALL XLOCTP(IVALUE)
CALL YLOCTP(IVALUE)

Figure 9.16 demonstrates the use of XLOCTP.

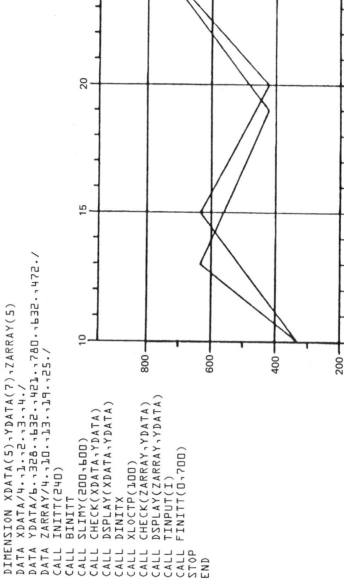

```
DIMENSION XDATA(5),YDATA(7),ZARRAY(5)
DATA XDATA/4.,1.,2.,3.,4./
DATA YDATA/6.,328.,421.,780.,632.,472./
DATA ZARRAY/4.,10.,13.,19.,25./
CALL INITT(240)
CALL BINITT
CALL SLIMY(200,600)
CALL CHECK(XDATA,YDATA)
CALL DSPLAY(XDATA,YDATA)
CALL DINITX
CALL XLOCTP(100)
CALL CHECK(ZARRAY,YDATA)
CALL DSPLAY(ZARRAY,YDATA)
CALL TINPUT(I)
CALL FINITT(0,700)
STOP
END
```

Figure 9.16 Axis location variation. (Copyright 1985 Tektronix, Inc., used with permission.)

Graphical data are plotted in reference to the graduations of the axes. These graduations are called tick marks. X and Y axes may be graduated differently by the use of

CALL XLAB(IVALUE)
CALL YLAB(IVALUE)

where IVALUE is an arbitrary integer value which refers to a label type shown in the accompanying table.

Integer	Type
0	None
1	Default value
2	Logarithmic
3	Days
4	Weeks
5	Periods
6	Months
7	Quarters
8	Years
Any negative	User written

Figure 9.17 illustrates two of the types shown in the table. Tick marks may be changed in the following ways:

1. Tick mark density: XDEN, YDEN
2. Tick mark intervals: XTICS, YTICS
3. Tick mark length: XLEN, YLEN
4. Tick mark form: XFRM, YFRM
5. Tick mark intevals and form: XMTCS, YMTCS

After the axes have been graduated the graph can be placed anywhere on the terminal screen. This done by

CALL PLACE(LIT)

where LIT is a literal string of three characters specifying the window location desired: STD, UPH, LOH, UL4, LL4, LR4, UL6, UC6, UR6, LL6, LC6, and LR6. Screen locations for each of these are given in Table 9.2. Now the graph

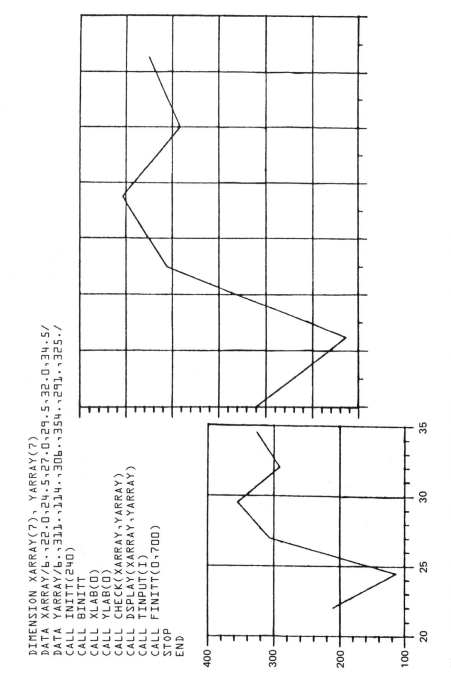

```
DIMENSION XARRAY(7), YARRAY(7)
DATA XARRAY/b.,22.0,24.5,27.0,29.5,32.0,34.5/
DATA YARRAY/b.,311.,114.,306.,354.,291.,325./
CALL INITT(240)
CALL BINITT
CALL XLAB(0)
CALL YLAB(0)
CALL CHECK(XARRAY,YARRAY)
CALL DSPLAY(XARRAY,YARRAY)
CALL TINPUT(I)
CALL FINITT(0,700)
STOP
END
```

Figure 9.17 Changing axes. (Copyright 1985 Tektronix, Inc., used with permission.)

Table 9.2 Screen Locations

Location	Value	Screen coordinates			
		XMIN	XMAX	YMIN	YMAX
STD (standard)	1	150	900	150	700
UPH (upper half)	2	150	850	525	700
LOH (lower half)	3	150	850	150	325
UL4 (upper left quarter)	4	150	450	525	700
UR4 (upper right quarter)	5	650	950	525	700
LL4 (lower left quarter)	6	150	450	150	325
LR4 (lower right quarter)	7	650	950	150	325
UL6 (upper left sixth)	8	150	150	525	700
UC6 (upper center sixth)	9	475	475	525	700
UR6 (upper right sixth)	10	800	975	525	700
LL6 (lower left sixth)	11	150	325	150	325
LC6 (lower center sixth)	12	475	650	150	325
LR6 (lower right sixth)	13	800	975	150	325

plotting is done. A review of all the subroutines necessary to plot the graph, in outline form might look as follows for Tektronix AG-II subroutines,

1. Data plotting routines:
   A. LINE: type of line uses in plots
   B. SYMBL: symbols used for point plotting
   C. STEPS: increment between symbols
   D. INFIN: infinity
   E. NUMBER: actual number of points in graph
   F. SIZES: symbol size changes
   G. SIZEL: line thickness

2. Axis plotting routines:
   A. NEAT: tick marks
   B. ZERO: zero suppression flag
   C. Y-LOC: location of axis
   D. X-YLAB: type of labels
   E. X-YDEN: density of tick marks

F. Y-YTICS: number of tick marks
G. X-YLEN: length of tick marks
H. X-YFRM: form of tick marks
I. XDMIN: data minimum
J. XDMAX: data maximum
K. PLACE: location of graph

LOGARITHMIC GRAPHS

Logarithmic plots may be created by entering data in the manner described in
the earlier sections of this chapter and specifying YTYPE or XTYPE of 2.
XTYPE and YTYPE are described as

        CALL XTYPE(IVALUE)
        CALL YTYPE(IVALUE)

where IVALUE is 2 of a logarithmic graph is desired. Figure 9.18 shows the output needed to create a comparison of a logarithmic and linear graph. Figure 9.19
indicates log output on the Y axis only.

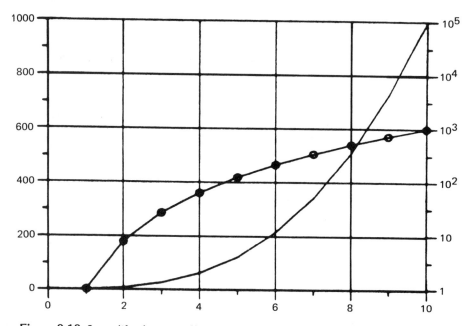

Figure 9.18 Logarithmic versus linear graph. (Copyright 1985 Tektronix Inc.,
used with permission.)

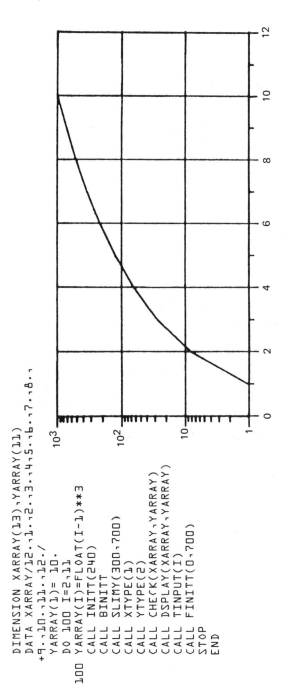

Figure 9.19 Logarithmic plot. (Copyright 1985 Tektronix, Inc., used with permission.)

Several routines have been developed for use with log graphs or semilog outputs:

1. Least significant digit: XLSIG, YLSIG
2. Transformation types: XTYPE, YTYPE
3. Tick mark labeling: XWIDTH, YWIDTH
4. Remote exponent values: XEPON, YEPON
5. Label frequency: XSTEP, YSTEP
6. Staggered labels: XSTAG, YSTAG
7. Remote exponent type: XETYP, YETYP

BAR GRAPHS

Bar graphs may be specified by using one of two routines: Tektronix HBARST
and VBARST or CalComp "Compbar" routines.

The Tektronix subroutines

CALL HBARST(ISHADE, IWBAR, IDBAR)
CALL VBARST(ISHADE, IWBAR, IDBAR)

are used. ISHADE is the integer value of the type of shading to fill in the bar.
Figure 9.20 illustrates the type of cross-hatching available. IWBAR is the width
of the bar in tek-point units. The width of the bar must be greater than 1, while
0 will result in a default value of forty tek-point units. IDBAR is the distance between the shading lines in tek points. Figure 9.11 is an example of this type of
output. Figure 9.21 is a display using the VBARST routine.

EXERCISES

1. Using Figure 9.1 as a guide, input the existing program and add a third line to
   the graph with YDATA3/6., 300., 250., 225., 300., 250., 200./.
2. Modify Figure 9.2 so that a line connects the scatter plot. Change the symbol
   from 6 to 3.
3. Correct the dashed line in Fig. 9.12 to data points 350., 395., 250., 225.,
   400., and 200. Check by displaying on the CRT.
4. Using Figure 9.15 as a guide, label the graph in exercise 3 "total number of
   units by two-month periods." Direct the output to the plotter.
5. Remove the linear portion of Figure 9.18 and display as a logarithmic graph.
   Make a hard copy of this graph.
6. Change the bar chart shown in Fig. 9.21 from VBARST 8 to 12.
7. Locate a chart or graph from a local newspaper. Write a program for displaying this graph on the CRT. Direct a copy to the hard copy unit.

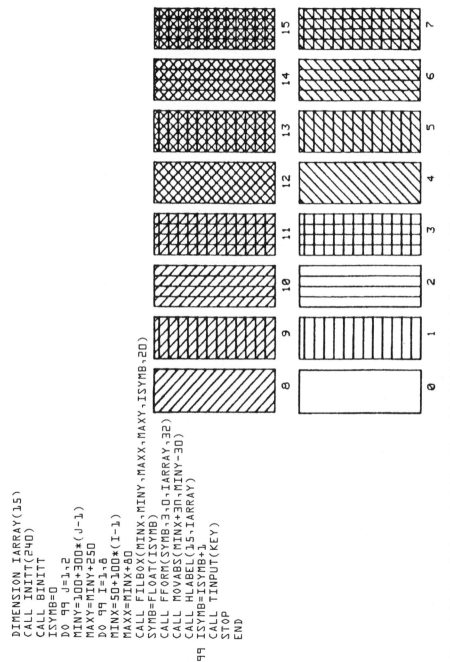

```
DIMENSION IARRAY(15)
CALL INITT(240)
CALL BINITT
ISYMB=0
DO 99  J=1,2
MINY=100+300*(J-1)
MAXY=MINY+250
DO 99  I=1,8
MINX=50+100*(I-1)
MAXX=MINX+80
CALL FILBOX(MINX,MINY,MAXX,MAXY,ISYMB,20)
SYMB=FLOAT(ISYMB)
CALL FFORM(SYMB,3,0,IARRAY,32)
CALL MOVABS(MINX+30,MINY-30)
CALL HLABEL(15,IARRAY)
99 ISYMB=ISYMB+1
CALL TINPUT(KEY)
STOP
END
```

Figure 9.20 Bar chart cross-hatching. (Copyright 1985, Tektronix, Inc., used with permission.)

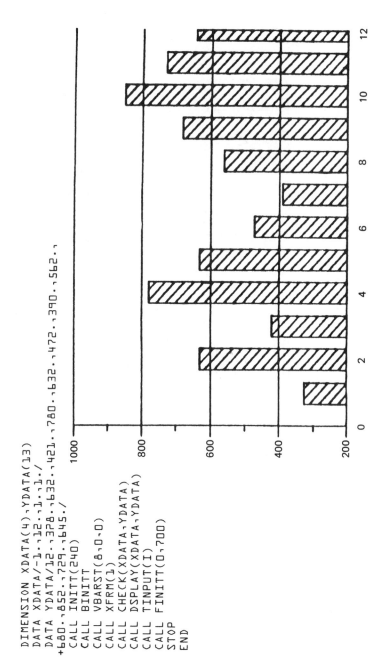

```
DIMENSION XDATA(4),YDATA(13)
DATA XDATA/-1.,12.,1.,1./
DATA YDATA/12.,328.,632.,421.,780.,632.,472.,390.,562.,
+680.,852.,729.,645./
CALL INITT(240)
CALL BINITT
CALL VBARST(8,0,0)
CALL XFRM(1)
CALL CHECK(XDATA,YDATA)
CALL DSPLAY(XDATA,YDATA)
CALL TINPUT(I)
CALL FINITT(0,700)
STOP
END
```

Figure 9.21 Bar chart example. (Copyright 1985. Tektronix, Inc., used with permission.)

10

Sample Programs and User Problems

Computer-aided graphics and design have been categorized in the first nine chapters of this text as human-machine communication. What goes on inside the computer between a human's input and the machine's output is called processing. This takes place according to the programs placed in the computer's processing unit. The devices with which the computer receives graphic input and creates graphic output have been presented in detail. In summary, the earlier chapters considered how a human handles pictorial information so that a computer can process the drawing, sketch, or photograph in a variety of ways. In previous chapters we also studied the hardware elements of computer graphics systems in relation to the user's requirements. After selecting the hardware, the software elements of these systems in relation to the applications in which they were used were presented. Within these descriptions other ideas were introduced which were not immediately involved with the hardware or software; these were graphical structures and data structures.

Some confusion may arise from the treatment of graphical and data structures. An explanatory note is appropriate. Although these two structures are related in a computer-aided graphics system, they are logically distinct. A graphical structure for problem solving had been used throughout the nineteenth century and the first half of this century. During the latter half of this century, engineers moved to a data structure for problem solving, keeping parts of the graphical structure for the presentation of engineering drawings. Unfortunately this situation can cause confusion in a computer-aided graphics and design problem-solving method because the same entity is often used for both. Throughout this text graphical structures were presented separately from data structures to try and avoid confusion.

Week 1   Introduction and orientation to the course, JCL and terminology. As-
          signment: Read Chapter 1. Write a subroutine for a title block that
          will be used for all assignments.

Week 2   Straight lines, angles, circles and arcs, geometric constructions. As-
          signment: Read Chapter 2. Select one of the problems on the handout
          sheet, write a FORTRAN program for plotting, submit it to the
          computer center.

Week 3   Selecting views, standard template parts, sheet arrangement. Assign-
          ment: Finish Chapter 2, work case study 3.

Week 4   Computerizing the drafting process. Assignment: Read Chapter 3,
          select one of the engineering drawings from the handout sheet, work
          case study 4.

Week 5   Drafting systems and programming. Assignment: Read Chapter 4,
          develop a subroutine for plotting one of the symbols on the handout
          sheet, use it to complete case study 5.

Week 6   Computer applications for detail drawings. Assignment: Finish reading
          Chapter 4. Select one or more of the piping symbols shown, and
          write a subroutine, use this in completion of case study 6.

Week 7   Equation plotting and surface description. Assignment: Read Chapter 5,
          use both the IBM 370 and the interactive HP 7202 plotter, plot only
          one in ten points for cam.

Week 8   Midterm examination.

Week 9   Computerized descriptive geometry. Assignment: Read Chapter 6,
          work case study 8.

Week 10   Spring break.

Week 11   Three-dimensional rotation of solid objects, shading techniques. As-
          signment: Finish reading Chapter 5, work simple animation job
          (case study 9).

Week 12   Pictorial representation. Assignment: Read Chapter 7, continue work-
          ing on case study 9.

Week 13   Surface description and computer-aided design programs. Assignment:
          Read Chapters 8 through 9, work case study 10.

Week 14   Continuation of week 13.

Week 15   Collection of data for notebooks and example problems.

Week 16   Final examination.

Figure 10.1 Typical assignment sheet for semester course.

The purpose of this chapter is to present a series of user case studies based on the concepts presented in earlier chapters. In each study the problem is discussed in step-by-step fashion followed by the programming steps necessary to create the output. Students of computer-aided graphics will learn much from studying each of these examples. These user problems are assigned during a normal semester as shown in Figure 10.1.

USING GRAPHICAL STRUCTURES

The design of the graphical structure of a computer-aided graphics and design system depends ultimately on the input/output requirements of the applications programming. Some programs have little application other than automated drawing aids (case study 1), but usually the graphics structure is subordinate to the data application. Graphics is, however, very important because it forms the interface between the user and the application of data.

Graphical structures have their main impact as an output device for the display of the engineering drawing. Before the final drawing is displayed the structure can also be used in the design cycle because the human brain is adept at the processing of visual information. The designer can perceive visually the effects of the data application. This procedure starts at the graphical display. The user selects a hardware device and points at the display; this point on the graphical display must be identified in the data structure. There are two ways of doing this:

1. The data structure list is sorted by the computer program until an output display point is located that "matches" the desired input location (case study 2).
2. Each geometric construction command given to the display hardware is compared with the desired input location. This command information is then stored as input commands. A graphical input can then be related back to the application program as shown in case study 3.

Always remember that the prime function of a graphical structure is to transfer data between the applications program and the display hardware. The applications program may output graphical points by issuing commands or by building some sort of data list. In either method, the output relates to the application program, not the final engineering drawing. For example, an electronics circuit analysis program may use graphics to build up a picture of the circuit to be analyzed. The display is composed of connected electronic symbols, described in Figure 10.2. The applications program shown in Figure 10.3 is concerned only

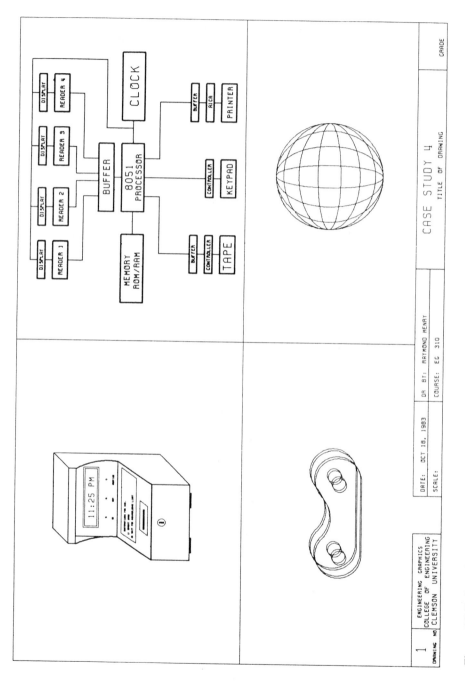

Figure 10.2 Sample case study four.

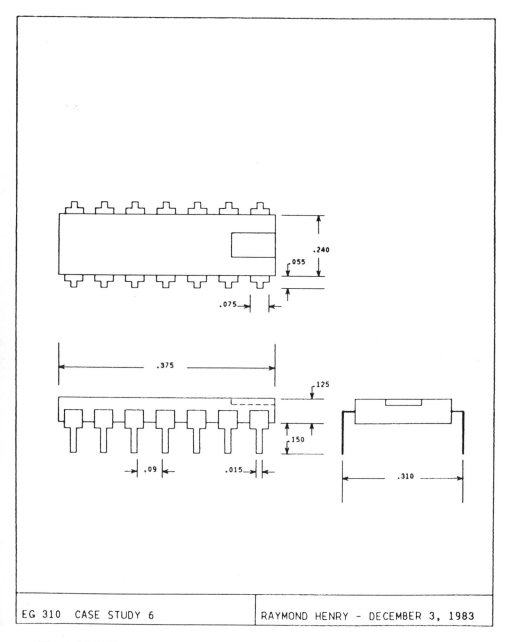

EG 310   CASE STUDY 6   RAYMOND HENRY - DECEMBER 3, 1983

Figure 10.3 Electronic component design.

with the connections between the components and the notation of the components, while the graphical structure of case study 5 is concerned with the position of the symbols on the display hardware and the shape, size, and location.

The application-dependent part of the graphical structure accepts commands from the program or sorts a data list produced by the program and provides a 2-dimensional drawing as an output. This may involve very little computer processing, as shown in case study 4, or more complicated treatment, such as case studies 5 and 6. Some of the ANSI symbols from which one selects in case study 6 are contained in Figure 10.5. Case studies 5 and 6 must be used together because case study 5 specifies the kind of symbol and the points to which it is connected. Case study 5 has to generate the shape for each component in the right place and in the right orientation. To do this, case study 6 uses the "master files" of the shape of each component which is rotated to the right orientation and placed in the proper location of the 2-dimensional drawing.

DATA MANIPULATION

The data structure specifies what is to be displayed. This is contrasted by the graphical structure, which tells how the program will display the drawing. The degree of data manipulation done by the applications program to describe the drawing depends purely on the application itself. The drawing may have no particular data structure, as in the case study 7. Other examples of this sort of problem include automative body shapes, contour lines on maps, and mathematical graphs and charts. Most engineering drawings have a definite structure. Points form lines, lines form planes, and planes form objects. Within an object, points and lines sharing a common plane have a closer association than other features of the same object.

The best way of structuring points, lines, and planes in an engineering drawing is to associate them into sets, as shown in the case study 8. The program deals with sets instead of points or lines. The sets are XARRAY, YARRAY, and ZARRAY. When a transformation (shift, rotation, or scaling) is applied to a set, it is applied to all the points of that array.

To produce an orthographic drawing, the sets shown below are plotted:

View	Arrays plotted
Horizontal	X and Z
Frontal	X and Y
Right profile	Z and Y

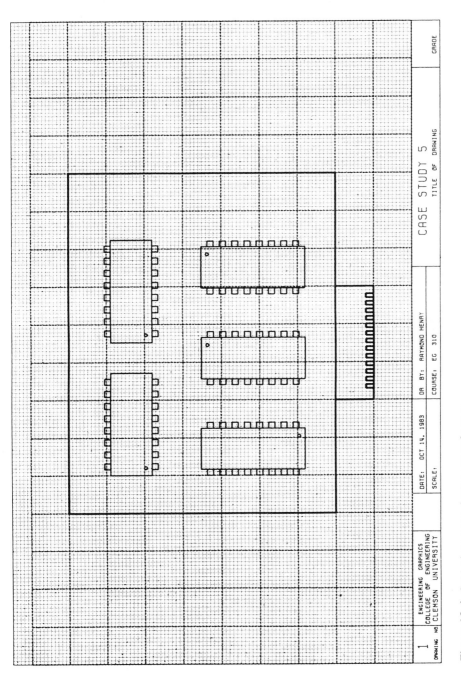

Figure 10.4 Grid placement during manufacture.

TRANSFORMATIONS

The set data manipulation or reordering of data structures is referred to as a transformation. This applies to the coordinates of all of the points determining the set. The coordinates of a point prior to transformation are X, Y, and Z and after transformation are XPLOT and YPLOT. Three-dimensional set data cannot be displayed on conventional computer-aided graphics hardware, so transformation is a common element of data structures.

Shifting. An object is transformed in relation to the origin by a distance in the X direction and Y direction. These distances must be assigned prior to transformation and are assigned as

    XTRANS = 2.5
    YTRANS = 5.5

where XTRANS is the physical distance shifted along the X axis and YTRANS is the distance shifted along the Y axis. XTRANS and YTRANS need not be equal. The transformed point is calculated by

    XPLOT = X + XTRANS
    YPLOT = Y + YTRANS

Rotation. An object is rotated by selecting the angle of rotation (ANG) and converting it to radius (ANG/57.3). The angle of rotation must be assigned prior to rotation and is assigned as

    AND = 30.

where 30 is the amount of rotation in degrees. The transformed point is calculated by

    XPLOT = X + Z*COS(ANG/57.3)
    YPLOT = Y + Z*SIN(ANG/57.3)

Scaling. An object is scaled by multiplying its set by a scaling factor (SF). SF must be assigned prior to the scaling and is assigned as

    SF = 1.

The enlargement or reduction is relative to the origin after shifting (XTRANS, YTRANS) and rotation (COS(ANG/57.3)SIN(ANG/57.3)). The transformed point is calculated by

XPLOT = X + Z*SF*COS(ANG/57.3) + XTRANS
YPLOT = Y + Z*SF*(ANG/57.3) + YTRANS

CASE STUDIES

Each of the case studies presented is done so with reference to certain figures contained in the first nine chapters. Following this description, a discussion of the problem containing the computer program is presented. By using this format, the material presented in Chapter 1 through 9 is summarized in case study form.

Case Study 1. Automated Title Block

Statement of the Problem. Modify the subroutine shown in Figure 2.20 so that changes in sheet sizes can be made. The listing shown will plot a size B (11 X 17 inch) format. Make the changes necessary so that a size A, B, or C sheet border and title strip can be selected.

Discussion. Subroutines are written so that the user may simplify the mainline or "calling" program. Whenever possible the subroutine is made as useful and flexible as possible to fit a wide range of uses. To do this a list of parameters called arguments are placed after CALL TITLE. A simple method of solving the problem might be

CALL TITLE(SIZE)

where size is input as A, B, or C. The user places the desired format letter in place of SIZE. The input in this case is a letter, not a number, so the subroutine format for SIZE must be alpha (A), not integer (I) or floating (F). One new line of FORTRAN will enable us to read alpha:

REAL SIZE

Next a series of tests will have to be made for size:

IF(SIZE.EQ.A)GOTO 10
IF(SIZE.EQ.B)GOTO 11
IF(SIZE.EQ.C)GOTO 12
GOTO 99

The logical IF statements route size A to line 10, B to 11, and C to 12. All other inputs are not considered; the GOTO 99 ends the subroutine without action.

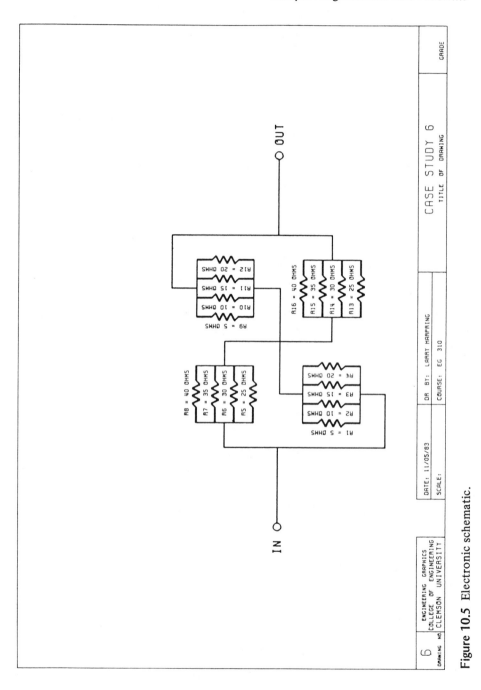

Figure 10.5 Electronic schematic.

```
10 CALL FACTOR(.5)
   GOTO 13
11 CALL FACTOR(1.)
   GOTO 13
12 CALL FACTOR(2.)
13 CONTINUE
```

Case Study 2. Digitizing Problem

Statement of the Problem. Digitize a simple object as described in Figure 1.26a. Prepare coordinate locations for the graphic shape selected. Prepare the coordinate list, as exercise 1.11 outlines. Use the simple program shown in Figure 1.26a for submitting digitized jobs to the CalComp plotter.

Discussion. The technique of describing a graphic shape by coordinate locations is called digitizing. There are two methods for locating the starting and stopping points of these shapes. They are "absolute" and "incremental." Either method can be used by a computer to store and supply drawing information called the database. The choice depends on the structure of the plotter.

Examples in Chapter 2 were digitized by counting the grid intersections in the horizontal and vertical directions and recording these as absolute amounts. Coordinate locations can be handwritten on a special form, or they can be read from an automatic locating device called a digitizer. This device will decrease the time spent in recording coordinates by about 50 percent. Either means can be used for problems of this type; the concept does not change.

Case Study 3. Geometric Constructions

Statement of the Problem. Choose one of the student exercises from Chapter 2. Write a FORTRAN program for any of exercises 2 through 13 or you may submit programs shown in exercises 2.17 through 2.22.

Discussion. In case study 2 the graphic input was broken into straight-line segments, each of which were represented by two pairs of digits. This is one of the oldest and most common means of graphic input; however, it is an extremely laborious process. To facilitate a faster form of graphic input, a series of geometric construction subroutines have been written and made commercially available.

You will use the thirty-five routines described in Chapter 2 to form shape descriptions that will replace the laborious manual procedure of mechanical detail drawing. As you progress through the ten case studies described in this chapter, one by one, the fundamentals will be laid for a system which permits a designer to create a design layout in real-time collaboration with a suitably programmed computer. After completion of the tenth case study, the human-machine system can automatically generate assembly drawings, parts lists, and detail drawings for the documentation of a design.

This is a formidable task, and only by the careful reading of the text materials, supported by computer programming experiences, can the user hope to master automated drafting.

Case Study 4. Piece Part Selection

Statement of the Problem. In Chapter 3, select four of the exercises and arrange a drawing sheet layout. Program a single sheet so that four different drawings can be placed inside the same title area. Use the CALL PLOT(X, Y, -3) technique for dividing the final output (see Figure 10.2).

Discussion. Case studies 1, 2, and 3 work admirably for drawings composed exclusively of straight lines, circles, and discrete points (such as locations for geometric construction routines); these techniques require painstaking effort on the part of the graphics programmer when circular arcs or other mathematically defined curves are to be displayed with precision by a computer. Case study 4 will be developed to permit curves and repetitive patterns to be described in compact, programmed statements called macros. These macros are composed of geometric construction routines connected together to form subpictures. These macros are placed at the end of the program and are read by the computer, which interprets them according to the subroutines called. The technician who writes the code describing the macro has come to be known as a part programmer.

Caution: The term part programmer is not the same as "N/C part programming" where the description of the part will be machined by numerical control. The concept beginning to form with this case study is the development of a graphics system that will enable the detail drawing to be computer-generated by software techniques from the design layout.

Case Study 5. Library of ANSI Symbols

Statement of the Problem. A library of ANSI symbols to automate an area of detailed drawing can be done. Two areas which contain symbols have been automated; the threads and fasteners symbols and piping symbols. Using exercises 8, 9, 10, and 11 as guides select one of the ANSI symbols not included and write a subroutine for it.

Discussion. In addition to various mechanical subpictures used in case study 4, optional features of macros abound. Of particular importance in manufacturing applications is the "grid recognition" capability of some macros. This is especially true in electronic schematic generation, where symbols are usually laid out so that all features are located to integer multiples of some grid spacing. Grid

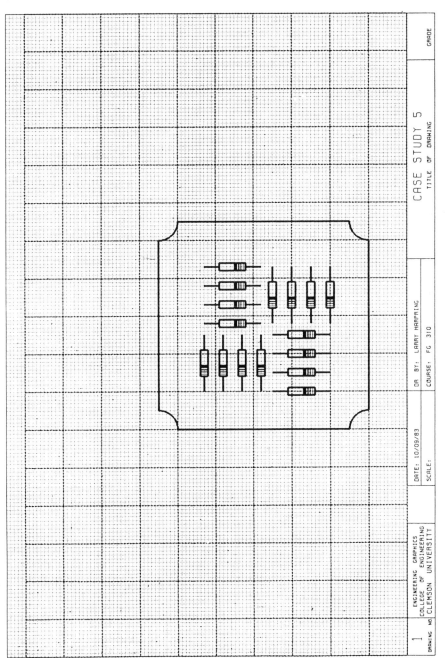

Figure 10.6 Grid recognition for schematic diagram.

378   Sample Programs and User Problems

recognition forces the coordinate measurement to be that of the nearest grid intersection. This then can be used for developing a computer-aided manufacturing data base. The grid information can be used to draw the design automatically and direct a machine operation (drill component locations). See Figures 10.3 and 10.4.

Case Study 6. Electronics Circuit Analysis

Statement of the Problem. Case study 5 can be used in the creation of an electronics schematic. Use as many of the macros as needed to complete the diagrams shown in Figures 10.5 and 10.6.

Discussion. All of the macros contained in the user's list have certain elements in common. Each has an X and Y starting location for page placement. The argument SIZE or GRID refers to the grid recognition capability of the macro. A grid size of 0.125, for instance, will yield a 1-inch symbol because of the 8 X 8 format of the macro.

Lines used to connect the symbols can be butted directly to a connection node of each symbol. Symbols are arranged according to an engineer's sketch or written description. Wiring is added, followed by the annotation for the diagram.

Case Study 7. Computer Modeling Techniques

Statement of the Problem. Design a program that will print a database for the profile of Figure 10.7. Four equations will be used in the solution: III is a

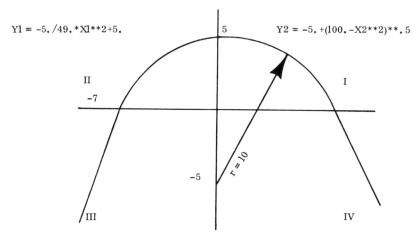

Y1 = -5./49.*X1**2+5.   5   Y2 = -5.+(100.-X2**2)**.5

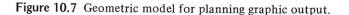

Y = 70./49.*X+10.   Y3 = -1.*3.**.5*X3+15.

Figure 10.7 Geometric model for planning graphic output.

straight line tangent at point -7 on the X axis, II is a parabola from the -7 to a +5 on the Y axis, I is a circle with a radius of 10 units, and IV is a straight-line segment tangent to the circle at the X axis. Modify the program so that the trial data can be plotted on the HP 7202 desk model.

Discussion. Having introduced the two other means for building a database, we are now ready to create a database by computer modeling. This is a method by which the pen path is described as the graph of a mathematical function. In this way we shall be able to get a "picture" of the function, and this picture allows us to guide the behavior of the plotted function.

The computer model of a function consists of all points whose coordinates (X, Y) staisfy the functional relationship $Y = f(X)$. By choosing a specific value for X and placing it in a graphics DO loop, we can then find the corresponding value for Y by evaluating $f(X)$ inside the computer model. In this manner we can obtain the coordinates of a point to place in a database. Repeating the process inside the DO loop, we obtain as many points as needed to plot the computer model.

The computer model for the second equation is determined from the general form of the equation for a parabola:

$$Y = MX^2 + B$$

$Y = -5./49.X^2 + 5$ would satisfy the constraints for the intercepts given (-7 and +5).

The computer model for the first quadrant equation is determined from the general form of the equation for a circle:

$$R^2 = (Y - k)^2 + (X - k)^2$$

$Y = -5 + (R^2 - X^2)^{1/2}$ would satisfy the constraints for the intercepts given (+8.67 and +5).

The straight-line segments are determined from the linear equation forms:

$$Y = aX + b$$

where a and b are constraints. It is called linear, since the output of such a model is always a straight line. See Figure 10.8.

Case Study 8. Computerized Path Specification

Statement of the Problem. Use the program shown in Figure 10.8 and design a simple machine path as illustrated in Figure 10.9. The database from case study 7 can be used for the basic shape if desired. Provide for at least one machined path by the use of CIRCL.

```
CALL PLOTS
CALL PLOT(12.,6.,-3)
X=-10.
Y=70./49.*X+10.
XA=X/4.+2.5
YA=Y/4.+1.071
CALL PLOT(XA,YA,3)
WRITE(3,*)XA,YA
X1=-7.
DO 4 I=1,100
X1=X1+.07
Y1=-5./49.*X1**2+5.
XB=X1/4.+2.5
YB=Y1/4.+1.071
CALL PLOT(XB,YB,2)
4 WRITE(3,*)XB,YB
X2=0.
DO 6 J=1,100
X2=X2+.086
Y2=-5.+(100.-X2**2)**.5
X4=X2/4.+2.5
Y4=Y2/4.+1.071
CALL PLOT(X4,Y4,2)
6 WRITE(3,*)X4,Y4
X3=10.
Y3=-1.*3.**.5*X3+15.
XC=X3/4.+2.5
YC=Y3/4.+1.071
CALL PLOT(XC,YC,2)
WRITE(3,*) XC,YC
CALL PLOT(12.,0.,999)
STOP
END
```

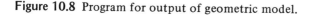

Figure 10.8 Program for output of geometric model.

Discussion. Use the programming techniques from Chapter 5 and the design skills from Chapters 6 and 7. A work-sheet format as illustrated in Figure 10.7 will prove helpful in the selection of points to input the application's program listed in Figure 10.8.

Case Study 9. Part Animation Studies

Statement of the Problem. The applications programming shown in Chapter 8 may be used to display the part specified in case study 8. Up to 100 separate views may be selected for display. Prepare the data for input to the animation program and output the piece part for rotation in the "free" space as shown in Figure 10.10.

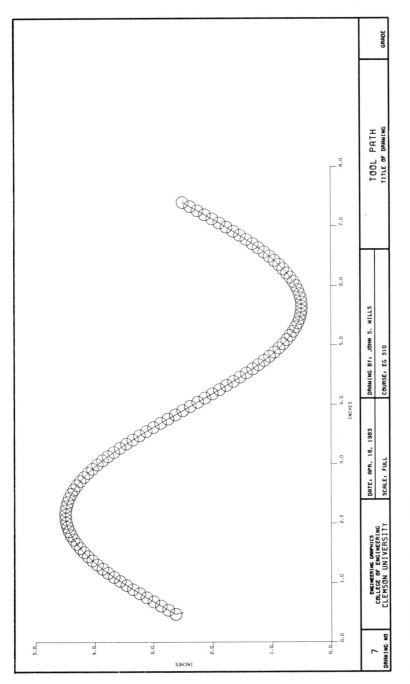

Figure 10.9 Total path specification.

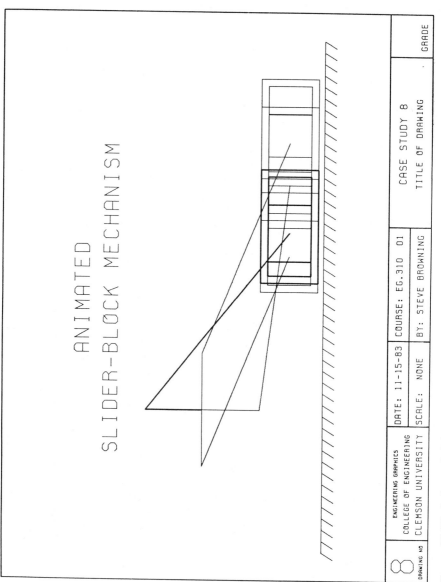

Figure 10.10 Animated slider-block specification.

Discussion. Refer to Chapter 5 for details on methods used in animation. Figure 10.11 represents the normal design datum of primary (X,Y), "table top surface," to be oriented the same as in case study 8. The database from case study 8 can be modified for input to the applications program output as shown in Figure 10.12. Notice that Figures 10.10-10.12 are progressive, illustrating complete movement of the part.

Case Study 10. Surface Descriptions

Statement of the Problem. Using the program listed in Figure 10.13 prepare the input data for the surface displayed in Figures 10.14, 15, 16, 17, and 18.

Discussion. Refer to Chapter 5 for the descriptions of patchwork surfaces. The applications program listed in Figure 10.13 may be run as a trial before the functions describing your surface input. During the trial display of Figure 10.13, use the DVST to preview the surface. Replace functions as desired to produce surface displays.

EXERCISES

1. Case study 1 is typical of a starter project in industry. New employees are given subroutine modifications and improvements while they are learning how to operate the computing equipment. Follow the steps in the discussion of the problem and complete this exercise during the first week of the course.
2. In case study 2 the student digitizes a simple object using common types of batch devices. Model numbers may be ignored, with substitution for local differences being made. This exercise is typical of the exercises in Chapter 2 and should be completed during the second week of the course.
3. A step forward in the programming level is the description of objects by the use of geometric construction techniques. Complete exercises at this level during the third week of the course.
4. The next level of drawing is known as subpictures. Case study 4 introduces this concept and is typical of exercises done in Chapter 3.
5. Case study 5 is typical of the techniques described in Chapter 4 and can be worked with any of the exercises in Chapter 4. In this case a library of symbols for electronics has been provided.
6. Select an example of an electrical exercise in Chapter 4 and work it along with case study 6.
7. Computer modeling, explained in case study 7, should be completed during the tenth week of the course. It is similar to the exercises in Chapter 6 or 7.
8. Case studies 8, 9, and 10 should be completed along with the exercises for Chapter 5. Follow the directions and complete them during the remainder of the first course.

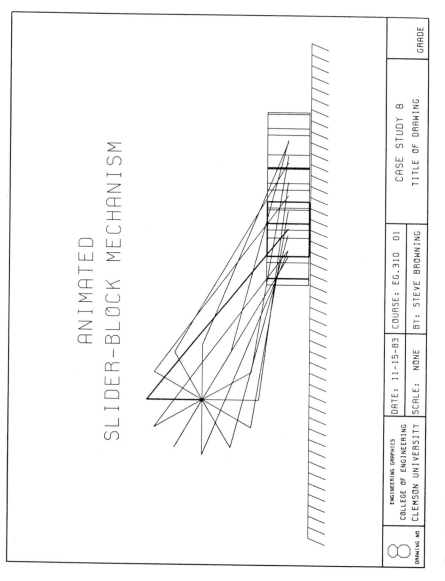

Figure 10.11 Animated slider-block specification.

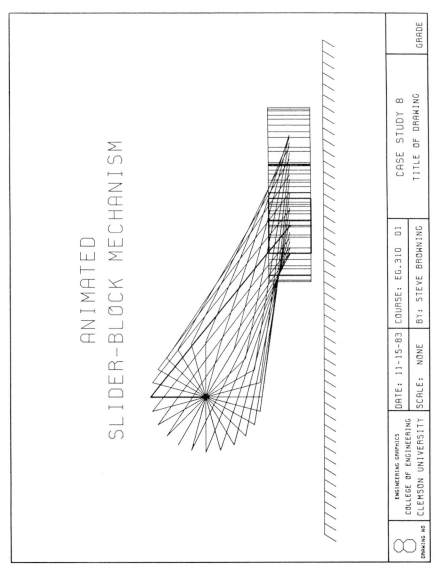

Figure 10.12 Animated slider-block specification.

```
DIMENSION WORK(42),IBUFF(2048)
INTEGER TITLE(13)
DATA TITLE/'LARRY HARPRING/EG 310/CASE STUDY 10/11-03-83'/
EXTERNAL Z
XMIN=-2.
YMIN=-1.5
ZMIN=0.
XMAX=3.
YMAX=1.7
ZMAX=4.
H=8.
Q=20.
NX=25
NY=25
N=0
IVIS =1
TH=210.
GM=85.
CALL PLOTS(IBUFF,2048,6)
CALL THREED(XMIN,YMIN,ZMIN,XMAX,YMAX,ZMAX,TITLE,Q,H,NX,NY,N,
+WORK,.5,Z)
GM=GM-15.
CALL VIEW(TH,GM,Q,IVIS)
CALL PLOT(0.,0.,999)
STOP
END
FUNCTION Z(X,Y)
REAL X,Y
Z=((Y**3)/3.3)*((X**2)/3.3))+.66
RETURN
END
```

Figure 10.13 Animated slider-block specification.

LARRY HARPRING / EG-310 / CASE STUDY 10 / 11-03-83

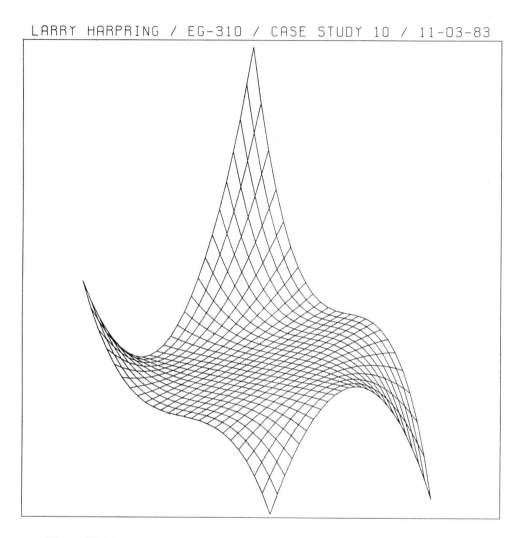

Figure 10.14 Display graphics from program, case study 10.

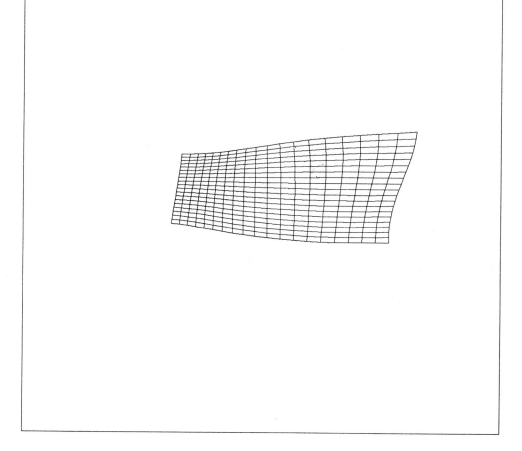

Figure 10.15 Changes in Z function.

CASE STUDY 10   STEVE BRØWNING

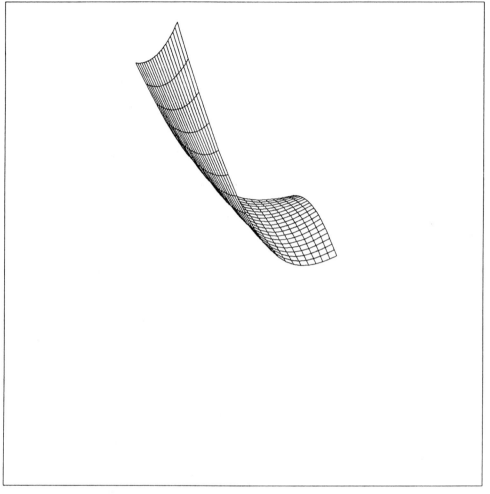

Figure 10.16 Changes in external Z and distance to viewpoint (Q).

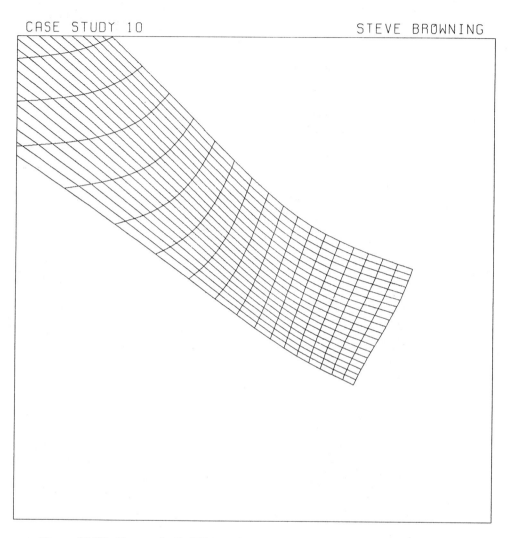

CASE STUDY 10   STEVE BROWNING

Figure 10.17 Changes in Q, IUIS, and N.

CASE STUDY 10 STEVE BRØWNING

Figure 10.18 Changes in TA.

Bibliography

Arthur, E. S. (April 1971). "Three-Dimensional-Plot Software Package," Houston Instruments.

Automated Drafting and Computer Graphics Seminar, November 17/18, 1983. Clemson University, Clemson, S. C.

Blinn, J. F. (August 1978). "Simulation of Wrinkled Surfaces," Computer Graphics *12*(3): 286-292.

Christensen, G. D. (March 1973). "Flying High with Computergraphics," Reprographics.

Coons, S. A. (1968). "Geometry for Construction and Display," IBM Systems Journal, 3(3, 4).

DiCurcio, R. A. (March 1972). "An Overview of Computer Graphics," Reprographics.

Faul, T. L. (March 1976). "The Coordinatograph: Precision Drafting Machine," Journal of the AIAA, 35(1): 18-20.

Feder, A. (August 1975). "Test Results on Computer Graphics Productivity," paper no. 75, AIAA, Los Angeles, CA.

Gain System (1978). Italcantieri Corp., Trieste.

Gilioi, W. (1978). "Interactive Computer Graphics," Prentice-Hall, Englewood Cliffs, NJ.

Interactive Graphics (1977). Gerber Scientific Instrument Co., Hartford, Conn.

Interactive Graphing Packages (1976). Tektronix Corp., Beaverton, Oreg.

Kelley, J. M. (March 1970). Remote FORTRAN Manual. UNO (University of Nebraska at Omaha) Press.

Kucks, J. D. (May 1975). Automated Drafting Notes. UNO (University of Nebraska at Omaha) Press.

Lans, C. A. (1973). "A Three-Dimensional Model Making Machine," in Computer Languages for Numerical Control, Proceedings of the IFIP/IFAC Conference.

Machover, C. Automated Design Seminar. University of Wisconsin, Madison. October 11/12, 1975.

Machover, C. (August 1977). "Graphic Displays," IEEE Spectrum 14(8): 24-32.

Newman, W. H., and Sproull, R. F. (1973). Principles of Interactive Computer Graphics. McGraw-Hill, New York.

PDS-4 System Description (1978). IMLAC Corp., Needham, Mass.

Prenis, John (1977). Computer Terms. Running Press, Philadelphia.

Ricci, A. (1973). "A Constructive Geometry for Computer Graphics," Computer Journal, 16(3).

Ryan, D. L. (1974). "The TTY and HP 7200 in an Image Display Process," Proceedings of the Computer Drafting Institute, Moorhead State University.

Ryan, D. L. (1975). "Automated Drafting and Computer Graphics," Journal of the AIAA, 34(7): 220-221.

Ryan, D. L. (1975). "Computer-Aided Design—How Can We Teach It?," Journal of the AIAA, 35(2): 56-57.

Ryan, D. L. and Davis, H. L. (1975). "Computer Drafting and Design," Journal of the AIAA, 35(1): 18-20.

Ryan, D. L. "Computer Graphics Made Painless," Technology Today, September/October 1977, 5-7.

Ryan, D. L. (1981). "Computer-Aided Kinetics for Machine Design," Marcel Dekker, Inc., New York, NY.

Ryan, D. L. (1984). "Principles of Automated Drafting," Marcel Dekker, Inc., New York, NY.

Sutherland, I. E. (1970). "Computer Displays," Special issue (July), Scientific American.

TEKTRONIX PLOT-10/Advanced Graphing-II Package Users Manual, copyright 1973. Portions of this manual have been used with permission of Tektronix Corp., Beaverton, Oreg.

Williams, R. (1971). "A Survey of Data Structures for Computer Graphics Systems," Computing Surveys, 3(1).

Woodworth, F. (1967). Graphical Simulation. International Textbook Co., Scranton, Pa.

Index

DATE DUE

DEMCO 38-297